The Handbook of Psyc[...]

This handbook provides a comprehensive introduction to the theory and practice of psychodrama, for professional and trainee psychodramatists.

The structure of the book innovatively reflects that of the classic psychodrama session – Warm-up, Action, Sharing and the subsequent Processing. Following an introduction to the history and philosophy of psychodrama the second section of the handbook focuses on the five instruments of psychodrama: the Stage, the Protagonist, the Group, the Auxiliary Ego and the Director. The theory of psychodrama is brought to life by detailed first-hand accounts of psychodrama sessions.

Chapters on psychodrama in action include discussion of the new use of psychodrama in the treatment of depression, and the relationship of the discipline to other group psychotherapies. The contributors illustrate how dramatic improvisation on stage contributes to emotional health.

Essential reading for practising and aspiring psychotherapists, this highly accessible and thorough introduction to psychodrama will also interest those working in allied mental health disciplines.

Marcia Karp is Director of the Holwell International Centre for Psychodrama and Sociodrama in Devon. **Paul Holmes** is a consultant child and adolescent psychiatrist and adult psychotherapist based in Brighton. **Kate Bradshaw Tauvon** is a psychotherapist in private practice in Stockholm, Sweden.

Contributors: Anne Bannister; Kate Bradshaw Tauvon; John Casson; Chris Farmer; Peter Haworth; Paul Holmes; Jinnie Jefferies; Marcia Karp; Dorothy Langley; Olivia Lousada; Zerka Moreno; Gillie Ruscombe-King; Anne Ancelin-Schützenberger; Ken Sprague; Susie Taylor.

The Handbook of Psychodrama

Edited by Marcia Karp, Paul Holmes
and Kate Bradshaw Tauvon

Preface by Zerka T. Moreno

Illustrated by Ken Sprague with original
drawings from psychodrama sessions

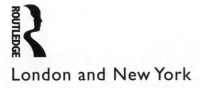

London and New York

First published 1998
by Routledge
11 New Fetter Lane, London EC4P 4EE

Simultaneously published in the USA and Canada
by Routledge
29 West 35th Street, New York, NY 10001

Typeset in Times by Keystroke, Jacaranda Lodge, Wolverhampton
Printed and bound in Great Britain by TJ International Ltd, Padstow, Cornwall

British Library Cataloguing in Publication Data
A catalogue record for this book is available from the British Library

Library of Congress Cataloguing in Publication Data
The handbook of psychodrama / edited by Marcia Karp, Paul Holmes, and
  Kate Bradshaw Tauvon ; drawings by Ken Sprague.
    Includes bibliographical references and index.
    1. Psychodrama. I. Karp, Marcia. II. Holmes, Paul.
  III. Tauvon, Kate Bradshaw.
  RC489.P7H355 1998
  616.89'1523–dc21   97–50005

ISBN 0–415–14845–6 (hbk)
ISBN 0–415–14846–4 (pbk)

Contents

List of contributors

Anne Bannister is a registered psychodrama psychotherapist and dramatherapist. She is a senior trainer with the Northern School of Psychodrama. She worked for many years with the NSPCC as a child sexual abuse consultant but is now a freelance trainer and supervisor. She has published widely including three books. Her latest book is *The Healing Drama: Psychodrama and Drama-therapy with Abused Children* (1997), Free Association Books.

Kate Bradshaw Tauvon, an occupational therapist and a trainer, educator and practitioner in psychodrama, sociometry and group psychotherapy examined by the Nordic Board of Examiners/Trainers (UKCP) is also a registered group analytic psychotherapist. She practises as a psychotherapist and supervisor in Stockholm and is a teacher and examiner with the Swedish Moreno Institute.

John Casson is a dramatherapist, psychodrama psychotherapist (UKCP registered), supervisor, trainer, is a Founder member of the Northern School of Psychodrama and of the Northern Trust for Dramatherapy; he is registered for doctoral research with people who hear voices at the Manchester Metropolitan University; and is in private practice.

Chris Farmer trained in psychiatry at the Maudsley Hospital and has practised as a consultant psychiatrist and psychotherapist in Guernsey's public mental health service. He employs psychodrama in general psychiatry and in family therapy. He qualified in psychodrama at the Holwell Centre and is the author of the book *Psychodrama and Systemic Therapy*.

Peter Haworth works as a clinical nurse specialist in psychodrama for Oxfordshire Mental Healthcare NHS Trust. He runs a number of psychodrama and integrated psychotherapy groups and supervises others. He obtained the diploma in psychodrama from the Holwell Centre in 1983. With Susie Taylor he runs the Oxford Psychodrama Group Psychodrama training programme.

Paul Holmes is a consultant child and adolescent psychiatrist, analytic psycho-therapist, and psychodramatist. He is an honorary member of the British Psychodrama Association and Fellow of the American Society for Group

Psychotherapy and Psychodrama and is the author or co-editor of a number of books on psychodrama.

Jinnie Jefferies is the director of the London Centre of Psychodrama and Group Psychotherapy; the Filyra Institute of Psychodrama, Greece and Senior Trainer for the Newtown House Psychodrama Centre, Ireland. She has made several programmes for the BBC and Channel 4 on using psychodrama with different client groups and has written about her work with the offender patient.

Marcia Karp pioneered the development of psychodrama in Britain and set up the first British training centre as well as trainings in other countries. She is on the Board of the International Association of Group Psychotherapists and is Co-Director of the Holwell International Centre for Psychodrama in Devon. She is co-editor of two previous books on psychodrama.

Dorothy Langley trained as a psychiatric social worker, later qualifying to teach drama to adults. From 1970 she developed dramatherapy, working with in- and out-patients in a psychiatric hospital. After training at Holwell, she introduced psychodrama to local hospitals. She teaches dramatherapy, psychodrama and supervision at South Devon College.

Olivia Lousada trained as a teacher, a group worker and a social worker. She is registered as a senior trainer in psychodrama, a dramatherapist and an accredited counsellor. She is the founding director of the London Institute for Psychodrama and Sociodrama and co-director of the London Centre of Psychodrama and Group Psychotherapy.

Zerka T. Moreno is the doyenne of psychodrama practice and has trained leading group psychotherapists and psychodramatists worldwide. Until 1982 she directed the Moreno Institute in Beacon, New York, founded by her husband J.L. Moreno, the original and world centre of psychodrama. In her eighty-first year she is as busy as ever worldwide.

Gillie Ruscombe-King trained as an occupational therapist and since completing her psychodrama training at the Holwell Centre she has worked with those struggling with drinking problems and acute psychiatric difficulties. She has a keen interest in the juxtaposition of the psychodramatic and group analytic process. She has had experience of both these methods and believes in helping those with whom she works to rediscover their creative potential.

Anne Ancelin Schützenberger, Professor Emeritus of Social and Clinical Psychology at Nice University, is one of the first twelve directors trained by Moreno. She organised the first International Congress of Psychodrama (1964, France). Her handbook on psychodrama has been translated into twelve languages. She specialises in geniosociograms. Her last book, *Aïe, Mes Aïeux!* has been translated into English and is a best-seller in France.

Ken Sprague is an accredited sociodrama director, psychodramatist and graphic artist. He is committed to the ongoing process of developing Morenian methods as life tools. He works to popularise action methods beyond the clinic and personal growth arena into the area of teaching, organisation or business management and community affairs. He runs the Four Seasons Arts School and contributed the drawings to this book.

Susie Taylor worked as an occupational therapist in a psychiatric hospital for nine years. She trained as a psychodramatist at the Holwell Centre and gained her diploma in 1983. Since 1985 she has worked as a freelance psycho-dramatist in both group and individual work. She is the co-founder of the Oxford Psychodrama Group which offers a training programme in this area. Susie has also run psychodrama training groups abroad on numerous occasions, with a regular commitment to Serbia and the Yugoslav Republic of Macedonia. Her present work in psychodrama includes a group at Grendon prison, and one for women who have experienced sexual abuse, training groups, open-weekend workshops, individual psychotherapy and supervision.

ZERKA TOEMAN MORENO

Preface

Zerka T. Moreno

If there is such a thing as a psychodramatic dynasty, this book may well represent one. All the contributors are graduates of the Holwell International Centre of Psychodrama and Sociodrama and thereby constitute a unique group of professional persons.

Although J.L. Moreno dreamt of his work circling the globe, he could not have foreseen that one day Marcia Karp would be the guiding spirit of a training centre in England. Her students come from many corners of the world and as the guiding spirit of that centre she holds an important international position in our midst. Together with her life partner, Ken Sprague, who also contributed to this book, she became a world traveller in psychodrama.

The *Handbook* is addressed to beginners and non-beginners. It serves as an introduction to the uninitiated and as a refreshing source of inspiration for those already exposed to and familiar with psychodrama. It focuses on four main stages in psychodrama: the Warm-Up, the Action, the Sharing and the Processing, as well as the five instruments of psychodrama, namely, the Stage or Setting, the Protagonist or Central Figure, the Group Present, the Auxiliary Ego(s) or Therapeutic Actor(s) and last but not least, the Director or Guide and Leader.

As to beginners, let me wish you a hearty 'Welcome'. It has been my particular pleasure to embrace what I have termed 'the psychodramatic Virgins'. The so-called Virgins ask the kind of important questions about our work that we may have long forgotten to think about. More significantly, these persons help us to maintain our very own 'virginality' or innocence. Marcia suggested the term 'virgin originality' and thereby indicated how important it is to stay close to our source of inspiration, our spontaneity and our creativity. We need to continue to ask questions of ourselves, such as: How is this working? What philosophical and theoretical basis do we have to understand and explain what is happening? What other sources do we need to attain the healing? How can I, the director, maximise the talents of the auxiliary egos and tap into the collective wisdom of the group? What kind of warm-up is most suitable for this particular group? How shall we select the protagonist from this group? How do we reach closure and what can we leave open for further exploration? How can the protagonist, the auxiliary egos and the group members carry the impact of the group experience into their own lives outside of the group? How can we guide that continuity?

Though just delineating these aspects of the director's task seems mind-boggling, we learn to deal with them. But it is only after many years of training and practice that we manage to put all these aspects into a cohesive whole and, almost unconsciously, use them naturally. I sense that the process becomes built in, organic.

One important thing I have learned about the warming-up process is that when the protagonist is fully warmed-up, no part of the self is available to stand aside, no part can only observe or record the action. Moreno believed that each of us has three components within us, the Director, the Actor and the Observer/Critic. The director tells us what to do: 'Make that phone call that you have not attended to'; the actor makes the phone call and engages in 'act-hunger'. The observer/critic cannot function and record what is happening if the actor is fully engaged. This means that the actor cannot recall what was said or done. It is only when the actor allows the observer/critic in, that the latter can record the interaction. The fully warmed-up actor component does not leave any room for the observer/critic. Thus, the not remembering is not repression because one can only repress that which has been recorded and no record was, in fact, made. Both the director and the observer/critic drop away when the actor takes over. It is a major reason why so many times we are unable to recall what was said or done in what I call the 'white heat of action'. Seeing ourselves later on videotape, for example, we are astounded: 'Did I really do that? Is that how I looked and behaved?' The white heat of action burned away the observer/critic. When the observer/critic is present you know it because of that small inner voice which says: 'You're not doing this very well, you know', or perhaps: 'That was not nearly as hard as you anticipated and feared it would be, you carried it off quite well.' The latter observation also showed that you did not lose your cool, literally and figuratively. But the implication of not remembering is that when we appear forgetful or absent-minded, it is because the actorial warm up was complete and took over. Indeed, many protagonists have exactly that experience of not remembering parts of their session. It could be that this 'losing one's so-called cool' is one of the major reasons why some members of the psychiatric profession have been and continue to be so fearful of psychodrama. It appears dangerous until one understands the power of the act-hunger syndrome which we carry from childhood. Moreno frequently told us that he was accused numerous times of making his patients 'sicker', that is, less in control. He countered this argument first of all by agreeing and responding:

> I give them a small dose of insanity under conditions of control. It is not the insanity I fear, it is the lack of control. Here they can learn that behaving that way outside is dangerous to themselves and to others. But they cannot learn control of their emotions until they have fully experienced them. In

psychodrama they can fully live out their emotions and then learn to control them.

(personal communication)

It is incumbent upon the director to see that the protagonist is safely returned to the group and that sharing from the group is carried out lovingly. This sharing enables the protagonist to feel supported and to build a cognitive grasp of some of the experience in a humane, non-critical way: 'Your experience reminds me of my own . . . etc.'

Moreno taught us that affirmation of the other, however bizarre that person's ideation, comes before denial. With that affirmation it is possible to reach *tele*. Tele is best understood as reaching into the feelings of another person, accepting and sharing the reality of those feelings in a mutual recognition of truth. Tele operates between the director and the protagonist, the auxiliary egos and the protagonist, the group members and the protagonist as well as between the members of the group. It never ceases to amaze me, after working in the field for more than fifty years, how tele operates invisibly. For example, the protagonist, unknowingly, picks an auxiliary ego whose own life reflects an identical experience. It happens over and over again. Recently, a young woman protagonist chose for her father who had died just a few months ago a young man who worked in the same mental health clinic. She had never discussed her father's death with him although that death had some unusual features. In enacting the scene she showed that her father died while sleeping next to her mother, of a massive heart attack. Her mother was not aware of what had happened because they slept with pillows between them to facilitate peaceful sleep. The protagonist was able to complete her farewell to her father, a profoundly meaningful act of which life had deprived her. Imagine our astonishment when the auxiliary ego's sharing started with: 'We never talked about this, but my father died exactly the same way.' From among 45 persons she picked the only other person who completely shared her experience. He too, had a fine catharsis, adding: 'You did my psychodrama for me. Many of the group members too, were able to share; a number among them never had a chance to make a loving farewell to a parent who had died, for a variety of reasons. Life is, after all, very complicated. But the specifics of the situation belonged only to these two group members who were invisibly tied together. It is not synchronicity, it is tele which is responsible for many of our subtle, invisible interactions and we need to become far more aware of and sensitive to, its impact.

Throughout this book, tele will be touched upon. Allow me to add that the existence of tele has been experimentally validated by J.L. Moreno and reported on by him in his magnum opus *Who Shall Survive?* (1953). It is abstracted in the current Student Edition (1993: 187), in which it is clearly demonstrated that a group of 26 girls who were given a chance to pick their mealtime table mates under the criterion: 'Who do you choose to sit with at your dining room table?' showed a far larger number of mutual choices (mutuality of choice is the simplest, most observable effect of tele in action) than could be predicted by chance alone: 'In the sample studied the probability of mutual structures is 213% greater in the actual sociometric configurations than in the chance configurations and the number of unreciprocated structures is 35.8% greater than actually.' This means that mutuality of choice, as explained above, is the essential expression of the tele in operation, and it is far more operative in life than we can begin to guess. Hence it also means that we need to study our own interpersonal relations with far greater refinement, utilising this awareness, because it is our ability to reach out productively to our fellow beings which establishes our security in life itself and keeps our socio-emotional environment in balance.

You will be reading about the importance of the role concept and how roles we play or need to play and don't, impact upon our mutual well-being. Thinking about ourselves as improvising actors on the stage of life helps us because, as we improvise, we can observe if we are interacting productively or counterproductively. As we engage ourselves in this learning, spontaneity and creativity are lurking in the background. Psychodrama is about doing, undoing and doing again, differently. That is where spontaneity and creativity, twin principles, can be mastered.

You will begin to understand that the reality in which we live may not be the reality of someone else and that this is a source of great interpersonal struggle and conflict. The main way to avoid some of the hurt of the variation of these realities is to remain aware that what each of us is dealing with is our 'subjective perception' of these realities, which are often disjointed. You will be asked, in psychodrama as in art, to suspend critical judgement for a while, to let your heart speak and not only your head. Cleverness and intellectuality, in psychodrama, are traps. This idea of 'subjective perception' gives us hope, because perception is always subject to change and re-evaluation in light of new findings. Do you recall, when you first went away to summer camp, or to school or university? You returned home after a while and it seemed as if your house had 'shrunk'. Does a house really shrink or was it your subjective perception that had changed? Have you recently found out something surprisingly different in some person or friend you thought you really knew well? Did that discovery make a difference in your relationship? The awareness of new aspects or new roles, in self or in the other, is what creates this change or moves the subjective perception to a different perspective. There is the apocryphal story of the young man who left his paternal home at age 18, only to discover upon returning home at age 25, how much his father had learned in those seven years!

I tell my students repeatedly: remember, none of us have total awareness of another human being; it is not given to us humans. Indeed, we do not have total awareness of ourselves, either. Profound learning in psychodrama means being humble about what we know and staying open to and eager for the new learning it offers. Such techniques as doubling, role reversal, the mirror and soliloquy, among others, are all ways to assist us in this learning.

This book is a guide to the world of psychodrama. May you find yourselves soon at home in it.

BIBLIOGRAPHY

Moreno, J.L. (1953/1993) *Who Shall Survive?*, Student edition, Roanoke, VA: Royal Publishing Co.

MARCIA KARP AND ZERKA MORENO

Introduction to the *Handbook*

Marcia Karp

A current illness in our society is 'compulsive conformity' (Moreno: 1965). People imitate others rather than being themselves, yet one of the most common statements made in therapy is, 'I just want to be myself.'

The precursor to psychodrama was spontaneity training, introduced by the founder of psychodrama, J.L. Moreno. He believed that spontaneity and creativity were the cornerstones of human existence. Without creativity, where would the world be? There is always a creator and the thing created. One could say about spontaneity and creativity: it's not that spontaneity and creativity are everything, it's just that there's not much else without it.

The Handbook of Psychodrama came about as a request from Routledge to the co-editors to present a simple, basic book on psychodrama, answering the questions, what is psychodrama and how is it used?

Our two prior collaborative efforts, *Psychodrama: Inspiration and Technique* (1991) and *Psychodrama since Moreno* (1994) are collected works by, and mostly for, psychodrama and psychotherapy practitioners. The *Handbook* is focused on beginners, refreshers and those leaders looking for an inspirational overview. We hope it is that.

The contributors are all graduates of the Holwell International Centre for Psychodrama and Sociodrama, Barnstaple, North Devon, England. I have been privileged to be the trainer to my two co-editors and to the twelve authors. It is a rare experience for the mother and children to give birth together but that is somewhat what we are doing in producing the *Handbook*. Each of the graduates of Holwell have become distinguished in their own field and have made unique contributions to psychodrama.

I envy anyone reading about psychodrama for the first time. Some thirty-five years ago, reading about psychodrama, was my own introduction. I discovered a book, *Who Shall Survive?* by Moreno, which was by accident or divine ordinance, sitting on a shelf above my head while I studied as a 21-year-old university student. Since often the best things in life happen by accident, I hope you, the reader, will accidentally discover your own hands, your own maker of things, your own creator, in this book made by us. Let the words stand as they are.

These days, whatever you have to say, leave the roots on,
  let them dangle . . . and the dirt,
Just to make clear where they came from.

(Charles Olson 1987)

BIBLIOGRAPHY

Holmes, P. and Karp, M. (eds) (1991) *Psychodrama: Inspiration and Technique*, London: Routledge.

Holmes, P., Karp, M. and Watson, M. (eds) (1994) *Innovations in Theory and Practice: Psychodrama since Moreno*, London: Routledge.

Moreno, J.L. (1953) *Who Shall Survive?*, Beacon, NY: Beacon House.

Moreno, J.L. (1995) *The Voice of J.L. Moreno M.D.*, audio tape recorded in 1965 and published by M. Karp, Barnstaple, England.

Olson, Charles (1987) *Collected Poetry of Charles Olson*, Los Angeles: University of California Press.

A note on the illustrations

The drawings in this book were made in psychodrama sessions all over the world during the past twenty-five years.

The only exception is the drawing for the sociodrama chapter. This was made after a sociodrama session at a street demonstration in the Playa de Mayo, Buenos Aires, where mothers danced in memory of their 'disappeared' sons and daughters.

I have not attempted to 'illustrate' the authors' words but to evoke the theme of each chapter. My aim is to contribute an additional chapter in the language of drawing, not words.

Ken Sprague
Holwell International Centre, 1997

Part I

The warm-up – what is psychodrama

INTRODUCTION TO PSYCHODRAMA

Chapter 1

An introduction to psychodrama

Marcia Karp

Psychodrama has been defined as a way of practising living without being punished for making mistakes. The action that takes place in a group is a way of looking at one's life as it moves. It is a way of experiencing what happened and what did not happen in a given situation. All scenes take place in the present, even though a person may want to enact something from the past or something in the future. The group enacts a portion of life seen through the eyes of the protagonist (or subject of the session). The personal representation of truth by the protagonist can be eye-opening for someone else watching, who may see themselves reflected in the struggle to express what is real. J.L. Moreno, who founded psychodrama in Vienna in the early 1900s, described it as 'a scientific exploration of truth through dramatic method'. Moreno (1953: 81) had observed that thus far there was a science without religion and religion without science. He felt that the way forward was a combination; 'A truly therapeutic procedure cannot have less an objective than the whole of mankind' Moreno (1953: 3). Each member of the group is a therapeutic agent of the other. To be understood and held emotionally and physically by a group member who is not previously enmeshed in the story, can be a healing experience in itself.

The psychodrama session has three parts: the warm-up, the action and the sharing. A fourth part, which is used for training purposes, is called the processing. In this chapter, I would like to describe these parts to you as well as discuss some practical considerations in using the method, the training of practitioners, the literature and the research in psychodrama.

THE WARM-UP

The warm-up serves to produce an atmosphere of creative possibility. This first phase weaves a basket of safety from which the individual can begin to trust the director, the group and the method of psychodrama. When the room has its arms around you it is possible to be that which you thought you could not be, and to express that which seemed impossible to express.

There are many ways to warm up a group. Moreno often encountered each person and enabled people to talk easily to each other. An individual person with a particular life issue was accepted by the group as their protagonist. Another way of warming up is for the director to select a protagonist, one who s/he thinks is ready to work. Another alternative is creative group exercise from which the subject of the session emerges. This is called a protagonist-centred warm-up. In a self-nomination warm-up, people can put themselves forward to be the subject. These suggestions are ways of protagonist selection which come from the warm-up while the warm-up itself makes it possible for people to feel freer to trust the group, and to present their problems in an atmosphere of love, caring and creativity. It is important to remember that each individual comes with their own warm-up. Group discussion may be an expedient catalyst to get the group into action.

ACTION

After the warm-up, the director and the selected protagonist take the work forward from the periphery of the problem to the core. Psychodrama means literally action of the mind, and it brings out the internal drama, so that the drama within becomes the drama outside oneself. The director uses the group members to play auxiliary egos who represent significant people in the drama. The design of the original psychodrama stage consisted of a circle with three tiers. The first level was for the audience, the second for soliloquy and represented the space outside the heat of the drama, and the top level was for the drama to be enacted. The design was for the work to go from the periphery to the core of the problem.

Enactment in most psychodramatic sessions takes place in a designated stage area. During the drama other group members do not sit in that space unless they are playing a role. The stage feels like a ritualised space once the drama begins: that is to say, the event that is meant to take place in that space takes place only there. Psychodrama that is attempted within the group space with no designated stage area, may fall flat because there are no boundaries spatially or methodologically.

Within the action there are five main tools or instruments that distinguish the method of psychodrama from other group methods. Moreno (1953: 81) said:

> The *stage* provides the actor with a living space which is multi-dimensional and flexible to the maximum; the *subject* or actor is asked to be himself on the stage, to portray his own private life; the *audience* is a sounding board of public opinion as well as the subject itself – it becomes healed by taking part; the *auxiliary egos* have a double significance, they are extensions of the director, exploratory and guiding, and extensions of the subject, portraying the actual or imagined. The *director* has three functions: producer, counsellor and analyst.

The stage

Psychodrama is based on life itself. The space a person moves in is reproduced on stage. If a conversation takes place in the kitchen, we set out the tables and chairs and give imaginative space to a window, sink, door, fridge, and other objects. The time, daytime or night-time; the atmosphere, warm, cold, hostile or friendly; and the space, the distance between people and objects are all important in staging a drama. Constructing the reality of an individual's space helps the person to really be there and warms them up to produce the feelings that do or do not exist in that space. When someone remembers a conversation that took place at the table, in childhood, it is often important to have the people in the scene played by selected members of the group. We can often learn more by looking in this way at a person's living space than we can in months of interview. I once was invited into a created space of a young man's apartment. He walked in by lifting his feet unusually high as if carefully tiptoeing. I asked why. He said, 'I throw my old milk cartons on the floor; they are everywhere.' That spoke of isolation, not many visitors, a lack of care for the smell and look. An important clue to his alienation was his living space. Our task, then, was to look at why he had no friends and why he became a recluse. His words, up until then, belied his reality, but showing the 'stage' upon which he lived gave us a truer reality to begin to assess our task together.

The protagonist

I used to work in a public theatre in New York at 78th and Broadway called the Moreno Institute. Seven nights a week there was a public audience, a circular wooden stage and a director. A person seated in the front, middle or back of the theatre, a professor, housewife or carpenter, could be a subject of the psychodrama session which each had chosen to attend. It could be anyone.

Human beings have problems. Normosis, a word coined by Moreno, meaning the struggle to be normal, confounds the best of us. Though psychodrama was designed to help psychotics, for many people it has evolved into a therapy of relationships for many people. The protagonist, meaning the first in action, is a representative voice through which other group members can do their own work. The protagonist simply states an aspect of life s/he wants to work on: my fear of death, my relationship with my daughter, my authority problem at work. The director, with the protagonist, sets out to create scenes that give examples of the problem in the present, past or future with an eye to a possible behavioural pattern. Seeing the problem in the present, seeing the problem as it exists in the past and trying to resolve the problem by establishing the core or roots of the issue, is the aim. Future behaviour may then contain a more adequate approach. The 'spontaneity' that is sought is defined as a fresh response to an old situation or an adequate response to a new situation. The idea of throwing away the script is crucial to the conceptualisation of psychodrama as an action method. The protagonist has a chance to review the life script that s/he is using, which may have been handed down for good reason, but fails to be adequate for present life requirements. A person who was handed a script 'Do not cry' may feel that it doesn't serve in present-day functioning. One who has never grieved for the loss of a parent because they bought the 'brave' script may feel the relief of crying, as grief is let go. The person may find a new definition of brave – one who has the courage to face what really exists within. That courage may not have been within the role repertoire of one's parents, but within this new 'family' group, bravery may find a new climate to encourage self-expression, which may have lain dormant for years.

The group

The average size of a psychodrama group is between five to fifteen people. I have seen groups of as small as three and as large as 500. The emotional material in large groups seems to transcend the numbers and often people feel the group shrinks in size. They are astounded that in a group of twenty-five they are able spontaneously to be themselves. The spontaneity of the director evokes authenticity in group members which in turn creates intimacy, which, ironically, makes the group feel smaller.

There are many societal roles represented in any given group. If, for example, the protagonist is an alcoholic, there may be a mother, sibling, partner or therapist in the group who, in the sharing, can present their own view of what happened to them in relation to an alcoholic family member. This feedback from other roles, in relation to the problem enacted, can be an invaluable insight for the protagonist. The socially investigative dimension of the problem is better researched in the session when many roles are represented. One of the aspects of a psychodrama group that sets it apart from other groups is the multiplicity of roles that are represented by each person in the group. We each play a staggering variety of roles each day: parent, son or daughter, professional, friend, lover, citizen, boss, student, not to mention all the somatic roles such as sleeping, eating, crying. Separate from the many roles we play in our own lives, we may be asked to play a role for someone else in the group – a dying mother, for example. If the person selected to play the dying mother has previously been seen as the group scapegoat, the role-structure can change drastically in a psycho-drama group, allowing a positive alliance to form between protagonist and person playing the dying mother; an alliance which previously did not exist. This constant change of role structure in a psychodrama group helps prevent the role rigidity that may occur in other groups. The role repertoire is expanded by each group member playing a different kind of role in the drama than s/he may be seen to play in the group. A member of the group with low self-esteem may be stretched to play a courageous role, surprising both themselves and the group by the release of creativity hidden in problematic, learned behaviour. The glimpse of courage motivates the player to produce more courageous behaviour and encourages group members to relate to them in a different way.

The auxiliary ego

In the very first group I joined, there was a psychiatric nurse for whom I formed an immediate dislike. While she was protagonist, she was asked to choose someone in the group who could understand her inner thoughts and could help her express what she was not able to say. She chose me to be her double. I was astonished at her choice, but found, once I stood next to her and we worked as a team trying to explore her inner truth, that I could understand her very well and I stopped disliking her. She taught me how much of me was in her and introduced me to the reality that the people we dislike usually display behaviour that strikes close to home; therefore we are warding off the very thing we cannot deal with in ourselves.

The auxiliary ego is anyone in the group who plays a role representing a significant other in the life of the protagonist. This may be a role external to the protagonist, such as a family member or colleague at work. It may be an internal role such as one's fearful self, child self or one's inner voice. This voice may be represented by an auxiliary ego playing the double. The double helps express that which is not being expressed, with or without words. Because Moreno felt that the royal route to the psyche is not the word but non-verbal expression, the auxiliary ego can express, by gesture, posture or distance, those unspoken secrets in relation to the protagonist. I once was a double for a man who was having a quite a normal dinner conversation with his wife of twenty years. He was telling her he did not like to eat liver and clenched his fist as he spoke. As his double, I also clenched my fist and went a step further. I slammed my fist down on the table and said, 'I've had enough of not being understood, I want a divorce.' He looked at me, shocked, and said to her, 'So do I!' It was the non-verbal clue that spoke the truth, not his words. His body conveyed the truth while his words masked it. He then chose to express his actual feelings. The body remembers what the mind forgets.

The auxiliary ego who plays a dying parent may reach out with arms to say goodbye to the protagonist caught in a web of unexpressed emotion. Those very arms may represent years of love that was also unexpressed. If the protagonist reverses roles and is able to speak or show what has not been said all those years, the role-reversal can release spontaneity that was dammed or blocked in his own role as son. He can express love in another role, as the parent.

Often people are more spontaneous in the role of someone else than in their own role. Role reversal is the engine that drives the psychodrama. The role of significant other in the drama is modelled by the protagonist and a group member then moves in to play that role. Through crucial role reversals, the protagonist experiences a shift in role boundary by playing another person. The person being the auxiliary ego holds the role that has been set and creates within it. They imagine how the person in that role would play it. The role is played through the perception of the protagonist which is a constant reference. The auxiliary ego is a therapeutic agent of the director and takes direction therein.

The director

In most therapies this is the therapist, facilitator or group leader. The director is a trained person who helps guide the action. The director is a co-producer of the drama, taking clues from the perceptions of the person seeking help. The following are some of the director's tasks which are expanded in Chapter 9:

- To build sufficient cohesion and a constructive working group climate.
- To stimulate individual group members sufficiently and warm them up for action. Authenticity and spontaneity are the golden rules of the director.
- To consider group dynamics and measure group interaction, preferably by sociometry.
- To guide the appropriate selection of a protagonist and take care of others in the group who are considered but not chosen to be a subject of the session.
- To make a treatment contract for the session which is an action-preparation negotiated with the protagonist.
- To establish a therapeutic alliance.
- To prepare the action-space or stage on which the therapeutic drama takes place.
- To intervene but to give the protagonist sufficient freedom to select the focus of exploration.
- To identify non-verbal messages of the protagonist, as well as the verbal communication.
- To anchor each scene setting in the appropriate time and place.
- To help put auxiliary egos into role.
- To identify central issues in the enactment and to help the protagonist show the group what happened rather than talk about it.
- To use psychodramatic techniques such as role reversal; to move the action from the periphery of the problem to the core of the issue.
- The core of the issue may involve a catharsis of emotion, insight catharsis, catharsis of laughter or catharsis of integration which the director maximises appropriately.
- To create sufficient safety for the protagonist and the group.
- To ensure confidentiality in the group as well as physical safety for all group members and the director.
- To ensure that the psychodrama is a group process and not one-to-one therapy in a group.
- To create sufficient closure so that the protagonist and group integrate the material presented in the session.
- To help the protagonist re-enter the group after the action portion of the session. 'She sees again, one by one, strangers and friends. Feelings of shame and guilt reach their climax. The tele-empathy transference complex moves from the stage to the audience. A group catharsis is gained' (Moreno 1953: 86).

- To facilitate role feedback from group members who played auxiliary roles in the session.
- To allow catharsis and integration of group members, who identify with the protagonist, and can share from their own experience.
- To protect the protagonist from distorted responses or analysis of the group. To attend to each member who shares similar experiences or moments.
- To share from his/her life history, if appropriate. The sharing of the director should not be done for the director to meet her own therapeutic needs. It should be focused more on constructive modelling for the protagonist.

SHARING

Sharing is a time for group catharsis and integration. It was meant as a 'love-back' rather than a feedback, discouraging analysis of the event and encouraging identifications. Points of most involvement by individual group members are identified, and each member finds out how he or she is like or unlike the protagonist. People are much more alike than different in behavioural responses. Often, as in Greek drama, the audience member is purged by watching the enactment of another's life story. The sharing is meant to capture this learning process and allow the group members to purge themselves of emotions or insights gained. It is also aimed at normalising the protagonist's experience by hearing how others are similarly involved at different levels of the same process. Sometimes, the effectiveness of the overall session can be measured by the depth of the sharing session. A further function of the sharing is a cool-down, a way of re-entering our individual realities after the group enactment. Appropriate closure is accomplished during this phase of the drama.

PROCESSING

Processing looks at the handling and processing of information after the psychodrama journey is completed. Learning takes place for the group, the protagonist and the director, particularly for those directors in training. During the processing phase, theoretical assumptions, clear rationale and therapeutic contract are discussed as part of directing the drama. The technical aspects are reviewed by the director, trainer and group members. How the director guided the protagonist from scene to scene, which therapeutic manoeuvres were successfully or unsuccessfully employed, why did they work and what could have been done differently, are all part of the processing discussion.

Feedback for the trainee director, as well as self and peer assessment, are invaluable. Though the processing is geared for the trainee director, protagonists report that they received a much clearer understanding from the processing than they did from the session itself. It is the cognitive unpacking of the session, aimed at the director's work, which helps group members, including the protagonist, understand scene by scene, intervention by intervention, what actually happened as the session went along. The protagonist may or may not attend, as they wish. Most would not miss it but for some it may be more input than they can take at that time. The length of time between the session and the time that the processing is done varies from country to country. For example, Giovanni Boria, from Milan, reports that their trainee directors often go home with a video of their direction and discuss it with their training group one month later. However, in most groups the processing is done within 24 hours of the psychodrama session.

TRAINING IN PSYCHODRAMA

Psychodrama training, which occurs at a postgraduate level, takes several years to complete. Psychodramatists have their own therapy and supervision as well as trainers who follow their clinical practice as well as their understanding of the process. Because psychodrama is a powerful therapeutic tool, only those trained in its use should be practising it. Trainee practitioners and trainers in Britain must be members of the British Psychodrama Association. Practitioners should be registered at their level of practice, with the BPA and the United Kingdom Council for Psychotherapy (UKCP). The situation is comparable in countries outside the UK with cultural differences. It is imperative that a Code of Ethics, which guides and protects both the client and the practitioner or trainer, is followed.

PRACTICAL CONSIDERATIONS IN USING PSYCHODRAMA

In psychodrama, as in other effective therapies, good training, ethical and physical safety precautions prevail. There are many issues to be handled with care, regarding the use of psychodrama as a method and many of the individual techniques (Karp: 1996).

First and foremost, it is important to have a purpose for using a specific technique within the method. Using a technique without purpose and forethought can be dangerous for the protagonist. Some techniques may be too powerful for a particular individual, some may be too esoteric and some too frightening. It is important to be aware of the ease with which an individual may be opened up by using this method as well as the difficulty and necessity of achieving closure. The psychodramatist must be careful not to provide a fantasy happy ending for a session that lacks a reality base. Cognition and theory is as important as expression and letting go.

There are scenes that require extreme sensitivity in their enactment, such as abortion, rape, incest and sexual abuse. In order to accomplish that which is necessary for the protagonist and still keep him/her intact, we must use care and discretion (Goldman and Morrison: 1984).

LITERATURE AND RESEARCH

A large body of literature has been published on therapeutic factors in group psychotherapy (Bloch and Crouch: 1985). Yalom (1975) found that interpersonal learning together with catharsis, cohesiveness and insight were the factors most valued by group members. Research into psychodrama is expanding, although limited, compared with some other forms of therapy.

Stuart Walsh (1996) observes that research into psychodrama has thus far focused on outcome research and positivistic paradigms such as those of Kellermann (1987, 1992) and Kipper (1978, 1989). Walsh suggests that psychodramatic research does not address itself to current non-outcome-oriented research paradigms which may be more relevant to assess and understand the process of psychodrama as well as measure the effects of that process. As Bradbury points out:

> the answer to a criticism of the validity of psychodrama lies in the cumulative evidence from both. Walsh points out that there is little guidance on how to conduct non-outcome-oriented research in psychodrama. This fact creates an open field for current researchers to generate ideas, define how it may be done; and to find their own integrative research practices. Walsh concludes that the quantum leap that has now to be made is in recognising that there are clear research grounds for treating these case studies less as simple anecdotes and formulate methods by which they can be actively researched and this research evaluated.
>
> (Bradbury 1995, p. 3)

Peter Kellerman (1992) found in two studies that insight, catharsis and interpersonal relations are therapeutic factors central to psychodramatic group psychotherapy. Grete Leutz suggests that making a conflict conscious, tangible, concrete and visible also makes it dispensable and thus the person can change (Leutz: 1985).

Adam Blatner (1996) has recently researched major psychodrama articles from books and journals not readily available. Some are from the American Society of Group Psychotherapy and Psychodrama journals. He has bound them into ten available notebooks containing the articles. James Sacks and colleagues (1995) have compiled a bibliography of all books and articles written on psychodrama. This catalogue, also available on computer disc, is indexed by subject and author. Both Blatner and Sacks et al. have made a major contribution to psychodramatic research and scholarship.

APPLICATION

Some professionals who have never experienced psychodrama for any substantial length of time, are afraid of it as a therapeutic method. Many tend to over-dramatise its process and emphasise its presumed dangers. Others exaggerate its virtues in a naive, superficial manner which violates the most elementary precepts of social psychology. Both groups are unaware of the relatively recent attempts that have been made to investigate, scientifically, psychodrama's therapeutic potential.

Kellerman (1992) stated that psychodrama, whether behaviouristic, psycho-analytic or existential-humanistic can make a contribution either on its own or as an adjunct to many branches of psychotherapy. He has emphasised that the method should be used with individuals who have adequate ego-strength, psychological-mindedness and a capacity for adaptive regression.

Psychodrama may be helpful for a wide variety of disorders including: relational, neurotic, psychotic and psychosomatic problems (Holmes *et al.* 1994; Leutz: 1985). Psychodrama is utilised for long-term, on-going groups, and individually or in groups, as a brief method of psychotherapy sharing many of the characteristics of crisis-oriented and focused therapy.

We hope you enjoy this book and its application.

BIBLIOGRAPHY

Blatner, A. (1996) *Psychodrama Papers*, private publication, 103 Crystal Springs Dr., Georgetown, Texas, USA.

Bloch, S. and Crouch, E. (1985) *Therapeutic Factors in Group Psychotherapy*, Oxford: Oxford University Press.

Bradbury, S. (1995) 'What Does Psychodrama Do? Using the Repertory Grid to Measure Change', *The British Journal of Psychodrama and Sociodrama*, Vol. 10 (BPA, Oxford).

Goldman, E. and Morrison, D. (1984) *Psychodrama: Experience and Process*, Dubuque, IA: Kendall Hunt.

Holmes, P. and Karp, M. (eds) (1991) *Psychodrama: Inspiration and Technique*, London: Routledge.

Holmes, P., Karp, M. and Watson, M. (eds) (1994) *Psychodrama since Moreno*, London: Routledge.

Karp, M. (1996) 'Introduction to Psychodrama', *Forum Journal of the International Association of Group Psychotherapy* (IAGP) vol. 5, 2, pp. 8–12.

Kellermann, P. (1987) 'Outcome Research in Classical Psychodrama', *Small Group Behaviours*, Vol. 18, Nov. (Sage Publications, London).

Kellermann, P. (1992) *Focus on Psychodrama*, London: Jessica Kingsley.

Kipper, D. (1978) 'Trends in the Research of the Effectiveness of Psychodrama: Retrospective and Prospective', *Journal of Group Psychotherapy, Psychodrama and Sociometry*, Vol. 31 (Heldref, McLean, VA).

Kipper, D. (1989) 'Psychodrama Research and the Study of Small Groups', International Journal of Small Group Research, vol. 5, pp. 4–27.

Leutz, G. (1985) 'What is Effective in Psychodrama?', in *Mettre sa vie en scène*, Paris, EPi-DDB.

Moreno, J.L. (1953) *Who Shall Survive?*, Beacon, NY: Beacon House.

Sacks, J., Bilaniuk, M. and Gendron, J. (1995) *Bibliography of Psychodrama*, New York Psychodrama Centre (71 Washington Place, NY, NY 10011–9184).

Walsh, S. (1996) 'A Review of Philosophical Paradigms and Methodological Views Expressed in Psychodramatic and Allied Literature', *British Journal of Psychodrama and Sociodrama*, Vol. 11 (BPA, Oxford).

Yalom, I.D. (1975) *The Theory and Practice of Group Psychotherapy*, 2nd rev. edn, New York: Basic Books.

DR JACOB LEVY MORENO

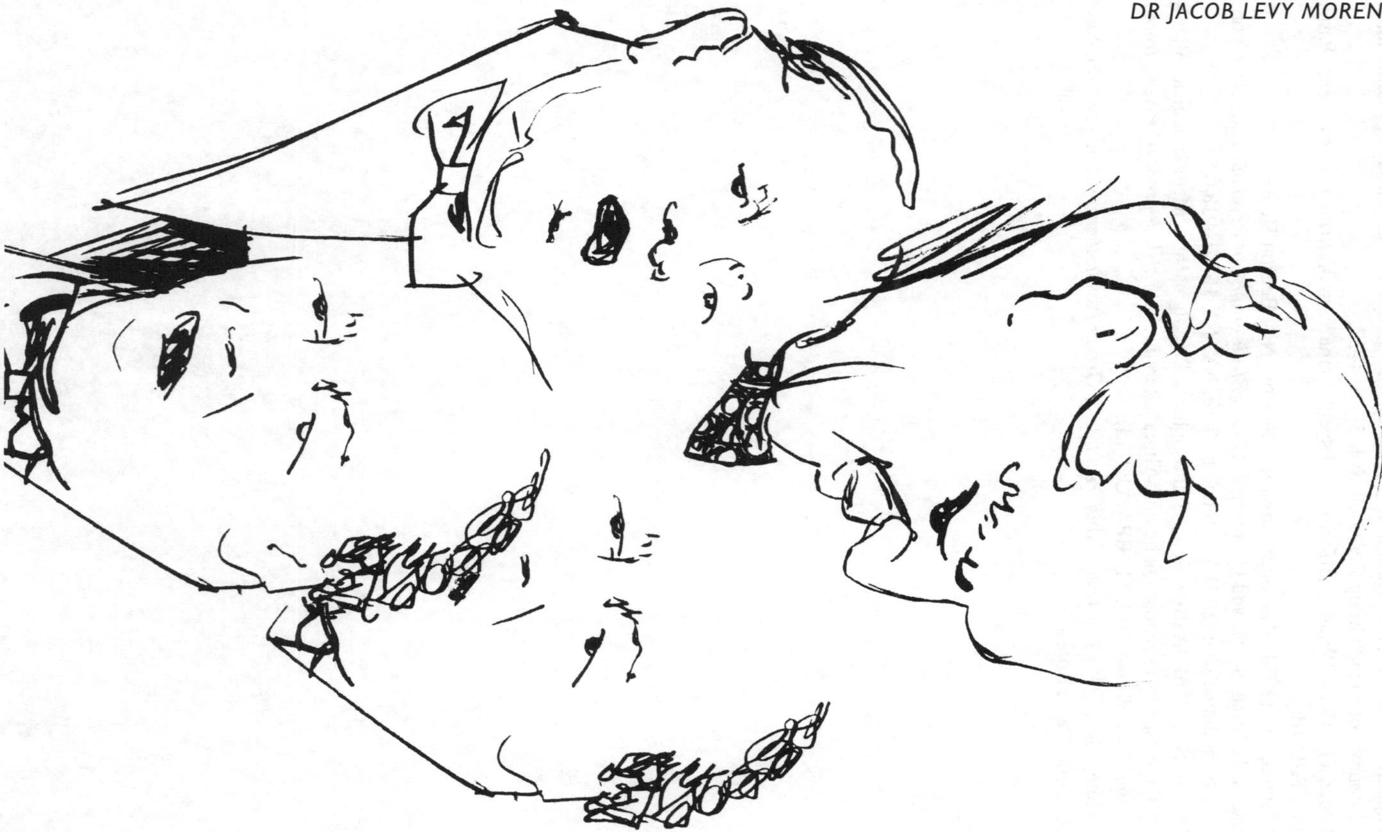

Chapter 2

The historical background of psychodrama

Peter Haworth

The central theme of this chapter is the philosophy and historical context behind the development of psychodrama, at a time when Europe had been torn apart by the ravages of the First World War. This period of history also saw the beginning of the rise of fascism. Moreno's development of group psychotherapy, psychodrama and sociometry drew together the social and psychological dimensions of human conflict. I will explore the historical roots of psychodrama in theatre and therapy, with a brief biography and social context of Moreno in Vienna in the 1920s. During this time, and since his death in 1974, psychodrama has become one of the major schools of psychotherapy, practised all over the world. I have chosen to cover the early philosophical roots of psychodrama in order to emphasise the fact that psychodrama is much more than a series of techniques. It is a method of exploration that includes psychotherapy but may also be used in other contexts. It arose from a particular historical period and it has a philosophical and psychological basis different from although connected with other psychotherapeutic methods. One important aspect of this difference is its positive view of humankind and its consequent emphasis on the exploration of social and political forms of human conflict as well as personal and familial pathology.

WHAT IS PSYCHODRAMA?

I am often asked the question, what is psychodrama? This may happen in a variety of different contexts and will therefore result in a number of different explanations. In an introductory talk on psychodrama to a group of clinical psychology trainees my opening sentence might be 'Psychodrama is a method of group psychotherapy developed by the Viennese psychiatrist, J.L. Moreno.' In conversations with a visiting plumber, come to fix the central heating, I could say that 'Psychodrama is a therapy that helps people try out different ways of dealing with problems without being punished for making mistakes.' To a client who has been referred to me by a GP for a psychotherapy assessment I might talk about psychodrama in terms of his/her own difficulties, 'You may set up a scene where you can tell your mother what you feel rather than pretending all is well.' In this case a potential group member is able to make a personal connection with psychodrama before experiencing the group itself. Each psychodramatic enactment is unique as every individual is unique and is formed by the relationship between the protagonist, the director and the group, at the moment and in the space that it is produced.

In the course of this chapter on the philosophy and history of psychodrama, I hope to show that an understanding of the history of psychodrama can help to more fully answer the question: What *is* psychodrama? Psychodrama is not just an action-based method of group psychotherapy. This description misses one of the most important aspects of modern psychodrama practice. Moreno developed psychodrama along with sociometry, sociodrama and group psychotherapy as ways of addressing social as well as personal issues at a time when Vienna was buzzing with the revolutionary ideas of Sigmund Freud and Karl Marx. Moreno's passion throughout his life was to develop the methods of sociometry, psychodrama and sociodrama to tackle the problems of the world, of society and of human interactions, rather than just the individual. He started from a hope for a better world and went to each individual reality. This passion arose from Moreno's early experiences in Romania and Austria at the turn of the century. But the philosophical origins of psychodrama are more ancient than that.

Moreno first used the term 'psychodrama' in 1919 (Moreno and Moreno 1970) but these early 'psychodramas' were very different from the method of psychodrama that we know today. It brought together ideas from different areas of Moreno's personal and professional life. It combined story telling with the children in the gardens of Vienna, early sociometric explorations in Mittendorf, his experiences as a doctor in Bad Voslau, the ideas of Freud and Marx, and the philosophical discussions that were important to him in Vienna. All these were present, in embryo, in 'The Theatre of Spontaneity' (*'das Stegreiftheater'*) in Vienna from 1922 to 1925 (Moreno 1947). Initially, the psychodrama was an active story telling on the part of the protagonist. The director's role was confined to facilitating the production. In the setting of the theatre, the therapeutic nature of the re-enactment was initially secondary to the performance and the entertainment of the audience. It was Moreno's objection to the lack of spontaneity in the recitation of formal theatre scripts, that led to the development of improvisations of real life experiences. From there, Moreno encouraged actors to use their own experiences and personal conflicts as a basis for the theatrical performance. Through experiment and application of ideas, Moreno continued to develop psychodrama for more than fifty years, first in Vienna and New York and later all over the world, picking up new ideas as he travelled.

THE INFLUENCES OF J.L. MORENO

Socrates

Socrates (469–399 BC) was a Greek philosopher who is said to have marked a major change in Western thought, although he left no writings of his own. Knowledge of his ideas is available only through the work of his followers (Plato 1954). He challenged the dominant view of man at that time, which was that we are basically self-seeking and that actions are for the preservation of the self. Socrates believed that this could not explain the achievements of mankind even then and spent his life talking to ordinary Athenian citizens to discover the real meaning of the self. He was tried for 'impiety and corrupting the youth of Athens' (Plato 1954) and was executed in 399 BC. Socrates was in some ways the original founder of existential philosophy that was to be a major influence on Moreno (Marineau 1989; Moreno 1995). One of the most important aspects of Moreno's influence, which is an inherent part of the philosophy of psychodrama, was his ability to pass on his genius. Interestingly, this was also said of Socrates and is what made him so dangerous:

> I don't think the Athenians are particularly concerned if they believe some-one to be clever, as long as he's not inclined to teach these skills of his. But if they think anybody makes others as well just as clever, they get angry with him.
>
> (Plato 1954)

Socrates' influence on Moreno is best illustrated by his view of the importance of his work with children in the parks of Vienna during the development of the method of psychodrama. 'My most important beginning was however in the gardens of Vienna' (Moreno and Moreno 1970: 13). Moreno learned psycho-drama from watching children play, then intervened to organise and structure their play, encouraging them to take action to challenge their circumstances, sometimes also involving parents in the process. The children began to take on Moreno's ideas and to challenge the values they had been taught at home and in school. On one occasion a group of children refused to go to see a film, asking instead to go out and see the real world. They talked about a mysterious young man in the park who lived in a tree. The school administration and the police started to search for him and a rumour began to spread that he might be a pederast. Moreno decided it was unwise to continue talking to children in this way but always stressed the value of these experiences in the development of psychodrama (Marineau 1989: 39).

Jesus and Christian story telling

Jeshua Ben Joseph was a Jew, prophet, teacher, healer and story teller who lived in Palestine at around 30 AD and was another major influence on Moreno. He was very taken up with a combination of the desire to change the world and compassion towards individual human suffering. Jesus's gathering the local people to tell stories, engaging his audience in a meaningful dialogue about the great moral issues of his time, encouraging the people to go forth and change the world and spread the gospel, had an enormous appeal to the young Moreno. In addition, Jesus was a great healer; he made the time to stop and heal the suffering of the individuals he encountered. People brought their relatives to Jesus to be cured and at the same time received the gospel. Interestingly, Zerka Toeman, later to become Moreno's wife and partner, first met Moreno, when she accompanied her psychotic sister to his Beacon clinic. One of the basic tenets of Christianity was that Jesus was the Messiah, the son of God, who had been sent to save the world. At the dawning of the twentieth century, as today, the people of the world were certainly in need of saving.

Christopher Colombus

In 1492, Christoforo Colombo, an Italian-born navigator, left Barcelona in Spain to search for a western route to Asia. Instead he is popularly credited with the discovery of the New World. He left with a largely Jewish crew, keen to escape the persecution that was unfolding. Later thousands of Jews were forced to convert to Catholicism or leave the country. Similarly, Moreno's ancestors left Spain and settled in Turkey. Many others of the fleeing Jews were persecuted, many were enslaved, raped or killed. After Moreno arrived in America in 1925 he invented many versions of the following story of his birth. I quote here a more tongue-in-cheek version from *The First Psychodramatic Family* (Moreno *et al.* 1964: 7–9).

> Among the many pioneers who arrived in this country was Johnny Psychodramatist. As the story goes, he was born one stormy night on a ship sailing the Black Sea in the southern parts of Europe. He crossed the Atlantic and settled here on the shores of the Hudson River.

This version of the story, I believe demonstrates most clearly his identification and at times confusion, with his own history.

Sephardic Jews are those who strictly follow the customs developed by the Jews of medieval Spain and Portugal. After their expulsion from Spain in 1492, many moved to the Balkans. Moreno's ancestors were such people. The cultural history of being a refugee and vilified as *Marranos* (pigs) could well have influenced Moreno's view of the world.

Sigmund Freud

Freud (1856–1939) was the founder of psychoanalysis and certainly the most famous and influential of psychological theorists. He was a Jew, born in Moravia, now in the Czech Republic. His family moved to Germany and later to Vienna, where he lived for most of his life. Like Moreno, Freud's father was a struggling merchant and his mother had high hopes for her eldest son. Freud was responsible for the development of a whole new field of scientific enquiry into the internal world of the human mind. Freud's ideas have become so much part of our culture that even the most vehement anti-Freudians unwittingly use and are influenced by his ideas. He is often linked with Marx, Einstein and Picasso as having had a major impact on twentieth-century thought. Although sometimes negative, Freud's influence on Moreno was enormous. Unfortunately Moreno's inability to fully acknowledge and make explicit Freudian influences, in my opinion, has been one of the factors that held back the development of psychodramatic theory. Had Moreno been able to build on the enormous amount of theoretical work undertaken by psychoanalysts, he would have been able to develop sociometry and role theory, built on the foundations of psychoanalysis, yet differing in philosophy and technique. This lack of a solid theoretical basis has led to many practitioners uncritically incorporating other methods, particularly psycho-analysis, into psychodramatic work. The post-Freudian development of object relations theory, which is very easily applicable to psychodrama (Holmes 1992) has become widely incorporated into the language of psychodramatists.

JACOB LEVY – THE EARLY YEARS, FROM BUDAPEST TO VIENNA

Moreno was born Jacob Levy on 18 May 1889. His mother, Paulina Ianescu, was just 15 when he was born. His father, Moreno Levy, was a travelling salesman and spent very little time with his wife and children, leaving Paulina to fend for herself. Moreno's relationship with his mother was extraordinary in a number of ways, and along with his early idealised fantasy relationship with his absent father, formed a basis for his almost lifelong struggle to come to terms with his own identity. Although a practising Jew, Paulina was educated in a Catholic convent school, until she married Moreno's father when she was 14. Her experience, combining both Jewish and Christian traditions, was to have a major influence on Moreno. When Moreno was only twelve months old he became seriously ill from rickets. A gypsy told Paulina that he would recover if he was put on his back in sand warmed by the sun. She said that he would grow up to be a great man and that people would come from all over the world to see him. Paulina took this to heart and the boy grew with his mother's belief that he would be some kind of Messiah. Moreno's identification with Jesus remained an important issue throughout his life, but particularly in the early years. He continuously tried to live out his mother's fantasy with consequent periods of deep despair, when he inevitably failed. His father's absence, coupled with Moreno's idealisation of him, developed into a belief that he was his own father. This culminated with his gradual adoption of his father's first name as his surname. He also made up a story about his own birth that he repeats in several of his writings (Moreno *et al.* 1964: 7–10; Moreno 1985: 6).

His omnipotent wish to magically resolve conflicts internally and externally made Moreno's early life full of twists and changes in direction. Early in his days as a medical student in Vienna, as mentioned earlier, Moreno would spend time in the park telling stories to groups of children. He later encouraged them to stand up to the oppression of family and school and set up a children's theatre group, with presentations either in the park or in a small hall turned into a theatre.

In 1913, Moreno, accompanied by Dr Wilhelm Gruen, a specialist in venereal disease and Carl Colbert, a newspaperman, started working with the prostitutes in Vienna. Moreno was ' . . . not motivated by a desire to reform the girls . . . I had in mind what LaSalle and Marx had done for the working class . . . ' (Moreno 1953).

Moreno and Freud

As far as is known, Moreno only met Freud once whilst he was in Vienna. This 'encounter' is referred to by Moreno several times in his writings, but never by Freud (Marineau 1984). Moreno's hostility to psychoanalysis is clear from much of his writing. Moreno was, however, heavily influenced by Freud and psychoanalytic theory in positive as well as negative ways. He respected Freud as a scientist, acknowledging Freud's fundamental contribution to the development of theories of the mind (Moreno 1967). He had close friendships with some psychoanalysts and psychoanalytic psychotherapists, particularly Helene Deutch in Vienna and later S. Foulkes in London. Discussions with Foulkes led on to the establishment of the International Association of Group Psychotherapy, which Moreno founded in 1951.

Moreno's hostility to psychoanalysis as a method was inflamed in 1931 by the psychoanalyst Dr A. Brill's presentation of 'a psychoanalysis of Abraham Lincoln'. Moreno admired Lincoln as a leader. He saw Brill's 'psychoanalysis' of Lincoln as an attack on a man he had never met. This led to a valuable clarification of Moreno's views on psychoanalysis (and Brill), although it is titled, perhaps somewhat 'tongue in cheek', *The Psychodrama of Sigmund Freud*. Moreno's main criticism of psychoanalytic theory was its negativism, its 'tendency to associate the origins of life with calamity' (Moreno 1967: 10) and with the idea that 'pain and evil dominate the universe'. His other major criticism was that it 'permits analysis and excludes action' (Moreno 1967: 11). For Moreno, action was paramount.

Changing the world

An important concept of Moreno's original philosophy and the classical method is that it is not enough for psychotherapy to address the internal world only. Internal conflicts and individual pathology are the product of an interaction with the external world of family and society as a whole. 'A truly therapeutic procedure cannot have less an objective than the whole of mankind' (Moreno 1953: 3). With help, people can be encouraged to change their world. For Moreno this was, in his early life, often confused with an omnipotent fantasy of changing *the* world. Of course, the world is in need of change, and we are each responsible for enabling change but Moreno was often alone in his fantasy that he was the only one to effect that change.

Playing God or being God

Moreno struggled for much of his life with his own omnipotent and narcissistic fantasies. His mother's projection of her own desires perhaps fed his omnipotence. At times he played God and at times he became God. Perhaps one of his most important pieces of writing was *The Words of the Father* (Moreno 1971). Moreno role-reversed with God and wrote on the walls of his house in Bad Voslau, then published these writings as the words of God. Hidden in the 'madness' of hearing the voice of God are some important notions of the philosophy of psychodrama, which he struggled to hold on to at times of despair at his own failures. It is interesting to note that in later conversations with students he used to say: 'the difference between me and a psychotic is that I called in a publisher' (Marcia Karp, personal communication). It seems quite likely that Moreno's hearing voices was some sort of dissociative experience, perhaps related to his childhood relationship with his father. In the preface to the 1971 edition of *The Words of the Father* Moreno says: 'This book contains the words of God, our Father, the Creator of the Universe.' But this creator is a co-creator. 'How can one thing create another thing unless the other thing creates the one thing?' (Moreno 1971: 53). Moreno's philosophy holds that the central core is the relationship, not the self. No one can exist without the other. We are jointly and mutually responsible for each other and for each other's action. The child is creator of the parent and the parent is creator of the child. They are a role relationship, without one there cannot be the other. If Moreno is God, then we are all God. Moreno's struggle with his own megalomania was finally resolved by expanding it to the entire universe. Everyone is omnipotent. In his hospital in Beacon, everyone, patients and staff were called 'Doctor' (Moreno 1995).

Moreno and the theatre

As mentioned earlier, Moreno was involved in many different aspects of the theatre. He saw the theatre and later television as a way of reaching more people than was possible in one-to-one dyads. If he had lived today he would probably have been more interested in television for that reason. In Vienna, Moreno was unhappy about the way theatre was presented. He believed that the spontaneity was in the writing of the plays. It was wrong for actors to be given a script to read that was written by someone else. It squashed creativity and at times had a negative effect on their personality. In one of Moreno's 'stories' he got on to the stage in a performance of *Thus Spoke Zarathustra* and told the actors to speak their own words and not those of the script. He was thrown out! He set up his own theatre company and put forward his own radical new theatre design to facilitate spontaneous theatre and audience participation. The *Living Newspaper* brought the day's news on to the stage and was popular in Vienna and later on in the United States (Moreno 1946; Haworth 1988). As sociometry and therapeutic psychodrama began to occupy more of his time and energies, his direct involvement in the professional theatre ceased and he began to use it in his own work.

Jacob Moreno Levy – life in transition

As the years passed Moreno grew more distant from his father and at the same time he took on aspects of his father's identity. He became his own father, by incorporating his father's first name as his middle name and later as his surname. Many of the activities he engaged in were beginning to crumble and he was disturbed by the hostile reception he was receiving. He believed that Europe was no longer the place for new creative ideas. He was frustrated in every direction.

JACOB MORENO LEVY – THE LATER YEARS, VIENNA TO NEW YORK

In 1926 Moreno finally left Austria for the United States, leaving behind parts of his past that he wished to forget. With his new identity, Dr Moreno had become the father, a father to himself and would accept no man in the role of father. He was to be an all new, all spontaneous creative man. He moved through life from one idea, one creation to the next, with only psychodrama remaining throughout. Even the success of his method of sociometry was partially abandoned for others to continue without him.

Sociometry and group psychotherapy

It was to be sociometry, the science of interpersonal communication that first brought Moreno the public acclaim that he believed he deserved. In 1933, a few dozen sociometric charts were exhibited at a convention of the Medical Society of New York. Moreno described this event as the start of the sociometric movement (Moreno 1955: 5). The first sociometric exploration was in 1915 in Mittendorf, a refugee camp for Italian peasants. Moreno was a student Officer of Health. Here was an opportunity for the young Moreno to watch a community develop from its birth, its *status nascendi* (Moreno 1995). He observed the development of attractions and repulsions, of love and hate. Through this experience he developed the sociogram, as a method of measuring group interactions. This tool led him to offering solutions to social problems of the camp. Sadly, these were not taken up. Following his move to the United States ten years later, Moreno had much more success. In his major work *Who Shall Survive?* (1953) Moreno includes a massive 'Sociometric Exploration in a Girls School in Hudson'.

Moreno saw his development of psychodrama and group psychotherapy as separate methods (Moreno 1995). In New York, Moreno developed group psychotherapy using sociometric tests and explorations. Modern psychodrama has become primarily a group psychotherapy by developing the process to combine aspects of sociometry within the psychodrama sessions, for example in the protagonist selection, where group members are asked to choose the person who they most identify with. As mentioned earlier, Moreno is credited with the first use of group therapy, with a group of prostitutes in Vienna. Whilst he was a medical student, Moreno took part in a project to improve the health of prostitutes and to help prevent the spread of venereal diseases. Part of this process involved discussion groups, which were initially addressed by speakers on various health topics. The group, however, continued to meet and gained a lot from the support they received from each other in the group. Moreno saw the development of group psychotherapy as separate from psychodrama (Moreno 1995). Psychodrama was possible in pairs as well as groups. It was the active techniques from sociometry, that enable the measurement of group dynamics, which marks a major difference with analytic approaches. For Moreno, one major aim of group psychotherapy is social change, not simple analysis of the individual problems.

Psychiatry and Sociatry

Continuing the theme of developing and working with the social and political dimensions of human suffering, Moreno had a somewhat ambivalent relationship with fellow psychiatrists in the USA. He moved to the USA from Vienna to escape from religious and professional persecution. He had the idea that the 'New World' would be full of opportunities and interest in his new ideas of spontaneity and creativity. Instead he faced similar reactions to his ideas as in Vienna. Psychiatry, then even more than now, was dominated by the chemical or even surgical approach. The predominant view was that mental illness would eventually be cured by the discovery of a chemical cause, or of a specific diseased part of the brain. The one main challenge to these ideas came from psychoanalysis, not from Moreno. But psychoanalysis placed the causes of human misery on the basic destructiveness of human instincts from the 'id' that had to be mitigated by the actions of the 'superego', largely controlled by fear of father's retribution. For many of the reasons outlined earlier, Moreno vehemently rejected this notion. His antidote was the development of a new science, perhaps a new branch of medicine, the method of 'sociatry'. Sociatry would bring together sociometry, group psychotherapy, psychodrama and sociodrama into a study of and, more importantly, the resolution of the ills of society. Unfortunately the world was not yet ready, and still isn't, to accept such a radical step forward. In order to survive and to have some of his ideas practically used and valued, Moreno had to compromise and concentrate on areas that were acceptable. First and foremost among these was psychodrama. In my view, an important part of this decision to concentrate on psychodrama, rather than on some of the ideas that first excited him and first brought him recognition, was the influence of Zerka Moreno.

Sociodrama

Sociodrama was a consequent development, arising from psychodrama. Moreno first saw psychodrama as a special form of psychodrama rather than a method in its own right (Moreno 1946: 353). Moreno had realised that at times there were bigger social issues that prevented the resolution of an interpersonal conflict. Sociodrama was developed to address these wider social and cultural issues. Moreno gave an example of two neighbours arguing over the fence between their houses (1946: 353). Behind this was an inter-racial conflict about boundaries between countries. Sociodrama provides a framework for the exploration of inter-group conflicts of class, gender, race and religion using an action method similar to but different from psychodrama (Haworth 1984; Garcia and Sternberg 1988). In sociodrama, the group is the protagonist. In psychodrama, the individual is the protagonist.

ZERKA T. MORENO

No historical analysis, even as brief as this, could be complete without emphasising the central importance of the contribution played by Zerka Toeman Moreno, both in conjunction with J.L. and in her own right. She first met Moreno in 1941 when she accompanied her sister to the Beacon sanatorium. Moreno immediately recognised her potential both as a colleague and partner. They were eventually married in 1949. Zerka gradually came to play an increasing role in the development of psychodrama, eventually becoming director of training at Beacon. She played a central part initially as a 'translator' of his ideas. Later, she has become one of the greatest proponents of the method of psychodrama. She was particularly responsible for popularising the development of psychodrama in a clinical setting, setting the framework for psychodrama as it is known today. Her simple translation of Moreno's ideas is well illustrated in 'Psychodramatic Rules, Techniques and Adjunctive Methods' (in Moreno and Moreno 1969) and in 'The Psychodramatic Model of Madness' (Moreno and Moreno 1984). The first paper lays the framework for the philosophical, psychological and practical structure of psychodrama as it is today. Zerka became Moreno's translator from a dense Germanic philosophical presentation of his ideas, to plain simple English that is easy to understand. In addition, she has since his death in 1974 continued to travel the world, superbly demonstrating the method of classical psychodrama and promoting Moreno's ideas to further generations of psychodrama trainees.

PSYCHODRAMA IN BRITAIN

Psychodrama took some time to become firmly established in Britain. Moreno himself came to Britain, giving several demonstrations of his work at the Maudsley Hospital and elsewhere beginning in 1951. Later, several trainers from the USA came to Britain in the 1960s and 1970s but it was not until Marcia Karp moved to Britain to establish the Holwell Psychodrama Centre in 1974 (the same year as Moreno's death), that psychodrama was able to become an established method of psychotherapy. Psychodrama began to be accepted as a method in both clinical and non-clinical areas. Marcia Karp began to train others and to establish a training centre at Holwell. At around the same time, Doreen and Dean Elefthery ran European training groups in psychodrama. The Holwell Centre, however, awarded the first diplomas in psychodrama in 1981. The British Psychodrama Association was founded in the summer of 1984 by myself, Marcia Karp, Ken Sprague and Susie Taylor (then Coombes). Zerka Moreno enthusiastically launched the first British journal of psychodrama later that same year. By 1997 there were seven training organisations in Britain, with more than twenty trainers and seventy qualified practitioners. Psychodrama has become an established and respected method of psychotherapy especially in parts of the NHS. In 1991 the British Psychodrama Association was accepted into the Humanistic and Integrative Psychotherapy Section of the United Kingdom Council for Psychotherapy. The necessary concentration on the development of psychodrama psychotherapy has unfortunately led to a temporary neglect of the non-clinical use of psychodrama and sociodrama. Whilst it has been important to establish psychodrama's place in the world of psychotherapy, it is equally valuable to develop its non-clinical applications, particularly in education, industry and in other areas of life outside the clinic. Three different strands of clinical psychodrama have developed in Britain. The first, classical psychodrama has seen refinements of the process, with development of Moreno's role theory, with dialogue about the use of spontaneous doubles, and with the use of specific techniques in working with survivors of childhood sexual abuse. Developments have taken place along the same line and with a basically Morenian philosophy. Psychoanalytic psychodrama has incorporated different aspects of the psychodynamic method, particularly moving away from physical touch and director sharing and sometimes paying more attention to analysis of the group process using psychoanalytic rather than sociometric techniques. Person-centred psychodrama (mainly developed by Jenny Biancardi) has integrated aspects of Carl Rogers's approach and presents psychodrama in the round. It is less directed and encourages spontaneous group interaction, doubling and discussion. Although there has been a gradual introduction of other theories and developments of the method, most British practitioners have remained close to the classical method, although perhaps adapting it to their particular interests and client group.

The number of psychodrama practitioners is continuing to grow both nationally and internationally and Britain is taking its place in the international development of psychodrama.

The development of clinical psychodrama

Psychodrama therapy began to develop in Britain in the 1960s and 1970s as part of the personal growth movement, alongside Gestalt therapy, transactional analysis and Rogerian encounter groups. Often groups of people would meet as self-help groups, or led by someone who had attended a workshop or two and had seen the power of the method, or even just read about it in a book. This approach obviously had some dangers and it is likely that some people's negative experiences led to some suspicion of psychodrama as 'dangerous'.

Trainers from the United States, particularly Marcia Karp, stressed the need for a full training but also encouraged mental health professionals to use some of the techniques in their work. This led to a more professional approach to the development of psychodrama as a method of psychotherapy. By the end of the 1970s a number of Holwell trainees, mainly psychiatric nurses and occupational therapists, with some psychiatrists and clinical psychologists, had begun to introduce psychodrama into mental health settings, particularly day hospitals and day centres, usually as part of a programme of different therapeutic activities and groups.

Later in the 1980s, long-term out-patient groups were run, often from a model learnt from group-analytic psychotherapy. A few weekly private groups were also set up. Psychodrama psychotherapy has, however, remained very strongly linked to the NHS and there remain far more NHS groups than private groups. By the end of the 1990s psychodrama was being used with a wide variety of client groups including people with learning disabilities (Sprague 1991), families (Farmer 1995) and with survivors of sexual abuse (Karp 1991, Corti and Casson 1990).

In an exciting new development in Oxford (Haworth and Thomson 1997), a number of psychodrama groups have been run as part of a primary care-based mental health team at St Bartholomew's Medical Centre. Psychodrama has become a major part of the mental health provision with three general long-term psychodrama groups, a group for young women, a group for women survivors of sexual abuse and two integrated psychotherapy groups, combining psychodrama with other therapeutic methods.

BIBLIOGRAPHY

Corti, P. and Casson, J. (1990) 'Dramatherapy into Psychodrama: An Account of a Therapy Group for Women Survivors of Sexual Abuse', *Journal of the British Psychodrama Association*, 5(2): 37–53.

Farmer, C. (1995) *Psychodrama and Systemic Therapy*, London: Karnac Books.

Hare, P.A. and Hare, J.R. (1996) *J.L. Moreno*, London: Sage.

Haworth, P. (1984) 'Psychodrama and Sociodrama, a Comparison', *Journal of the British Psychodrama Association*, 1(1): 36–40.

Haworth, P. and Thomson, S. (1997) 'Psychodrama as a Major Component of a Primary Care-Based Community Mental Health Team', Oxford: Unpublished Paper.

Holmes, P. (1992) *The Inner World Outside: Object Relations Theory and Psychodrama*, London: Routledge.

Karp, M. (1991) 'Psychodrama and Piccalilli', in *Psychodrama: Inspiration and Technique*, edited by P. Holmes and M. Karp, London: Routledge.

Marineau, R. (1989) *Jacob Levy Moreno 1889–1974*, London: Routledge.

Moreno, J.L. (1941) *The Words of the Father*, New York: Beacon House.

Moreno, J.L. (1947) *The Theatre of Spontaneity*, New York: Beacon House.

Moreno, J.L. (1953) *Who Shall Survive?*, New York: Beacon House.

Moreno, J.L. (1955) *Preludes to My Autobiography*, New York: Beacon House.

Moreno, J.L. (1967) *The Psychodrama of Sigmund Freud*, New York: Beacon House.

Moreno, J.L. (1985) *The Autobiography of J.L. Moreno M.D.*, Moreno Archives, Harvard University, Boston, USA.

Moreno, J.L. (1995) 'The Voice of J.L. Moreno: Interview by James Sacks from 1965', Barnstaple, Devon: Holwell Centre Tape.

Moreno, J.L. and Moreno, Z.T. (1969) *Psychodrama: Third Volume*, New York: Beacon House.

Moreno, J.L. and Moreno, Z.T. (1970) *The Origins of the Encounter and Encounter Groups*, New York: Beacon House.

Moreno J.L., Moreno, Z.T. and Moreno, Jonathan (1964) *The First Psychodramatic Family*, New York: Beacon House.

Pitzele, M. (1980) 'Moreno's Chorus', *Group Psychotherapy, Psychodrama and Sociometry*, 23 (Washington: Heldref).

Plato (1954) *The Last Days of Socrates*, translated by Hugh Tredennick and Harold Tarrant, Harmondsworth: Penguin Books.

Scheff, T.J. (1979) *Catharsis in Healing, Ritual and Drama*, Berkeley: University of California Press.

Sprague, K. (1991) 'Everybody's a Somebody', in *Psychodrama: Inspiration and Technique*, edited by P. Holmes and M. Karp, London: Routledge.

PRINCIPLES OF PSYCHODRAMA

Chapter 3

Principles of psychodrama

Kate Bradshaw Tauvon

Am I only a corpse that will rot and turn into meaningless dust? Or is this consciousness that I now feel extending into the cosmos the most real thing there is? In other words, am I nothing or am I God?

(Moreno 1941 quoted in Holmes et al. 1994: 98)

Underpinning Moreno's 'Philosophy of the Moment' is a profound belief in the infinite spontaneity and creativity of human beings all of whom are considered equal in status. His first texts written between 1908–1919 – 'Homo Juvenis', 'Das Reich der Kinder' (The Realm of the Children), 'Die Gottheit als Komoediant' (The Godhead as Comedian), 'Die Gottheit als Autor' (The Godhead as Author) and 'Die Gottheit als Redner' (The Godhead as Orator or Preacher) (see Martineau 1989) – all reflect aspects of Moreno's philosophy and were the basis for his development of *axiodrama*, a forerunner of psychodrama which explores issues of ethics, cosmic relationships or values. Protagonists are, for instance, able to review their relationship with God, life, death, the universe, Satan, the future or perfection.

According to the principle of the I-god, a philosophy developed by Moreno around 1918 in post-war Vienna, each person is both the one who creates and the one who is created and is therefore responsible for the world which they have created and everyone and everything in it. It might be too simply expressed but may be of use to suggest that Moreno means that each of us tends to project our inner world on to the world around us and it is therefore up to each of us to correct the resulting distortions in our view of the world, by the reduction of transferential relationships and the development of *tele* (I define *tele* later in this chapter). Moreno promotes the development of each person's maximum involvement in life and every person's subjective reality is accepted as equally valid.

Philosophers who influenced Moreno are known to include Socrates, Dante, Kierkegaard and Nietzsche (see Marineau 1989: 49). From these philosophical roots, Moreno came to emphasise the primacy of the original encounter and to contend that human life develops against a background of the group in which one lives and action. He, among others, stressed the necessity to alter the form taken by culture to arrive at a more 'fruitful chaos'. Malcolm Pines, a British group-analytic psychotherapist, has pointed out that the schools of psychotherapy have different styles and metapsychologies. He likens Moreno's to the Dionysian:

> In Greek mythology . . . Dionysias, Pan . . . brings from his Asiatic sources a super-abundance of creative energy with which to celebrate life that leads to a desire for destruction in order to bring about change. . . . Dionysias is always surrounded by a Bacchantic crowd, bringing cathartic release from the oppression of individuality.
>
> (Pines 1987: 16–17)

Moreno also stressed the importance of 'experiencing' reality as a means of change rather than just talking about it, giving prime importance to the body. Moreno's sensitivity to bodily experience was important in the development of the concept of *tele*.

In a letter to an American psychodramatist, Ira Greenberg, dated 17 June 1970 (Greenberg 1974: 122) Moreno listed nine principal concepts of psychodrama: (1) warming-up principle, (2) creativity, (3) spontaneity, (4) encounter, (5) tele, (6) co-conscious and co-unconscious, (7) role, (8) role vs. ego and (9) role reversal which I will now use as a basis for describing the central principles of his theoretical frame. In addition to these nine concepts I will describe a tenth, the centrality of action: (10) action.

PRINCIPLE OF WARMING UP

Spontaneity shows itself through the warming up of a person to a new setting. All activities have a warming-up phase, before they are carried out. Take, for example, going to the cinema. Before you go, you think about the idea, think which film you would like to see and who you might go with. You may ring a friend, look in the newspaper to see what films are available and check times of buses. There are myriad small details you will attend to before you find yourself sitting in the cinema looking at the film. An inadequate warm-up will lead to an inadequately carried out activity. If you don't ring the friend they won't be there. If you don't check at which cinema your chosen film is being shown, you will probably not see the film of your choice.

In psychodrama the same can be said. The warming-up process includes details which promote an atmosphere within which a psychodrama can be enacted and is designed to increase the level of spontaneity in the group. An inadequate warm-up leads to an inadequate drama. Susie Taylor, in her chapter about the warm-up in this book, describes these processes in detail (Chapter 4).

Moreno called the warming-up process 'the *operational* expression of spontaneity' (Moreno 1953/1993: 14).

CREATIVITY AND SPONTANEITY

Moreno, in his letter to Greenberg, listed these two factors separately but as they are so intricately interconnected I will talk about them in relation to each other here.

Moreno (1953/1993: 13,19) taught us that spontaneity operates in the present, here and now. It is the energy which moves a person towards responding adequately in a situation they have not previously experienced or facilitates the capacity to come up with a new response in a familiar situation. Based on his experimental study, spontaneity came to be considered through its four characteristic expressions:

- the spontaneity which goes into the activation of cultural conserves and social stereotypes (the concept of cultural conserves are described later in this chapter);
- the spontaneity which goes into creating new organisms (considered later in this chapter, under the heading of 'co-conscious and co-unconscious'), new forms of art, and new patterns of environment;
- the spontaneity which goes into the formation of free expressions of personality;
- the spontaneity which goes into the formation of adequate responses to novel situations.

(Moreno 1946/1980: 89)

Creativity only comes to full fruition with the help of spontaneity as it is spontaneity which catalyses its substance. The degree of adequacy of response to events is brought about and facilitated by spontaneity and depends on the extent of familiarity with a situation. In a novel situation a person may have: (a) no response, (b) an old response, (c) a new response (Moreno 1946/1980: 92). An adequate new response requires a sense of timing, a sense of appropriateness and autonomy.

Spontaneity is a catalyst for creative activity. If placed on an imagined line representing a continuum, it would be positioned at the one end and anxiety at the other. Imagine a fulcrum now in the middle of the line, since they have a see-saw relationship, the higher a person's level of anxiety the lower the degree of spontaneity and vice-versa. Spontaneity should be differentiated from impulsivity, which lacks any form of creativity and can rather be described metaphorically as jumping from the frying pan into the fire. A person may have creative ideas but without spontaneity they cannot be put into practice and realised.

A creative act results often in a product: a poem, a symphony, a painting, a play; these are what Moreno called *cultural conserves.* In the moment they are complete the creative act is over and unless they are subsequently approached with spontaneity they may lose their creative quality. We have all heard a set piece of music played with varying degrees of spontaneity and the results can be disparate. Even our level of spontaneity when seeing for example the *Mona Lisa* can vary and what on one occasion can be a profound experience, on another leaves us flat. So creativity is catapulted into being by spontaneity. Spontaneity is not a pre-existent reservoir as libido is considered to be by psychoanalysts or as energy is deemed to be according to the law of the conservation of energy. 'It is not only the process within the person, but also the flow of feeling in the direction of the spontaneity state of another person' (Moreno 1946/1980: 81).

The idea of consciously developing spontaneity may seem paradoxical, since spontaneity is often equated with impulsiveness, but psychodrama predominantly works at the level of training up group members' spontaneity and creativity in order to more adequately respond in a given moment to life events. This can be done by continuously placing group members in situations which demand a response and providing the opportunity for them to try out a range of alternatives with the help of the director and the group. I am reminded here of Moreno's suggestion that what is functional in the free association in psychoanalysis is not the association of words but the spontaneity which propels them to associate (Moreno 1946/1980: xii).

ENCOUNTER

In the spring of 1914–15 Moreno published in three parts *Einladung zu einer Begegnung* (Invitation to an Encounter) which included his first written definition of encounter, the concept which became central to the existential movement. In his motto for *Psychodrama: First Volume*, he used the idea of two people exchanging eyes to comprehend and know each other.

> A meeting of two: eye to eye, face to face.
> And when you are near I will tear your eyes out
> and place them instead of mine
> and you will tear my eyes out
> and will place them instead of yours,
> then I will look at you with your eyes
> and you will look at me with mine.
>   (Moreno 1946/1980: preface)

The principle of encounter, is essential to the philosophy of psychodrama, the ability to meet others, being as present and aware as is possible and each being capable of mentally reversing roles with the other. The concept of encounter shifted the focus of psychotherapy from the separate individual level, to that of the primary dyad and in that way to the interpersonal level, the area between people. In this way Moreno's theory of interpersonal relations was to contribute to a new epoch in the history of psychotherapy. He writes:

The theory of interpersonal relations is based upon the 'primary dyad,' the idea and experience of the meeting of two actors, the concrete-situational event preliminary to all interpersonal relations. The limiting factor in the individual centred psychologies and mass centred psychologies is the non-presence of the 'other actor.'

(Moreno 1993: 36)

It was this shifting of focus which was to differentiate psychodrama at that time from other forms of psychotherapy.

Encounter is the experience which occurs when a person immediately and meaningfully confronts himself in relation to important people either in his life or as portrayed by *auxiliaries* on the psychodrama stage. Zerka Moreno has, in the last few years, preferred to use the simpler term 'auxiliary', without the added 'ego' and what she has referred to as the 'auxiliary world' (Blatner and Blatner 1988: 160). The auxiliary does not only represent aspects of the protagonist's ego but also other aspects of himself.

Within a psychodrama it is not only possible to encounter *the other* but even to encounter *the self* (see Williams 1989: 17). Through the use of the empty chair technique or with the help of auxiliaries, it is possible to *concretise* and dramatise the self. It soon becomes apparent that the self is not one figure but several, existing in what can be called a system of aspects of the self. This system can be represented on the stage where a dialogue can be created, between such parts, inevitably changing the quality of the relationship (or tele) between these aspects of the self. This improved inner tele occurs as the relationship becomes visible through the dramatic dialogue. The relationship between these inner aspects of self is known as *auto-tele*.

Concretisation is the term used to describe the act of converting the concept of a role, a figure, a metaphor or scene into a concrete image on the psychodrama stage. Aspects of a person or her world can be concretised on the psychodrama stage by dramatically focusing on her operational roles and the pattern of surrounding role-relations.

TELE AND TRANSFERENCE

Tele is a concept born of Moreno's work on *sociometry*, the measurement of relationships between people. Tele describes the flow of feeling between people and expresses itself in terms of authentic here-and-now exchanges, or encounter. It was deemed by Moreno to be the decisive factor for therapeutic progress (Moreno 1946/1980: xviii) and is the process which attracts individuals to one another or which repels them. Most communication contains a mixture of both transference and tele but a goal of psychodrama is to minimise transference aspects of a relationship and maximise authentic communication. I will describe tele in relation to transference in some depth as it is so central to Moreno's theoretical approach.

The etymological root of the word 'tele' is from the Greek and means 'far, influence into distance' (Moreno 1946/1980: xi). It represents the capacity to sense, without words, the relationship between people and is the invisible bond which holds groups together. It is a two-way process, in contrast to the one-way feeling of empathy.

Transference is a concept born of Freud's psychoanalytic theory. It refers to the process, both in therapy and in real life, of unconsciously re-enacting patterns of relating, in current relationships, which have been learnt in infancy and *repressed*. A useful discussion of the concept of transference from the perspective of a psychodramatist is taken up by Paul Holmes in *The Inner World Outside: Object Relations Theory and Psychodrama* (1992).

According to Moreno's theory of child development, tele is initially undifferentiated. He defines the infant's 'first universe' as the first two developmental phases, in which he goes through two periods: first the period of 'all identity' where all things including himself are not differentiated but are experienced as one total entity; the second period is that of 'differentiated all-identity' or 'all-reality' in which people and things including himself have become differentiated (Moreno 1946/1980: 68). There is as yet no significant difference made between the real and the imagined, between animated and dead, between appearances of things (mirror images) and things as they really are.

With time, a tele for objects differentiates itself from a tele for people, positive and negative tele become distinct, as do tele for real objects and tele of imagined objects. This occurs at the onset of what Moreno defines as the 'second universe' (1946/1980: 72), when the personality normally becomes divided into two parts or pathways; one which warms up to reality acts and another which warms up to fantasy acts. These parts organise themselves and, depending on their degree of separateness, a person has greater or lesser difficulty in switching between them in order to gain mastery over their life. No person can live in an entirely real world or in an entirely imagined world. The cosy uniformity of the first universe is gone and the remaining breach bears with it the risk of inertia, arising from a blocking of spontaneity. As long as a person lives he tries to merge the original breach and since this is rarely possible even when most integrated, 'the human personality has a tragic touch of *relative* imperfection' (Moreno 1946/1980: 73).

In psychodrama one moves easily between these two parts or pathways in the realm of *'surplus reality'*. One can enact not only scenes that involve actual events in one's life but also the scenes that, as Zerka Moreno has said, 'have never happened, will never happen, or can never happen' (personal communication). These inner scenes, which may represent hopes, fears or unfinished psychological business, often have a strong influence on our lives and are sometimes experienced as being more real than the events of everyday life. These imagined scenes can be concretised, placed over and above life and beyond the grip of the ego. Leif Dag Blomkvist, a Swedish psychodramatist, points out that within surplus reality scenes 'an object only represents itself and does not stand for any hidden thing. What is more important than explaining and interpreting is that one becomes involved in these new and unfamiliar experiences and bears the tension' (Blomkvist and Rützel 1994: 242). Psychodrama was also named 'the Theatre of Truth' by Moreno, since he saw the spheres of people's emotions, imagination *and* surplus realities as equally essential to their existential truths.

Transference is the repeating of a relationship pattern which is historic but which is played out in the present, whereby old patterns of relating are projected on to someone in the vicinity, in one-to-one analytic therapy, the therapist. Moreno considered that transference is not a one-way process even if an analyst tries as much as possible to be a 'blank screen' and described that the process does not occur in relation to a person but to a role (Moreno and Moreno 1959/1975: 8). The role which the therapist represents for the patient may be that of a parent, a higher authority, a lover, the perfectly adjusted individual and the therapist may fall into experiencing complementary roles.

It is not only in the protagonist's relationship with the director, that transference (a Freudian concept) and tele (a Morenian concept) can be observed but also in relation to group members or the group as an entity. An aim of psychodrama is to increase reality-based here-and-now communication and diminish *projection.* This is achieved by bringing into awareness the nature of the transference relationship largely via the auxiliaries. The etymological root of *projection* is the Latin for 'throwing in front of oneself' (Cox 1992: 165). It is the professional, psychological term which describes the process by which specific impulses, wishes, aspects of the self are felt to be located outside the self. In this way, ego-alien aspects of the self are often projected and displaced into other people. It is not unusual for alien aspects of the self to be projected into a part of the body, for example the stomach or back, which then is described as being 'the problem'.

Holmes gives us some tips on how to spot transference:

> The relationship between psychotherapist and patient in individual therapy can be considered to consist of three elements:
> 1. those (not reality-based) aspects of the relationship derived from the patient's inner world (transference);
> 2. those similar aspects based on the therapist's inner world (counter-transference);
> 3. additionally, as a rule, if the patient is not too deeply disturbed, a reality-based here-and-now relationship. Psychoanalysts call this the therapeutic or treatment alliance. It is an adult-to-adult contract and, in Moreno's terms, it is an encounter involving tele.
>
> (Holmes 1992: 46)

The example of Louise illustrates the interplay and differences between transference and tele:

Louise

Louise, who has recently joined an on-going therapy group, conveys what are experienced as excessively positive feelings towards the male therapist and excessively antagonistic feelings towards me and to a lesser extent the group. Her responses seem to be of a transferential nature. They have the quality of having to do with feelings she has towards other significant people in her life from long ago, rather than of a tele nature, which would have to do with feelings evoked in relation to the therapists and the group relevant to the here-and-now situation. She has experienced psychodrama before and is of the opinion that it is only in the protagonist position that she will gain anything from the group. She demonstrated this in early sessions by loudly criticising dramas and such like, when not selected to work on stage.

Often the protagonist of the previous session has the privilege of speaking first, allowing them to share reflections after their work. This time the group has just sat down in a circle at the beginning of a session when Louise, who was not the previous group's protagonist, lets fly a long harangue on how badly I had treated her in the previous session. What I had done was to set a very firm limit on her interventions in order to be able to work with another person on stage. Her anger is a direct response to my action but originated in deep-seated expectations of me, primed in her earlier relationship with her mother.

My co-therapist now asks her to reverse roles with me, a hard task when she is so angry. She accepts the direction and tries to go into my role. At first it is very difficult and she takes the opportunity of criticising the other group members. She persists though and after a while she gets in touch with what options a director might have in that situation. Through role reversal she can correct transferential distortions. She feels that she has gained some insight and is much calmer. My limit-setting had been frightening. She needed me in the role of 'good mother', did not trust me, as she had not been able to trust her mother and interpreted my limit-setting as a rejection of her. Understanding of the 'bad mother' transference was facilitated by looking at a tele relationship through role reversal.

Locus nascendi, matrix and *Status nascendi*

In psychodrama, the moment at which the tele relationship was harmed and a person's emotional development was arrested can be returned to in order to re-establish a healthy two-way relationship. Moreno used the terms, *locus nascendi*, *matrix* and *status nascendi* to describe respectively the place, surrounding conditions and specific moment when a response to a situation emerged (Moreno 1946/1980: 55). Survival techniques we learned as children represent the best response to a given situation we could achieve at that time but are often not the most creative response to similar events we experience as adults. Where a response to a situation is no longer adequate, the *status nascendi* can be approximated on the psychodrama stage in terms of time, place and person. The director can enable the protagonist to return to a scene to;

1   re-experience the original feelings;
2   bring into awareness the prevailing physical, emotional, spiritual and intellectual conditions;
3   creatively revise the scene;
4   experience catharsis and gain insight on all those levels;
5   thus providing an opportunity for re-integration.

The following example of Eve describes this process.

Eve

Eve talks about the loneliness she experiences in her work situation. As she works on stage the director asks her when was the first time that she recalls feeling so alone in her life. Eve sets a scene where she, aged 5, and her parents are sitting by a lake with her new baby brother lying in the arms of her mother. Her feelings of alienation arise in this place, the locus. The matrix in Morenian terms is the background of relationships and conditions surrounding Eve around the time of her brother's birth; the status nascendi is the temporal factor, the specific moment when the response emerged. In the scene Eve receives help from a double in expressing to her parents what she is feeling and what she needs. Eve's parents are able to explain why their attention is so much on the new baby; apologise for their neglect of Eve; express their love for her and introduce her to her new little brother, letting her know that there is a special place in the family for them both.

CO-CONSCIOUS AND CO-UNCONSCIOUS

The co-conscious and co-unconscious concepts of Moreno, are to be differentiated from the phenomenon of conscious and unconscious states described by
Freud and the collective unconscious defined by Jung. Moreno states that the
co-conscious and co-unconscious are phenomena which can be seen in relation
to what he termed the 'inter-psyche'. He defines a concept which describes
a two-way process whereby two or several individuals are interlocked within a
system of co-unconscious states (Moreno 1946/1980: vii). The inter-psyche of a
group can be made external and explicit through psychodrama techniques,
thereby making manifest the tele relations, the co-conscious and co-unconscious
states. These states have been experienced *jointly* by partners, family members
or closely connected group members and can therefore only be reproduced or re-
enacted jointly. 'A co-conscious or co-unconscious state cannot be the property
of one individual only, it is common property' (Moreno 1946/1980: vii).

> People who live in close symbiosis, like mother and child or like the
> famous couple of Greek folklore Philemon and Baucis, develop in the course
> of time a common content, or what might be called a 'co-unconscious'. I
> have frequently been confronted with emotional difficulties arising between
> individuals living in close proximity. I was not then treating one person or
> the other, but an inter-personal relationship or what one may call an inter-
> personal neurosis.
>
> (Moreno and Moreno 1959/1975: 50)

Within a group the intricate network of relationships formed between protagonists and auxiliaries is the foundation for the therapeutic work. A protagonist in
one drama may later play an auxiliary in another, building a shared network
of emotional and cognitive traces which are more or less conscious – the
co-conscious and co-unconscious. This network of traces is based on tele and is
often experienced without being named.

Monica Zuretti, an Argentinian psychodramatist who has developed these
concepts of Moreno, states (Holmes *et al.* 1994: 214): 'Man develops his life in
successive matrices – genetic, maternal, identity, family, social and cosmic'; this
network 'belongs to the secret realm of the genetic or cosmic knowledge'. Birth
occurs at a moment in time and space, when the co-unconscious forces merge,
in a place where a choice is made between life and death. This is what Moreno
referred to when he talked about 'the spontaneity which goes into creating new
organisms'. The first beginnings of roles, proto-roles, are expressed physiologi-
cally and are known as psychosomatic roles, such as that of eater, or sleeper. The
first psychosomatic role, or proto-role emerging from the cosmic co-unconscious
is that of 'contacter', enacted at the meeting of sperm and ovum, where tele
reveals itself at a microcosmic level. All creative acts occur at a junction of
holding relationships, both emotional and physical, where the co-unconscious

develops and nourishes the creative process. This is true within the psychodrama process too.

ROLE

> The word role has its etymological roots in old French being taken from the Latin 'rotula'. In Greece and also in ancient Rome, the parts of the theatre were written on 'rolls' and read by the prompters to the actors who tried to memorise their parts by heart. . . . Role is thus not by origin a sociological or psychiatric concept; it came into the scientific vocabulary via the drama. Role is the functioning form the individual assumes in the specific moment he reacts to a specific situation in which other persons or objects are involved.
>
> (Moreno 1946/1980: iv)

Moreno called the phase of development both before and after birth, when the infant lives in an undifferentiated world, 'the matrix of identity' (Moreno 1946/1980: iii). This may be considered to be the locus (place) from which the self and its manifest aspects, the roles, emerge. There are two main roles which arise early on during an infant's development: the role of giver and the role of receiver. A certain role expectancy results from the quality of interchange occurring between the infant and the carer, which lays the foundation stone for the capacity to give and take in all future relationships. Dalmiro Bustos, an Argentinian psychodramatist (1994: 70–71) has developed Moreno's theory of the development of self through role clusters and states that there are three role clusters. The earliest roles, defined by Bustos as Cluster One, have a dynamic which is passive-dependent-incorporative and they are learned mostly in relation to the mother figure. Roles in Cluster Two have to do with the performance of active roles which involve work, self-confidence, the capacity to achieve and to exercise power. They presuppose a prevalence of autonomy and activity and are learned mostly in relation to the father figure. The prototype of Cluster Three roles is the fraternal relationship where one learns to play, to compete, to rival and to share. Such roles have to do with imposing limits, taking care of possessions and attacking or defending one's self from aggression. Through developing these roles and expanding our role repertoire, that is to say the collection of roles one is able to play adequately; each of us learns to look after ourself more fully. All of us have experienced developmental obstacles through the excesses, failings or absences of others during our growing towards a mature self, which have left resulting scars. Thinking in terms of role clusters and identifying the areas requiring focus, can assist us in moving from transferential relationships towards tele relationships.

Role assessment is an integral part of this process of change. Max Clayton (1994: 139–142) has developed Moreno's theories concerning role assessment/role analysis. He has described role systems in terms of:

1 fragmenting and dysfunctional role system (archaic roles needed for survival but now undesirable),
2 coping role system (roles for dealing with situations in which survival is threatened),
3 progressive functional role system (desirable roles which are developing or well-developed).

By plotting roles within the various role systems a director can assist a protagonist in determining what is adequate, overdeveloped, underdeveloped, conflicted or absent in their role repertoire. Here it is role training, which aims to develop identified, limited aspects of a person's professional or personal functioning rather than a more wide-ranging psychotherapeutic process which psychodrama entails.

ROLE vs. EGO

Moreno argued that roles arise before the self and that they strive towards clustering and unification (Moreno 1946/1980: iii). Before a person is able to experience their unification, or what might be called a sense of self, operational links must be established between the physiological, social and psychological role clusters. Hypothetically the operational self emerges whilst the latent metapsychological self is still to emerge. Auto-tele is yet to be developed. 'The tangible aspects of what is known as "ego" are the roles in which he operates, with the pattern of role-relationships around an individual as their focus' (Moreno 1946/1980: v). Moreno states that, in the first stage of development after birth, the 'matrix of identity', no differentiation is made between internal and external, between objects and people, between psyche and environment, but all is one. The psychosomatic roles then help the infant experience their 'body', the psychodramatic roles facilitate the infant's experience of 'psyche' and the social roles to create what we call 'society'. *Body, psyche and society are then the intermediary parts of the self'* (Moreno 1946/1980: iii).

ROLE REVERSAL

Moreno describes the five stages which represent the psychological bases for all role processes and for such phenomena as imitation, identification, projection and transference (Moreno 1946/1980: 61–62). I have interpreted these stages in the following way:

1 *The stage of the matrix of identity* the stage of the all-identity or mother/baby unit. Moreno described the mother as the baby's natural double.
2 *The stage of the double* the infant focuses on the stranger part of himself or 'mother'. The baby is mother's natural double.

3 *The stage of the mirror* the infant focuses on the stranger part of himself which is lifted out and all the other parts, including himself are omitted.
4 *The stage of role reversal* the infant places himself actively in the other part and acts its role.
5 *The stage of reversal of identity* the infant acts in the role of the other towards someone else, who in turn acts his role. It is only after completion of this stage that he has the capacity to assume his own identity fully.

Moreno described role reversal as the fourth stage in his theory of childhood development; the first stage being that which he terms both the all-identity and the matrix of identity, where the infant and mother have a shared identity and where the mother is the child's natural double. During the second and third stages of development, the infant has begun to recognise himself as separate from others and has developed a concept of self; but the capacity for role reversal requires that the child has developed to the fourth stage. This occurs at the onset of the second universe, where the child has learned to differentiate in the areas of time, place and person, and is capable of moving out of his own position into the position of the other to be able to act his part. The final stage, that of reversal of identity, the precursor to assuming one's own identity, is not fully developed until the 'child' has completed the separation from the originally shared identity and as it were stepped into his own shoes. This last stage is perhaps rarely more than partially completed even in adulthood. Three of these stages, stages two, three and four, have their counterpart in the psychodramatic therapeutic techniques of the double, the mirror and the role reversal.

The double is a group member or person trained in the technique of doubling, who takes on the role of another person, with him. What you see, is two people, who represent one person. The double echoes the physical position of the person he doubles and tries to express what he experiences in that role.

The mirror technique involves a person (A) demonstrating that he has perceived and understood something that another person (B) has conveyed. Person (A) mirrors back through action, what he has witnessed, thereby letting person (B) know that he has been seen and to some extent understood. Person (B) recognises himself in the 'mirror'.

The act of reversing roles involves physically changing places and stance with another, who changes places with you and each goes into and explores the other's role. Effectively one can see oneself through the eyes of another. These techniques are described by Moreno in *The Essential Moreno* (Fox 1987: 130–132).

According to Morenian theory, unity and integration come first before there is differentiation; then comes the important discovery of the child of a sense of self and only then can one place oneself in someone else's shoes. Since the time when Moreno developed his theory of child development, much infant research has been carried out and new theories of child development have evolved. Olivia Lousada, in her chapter in this book on the clinical use of psychodrama, presents new theoretical developments and places the technique of role reversal within that frame of reference.

ACTION

The activity in the warm-up phase in psychodrama discloses the social structure between the group members by demonstrating their movement and positions in space with regard to one another. The movement stimulates energy and awakens body memories in each person and by focusing on and maximising what feels like a natural posture and pace, group members become more aware of what psychological processes are active in them at the moment. Additional to the social and psychological awakening and focusing, activity is considered to stimulate the functioning of the endocrine system which promotes the body's natural healing process. Peter Parkinson, an Australian General Practitioner and psychodramatist actively stimulates glandular function through the psychodramatic development of roles. When working with a patient with asthma, for example, he nurtures the adrenal gland.

> By nurturing the adrenal gland I mean to encourage it to secrete its hormones in appropriate amounts at appropriate times. In other words I am asking the hormones to play their part in facilitating spontaneity in the production of adequate and appropriate roles. By doing this the wheezing should be reduced to its psychosomatic purpose. There are two parts to the adrenal gland:
> * the medulla which secretes adrenaline and
> * the cortex that secretes steroids (Hydrocortisone among others) . . .
> Extremes of adrenaline production are achieved in the **Congruent Expression of Outrage**. It would seem prudent, therefore, to treasure this role in the development of a culture free of psychosocial wheezing.
> (Parkinson 1996: 38)

When one listens to a person talking about something that has happened, the story is told in the third person, past-tense. This distancing diminishes the intensity of experience in contrast to seeing the experience on-stage which heightens and clarifies the experience. It is easy to hide behind words, most of us are experts at it, but seeing our story in action is innovative. As Moreno (1946/1980: 65) points out, a child warms up to spontaneous acts with such a degree of intensity that every particle of his being participates in this experience and this intensity is reflected by the fully spontaneous subject on the psychodramatic stage. By involving the body in the psychotherapeutic process the experience is deepened and brings to the moment all the information the protagonist has stored in his being. The inclusion of touch in the process of the drama often contributes invaluably to the therapeutic process, whether inherently protective and nurturing, representative of the rough and tumble of siblings or outright aggressive (directed in a form that no one in the group is physically harmed). As in all forms of body therapy the leader has an awareness of and respects special ethical considerations in regard to physical contact.

Psychodrama can involve re-enacting events of the past in order to re-integrate them. Peter Felix Kellermann, a Swedish psychodramatist who lives in Israel, states that: 'this principle of "act-completion" is congruent with psychoanalytic practice, and . . . psychodramatic enactment is not defensive aggression opposed to working through but rather regression in the service of the ego, a therapeutic process of re-organisation' (Kellermann 1992: 129). He goes on to say that: 'No adequate therapy is possible unless all actions – whether emotional, cognitive or behavioural – are allowed to emerge within the therapeutic setting.'

Moreno's original term for what is now known as psychodramatic enactment, was 'acting out'. This term has since so often been used to describe the 'acting out' of unconscious behaviour elicited within analytic therapy but enacted outside the therapeutic environment that the term is seldom used in its original meaning.

Moreno said concerning acting out:

> When I introduced this term (1928), it meant acting *that* out which is within the patient, in contrast to acting a role which is assigned to the patient by an outsider. It did not mean that they should not be acted out because they camouflage a form of resistance (psychoanalytic view). I meant just the opposite – that they should be acted out because they may represent important inner experiences of the patient which otherwise remain camouflaged and difficult if not impossible to interpret. In psychodramatic thinking, acting from within, or acting out, is a necessary phase in the progress of therapy.
>
> (Moreno 1946/1980: x)

Here Moreno differentiates between 'irrational incalculable acting out in life itself, harmful to the patient or others, and therapeutic, controlled acting out taking place within the treatment setting.'

CONCLUSION

The *'philosophy of the moment'*, developed by J.L. Moreno, is psychodrama's foundation stone. Moreno propounded a world-view within which all human beings are considered infinitely spontaneous and creative and equal in status. This stance then should be the starting point for the director of any psychodrama session. The director should be aware of the physiological signals of the group members; she makes use of physical *warm-ups*; she has an awareness of group members' body tensions, and may facilitate their body memories; she aims to stimulate the body's healing processes; in a process of psychotherapeutic self-exploration through dramatic method in the here-and-now. This of course involves *action*.

Central to the method of psychodrama is Moreno's concept of *encounter*, which requires authenticity and the maximum of involvement in meeting oneself and others in the here-and-now. This leads to a greater awareness of *tele*, the flow of feeling between people, which in turn enables us to adequately respond to others. An awareness of the concepts of the *co-conscious* and *co-unconscious* provides us with the means to define problems in terms of interpersonal issues rather than those of an isolated individual. An understanding of *role theory* provides an instrument for the analysis of group members' *roles* and *role repertoires*, the quantity of available roles a person can enact with adequacy at a given time. An awareness of group members' role repertoires may guide a director when auxiliaries are being selected for a psychodrama, since a person's role repertoire can be expanded by playing roles which are underdeveloped. The capacity to *role reverse* enables us to see ourselves and others from new perspectives and facilitates moves towards self actualisation. The intermediary parts of the self are body, psyche and society.

Moreno wanted us to adopt his philosophy and principles, in order to work towards improving the world, by combating the negative effects of mechanisation, robotism in humanity and stereotypy – what he considered to be a living death or 'normosis'. It was his aim and can be ours, to develop spontaneity and creativity in order to co-create the world we live in.

> The infinite spaces and the starry sky above us have been symbols to our ancestors that there is a place for everyone to live. They have been a perennial challenge to the inventiveness of man to create the means necessary to the survival of all.
>
> (Moreno 1934/1953/1993: 246)

BIBLIOGRAPHY

Blatner, A. and Blatner, A. (1988) *Foundations of Psychodrama – History, Theory and Practice*, New York: Springer Publishing Company, Inc.

Blomkvist, L.D. and Rützel, T. (1994) 'Surplus Reality and Beyond', in P. Holmes, M. Karp and M. Watson (eds) *Innovations in Theory and Practice: Psychodrama since Moreno*, London: Routledge.

Boustos, Dalmiro (1994) 'Wings and Roots', in P. Holmes, M. Karp and M. Watson (eds) *Innovations in Theory and Practice: Psychodrama since Moreno*, London: Routledge.

Clayton, Max (1994) 'Role Theory and its Application in Clinical Practice', in P. Holmes, M. Karp and M. Watson (eds) *Innovations in Theory and Practice: Psychodrama since Moreno*, London: Routledge.

Cox, M. (1992) *Shakespeare Comes to Broadmoor*, London: Jessica Kingsley.

Fox, J. (ed.) (1987) *The Essential Moreno: Writings on Psychodrama, Group Method, and Spontaneity by J.L. Moreno, M.D.*, New York: Springer Publishing Company, Inc.

Greenberg, I. (1974) *Psychodrama Theory and Therapy*, New York: Behavioural Publications.

Holmes, P. (1992) *The Inner World Outside: Object Relations Theory and Psychodrama*, London: Routledge.

Holmes, P., Karp, M. and Watson, M. (eds) (1994) *Innovations in Theory and Practice: Psychodrama since Moreno*, London: Routledge.

Kellermann, P.F. (1992) *Focus on Psychodrama*, London: Jessica Kingsley.

Marineau, R.F. (1989) *Jacob Levy Moreno 1889–1974: Father of Psychodrama, Sociometry and Group Psychotherapy*, London: Routledge.

Moreno, J.L. (1914) *Einladung zu einer Begegnung*, part 1, Vienna/Leipzig: Anzengruber/Verlag Porüder Suschitzky.

Moreno, J.L. (1941) *The Words of the Father*, New York: Beacon House.

Moreno, J.L. (1946/1980) *Psychodrama, First Volume*, 6th edn, New York: Beacon House.

Moreno, J.L. (1934/1953/1993) *Who Shall Survive?*, Roanoke, VA: Royal Publishing Company.

Moreno, J.L. and Moreno, Z.T. (1959/1975) *Psychodrama, Second Volume*, New York: Beacon House.

Parkinson, P. (1996) 'The Contribution of Psychodrama to the Understanding and Treatment of Asthma', Psychodrama Thesis, Australia and New Zealand Psychodrama Association, ANZPA Press.

Pines, M. (1987) 'Psychoanalysis, Psychodrama and Group Psychotherapy: Step-children of Vienna', *Journal of the British Psychodrama Association*, 2(2): 15–23.

Williams, A. (1989) *The Passionate Technique: Strategic Psychodrama with Individuals, Families, and Groups*, London: Routledge.

Zuretti, M. (1994) 'The Co-Unconscious', in P. Holmes, M. Karp and M. Watson (eds) *Innovations in Theory and Practice: Psychodrama since Moreno*, London: Routledge.

Chapter 4

The warm-up

Susie Taylor

> The moment of birth is the maximum degree of warming up to the spontaneous act of being born into a new setting, to which he must make a rapid adjustment.
>
> (Moreno 1946: 54)

As an introduction to this chapter, which is in itself a warm-up to the continued reading of this book, I would like to look at Moreno's thinking of the warm-up process. I will then move on to look at the warm-up of the director and group. The final part of this chapter will concentrate on practical examples in certain situations. The element concerning warm-up that I wish to emphasise is that it is a process and not simply a technique.

MORENO AND WARM-UP

In his spontaneity theory of child development, Moreno says 'the first basic manifestation of spontaneity is the warming-up of the infant to the new setting' (Moreno 1946: 52). His definition of spontaneity is that of a new response to an old situation and an adequate response to a new situation. The link between spontaneity and the warm-up process is vital in terms of the child and adult's ability to engage and complete tasks in life. If an athlete does not complete his/her warm-up exercise before competing in the race, there is not only the possibility of a physical injury because the muscles have not been warmed, stretched and primed but also a 'mental injury' because the athlete has not made available his/her optimum level of spontaneity, or the 's' factor as Moreno called it.

PHYSICAL AND MENTAL STARTERS

Moreno goes on to describe physical and mental starters that are used by adults in order to begin the warm-up process:

- *Physical starters* These are present from the moment of birth, and maybe even before. They are bodily activities such as sucking – a baby warming-up to the act of feeding – walking, smelling etc. These starters continue to be important throughout life.
- *Mental starters* Development of these begins once the child is able to differentiate between the self and the environment. As the environment includes objects and people, these mental starters can also be referred to as interpersonal. Psychological triggers – fantasies, dreams, aspirations – and sociocultural triggers – social norms, group pressures, social status, moral and ethical codes – influence mental starters (Kipper 1986).

Moreno also includes social and psychochemical starters. The social starters correspond to the sociocultural ones described by Kipper. The psychochemical ones refer to substances used to enhance an individual's warm-up – drugs, alcohol, coffee, etc. It may be that these do not produce a positive effect, but then a warm-up may not result in a positive outcome itself.

These starters can be self-initiated – by the protagonist – or activated by some external person – the director – or other stimuli. Kipper (1986) categorises them as internal or external stimulations. It is useful to note Moreno's description of birth where the child – protagonist – is using its own physical starters but also needs the mental starters of mother, midwife, etc. – auxiliary egos – to enable its completion of the birth act. The implication here is that physical starters may not be enough to complete a given task, or to meet a situation adequately. Therefore the importance of the warming-up process to the whole group – in this case the child, mother, midwife, doctor, etc. – is vital. Each can then have available the maximum level of spontaneity to complete the act they are all engaged in – birth. This is also true for the director and group, from which will emerge the protagonist and auxiliary egos.

Zones

Moreno introduces the concept of *zones* which serve as physical starters to warming-up. Examples of these are the visual zone, nasal zone, mouth zone, etc. They are the somatic expression of the warming-up process to a spontaneous act.

To clarify this concept, let's take the act of the infant feeding. The warm-up to the act of feeding has a focus, in this case the zone of the mouth:

> The zone is, in this 'sociometric' sense, an area to which, for example, the mouth, the nipple of the mother's breast, the milk fluid, and the air between them are contributing factors. Whenever these components come to a focus, the zone emerges into action.
>
> (Moreno 1946: 57)

Different zones can be activated simultaneously and can work co-operatively, e.g. mouth and throat zones; as well as excluding one another. As the child matures, so he/she is able to warm up larger areas of the body, and so include more zones.

Moreno describes the dual warm-up for both mother and child in the feeding act: 'In the course of the two-way warming-up, with one aim – the satisfaction of the child's hunger, the physical adjustment efforts go hand in hand with mental adjustment efforts' (1946: 61). The mother and child will each have a different set of physical starters in the warming-up process to the act of feeding. If we take the analogy of mother/director and child/protagonist, the same is true. What is important is that they adjust to each other to complete the task at hand. 'One activity at a time excludes every other activity; one focus every other focus. He/she warms-up exclusively to immediate situations. He/she lives in immediate time' (Moreno 1946: 61).

The mother/director should be more available to adjustment than the child/protagonist, due to the fact that she has mental as well as physical starters, and her matrix of identity is well developed:

> This co-being, co-action and co-experience which, in the primary phase, exemplify the infant's relationship to the persons and things around him/her, are characteristics of the matrix of identity. This matrix of identity lays the foundation for the first emotional learning process of the infant.
>
> (Moreno 1946: 61)

The warm-up can be used to absorb and undo a small range of the personality that may cause the individual distress, by including that aspect in a warming-up process that has a wider range, and involves larger areas of the body/mind. The following is an example taken from Moreno's account about a man who complained of a 'drawn' feeling on the left side of his face. This became worse when a light was shone on that side, or when a woman sat on his left. He was able to combat this when he was asked to play different roles, particularly that of the aggressor. The warm-up to this role where he would be required to shout out loud commands, not only involved the left side of his face, but also more of his personality, and so enabled him to enact the role fully. Moreno later worked with this man helping him to understand the warm-up process he embarked on which would result in the 'drawn' feeling.

I have spent some time looking at Moreno's concept of warm-up because it is far more involved than the simplified idea of 'warm-up' in terms of the psychodramatic method. To have a broader understanding of this concept may enrich our use of this process. There seems to be a general appreciation that the warm-up phase of the psychodrama method is used to increase spontaneity, encourage trust and cohesion within a group, as well as the emergence of a protagonist. I feel it is important that the relationship between the warming-up process and spontaneity are well understood. If the director, group, protagonist and auxiliary egos do not have their maximum level of spontaneity available to them, any task they undertake will not be completed fully, and creativity will be minimal.

I will continue to discuss the warming-up process from a theoretical perspective before looking at particular types of warm-up exercises and examples of each.

PERIPHERY TO THE CENTRE

So, the warm-up process continues after the warm-up phase of the group? Yes. Every act we undertake has a warm-up to it. This is what is so important in understanding Moreno's concept of warm-up. Every scene entered into by the protagonist has its own warm-up. The setting of the scene will trigger both physical and mental starters for the protagonist. To start at the periphery and work towards the centre or core of the protagonist's issue is using the process of warm-up. 'The warm-up does not conclude when the action portion begins, but it continues throughout the session as it is necessary to warm the protagonist up to each time and place in the session' (Goldman and Morrison 1984: 6).

To underline this point, I include the fifth rule cited by Zerka Moreno in 'Psychodramatic Rules and Techniques and Adjunctive Methods' (Moreno and Moreno 1969: 235): 'The warming up process proceeds from the periphery to the centre'. She goes on to say:

> The director will, therefore, not begin with the most traumatic events in the patient's life. The commencement is on a more superficial level, allowing the self-involvement of the patient to carry him/her more deeply towards the core. The director's skills will be expressed in the construction of the scenes and the choice of persons or objects needed to assist the patient in his/her warm-up.
>
> (1969: 235)

The stage that Moreno used in his theatre in Beacon reflected this as it consisted of three concentric circles rising up. As the work began, he would move from the group to the stage area, and as the protagonist moved to the core of the work, so he/she would move towards the centre of the stage.

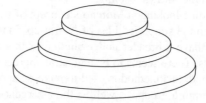

Elaine Goldman (Goldman and Morrison 1984) uses this image in her explanation of the method of psychodrama through tracking. The first scene will be a present situation, then moves to a recent past and so to the distant past. She

will always bring the protagonist back to the original scene to concretise what
has been worked on from the distant past.

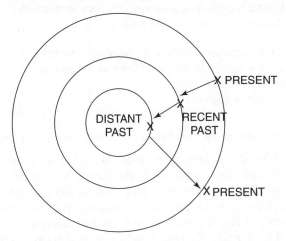

If the director tries to miss a stage in the enactment warm-up – working from
the periphery to the centre – the spontaneity level within the protagonist will
drop, and the emotional engagement will break.

Specific warm-up techniques – I shall now refer to these as structured warm-
ups – were not originally part of Moreno's thinking. His notion was that group
members came with their own warm-up and this needed to be facilitated so that
a protagonist would emerge from the group, and the warm-up to action would
begin once the protagonist and the director began their work. Structured warm-
ups were introduced into the method by James Sacks, adapted from theatre
games used with actors.

I hope the point that every time we go into action we have completed a warm-
up has been established. When we wake up and prepare to get up and go to work;
when we eat; when we prepare to be a member of a group or the director of that
group the warm-up is a continuing process.

THE WARM-UP OF THE DIRECTOR AND GROUP

This section of the chapter will look at the warming up process of the director
and the group.

The director's warm-up

The director should prepare him/herself for leading a group by undergoing
his/her own warm-up. He/she needs to develop his/her own spontaneity so as to
do the same for the group. He/she should be aware of any resistances he/she may

have, or expectations of him/herself or the group. His/her fears and anxieties must be dealt with constructively before entering the group, thus enabling him/her to facilitate the group to increase their own spontaneity.

I have divided this process into four aspects:

1   the director's warm-up to the act of directing – the role;
2   the director's warm-up to the group prior to entering it;
3   warm-up to the group *in situ*;
4   warm-up to the protagonist.

The director's warm-up to the act of directing – the role

Most of us will be able to identify the physical starters we experience, even to the point of the zones they centre on! If the director has not completed his/her warm-up to the role sufficiently, then they will not have an optimum level of spontaneity available to themselves and so to the group. Learning to contain and utilise the anxiety of this role seems to be a major component.

Moreno and Kipper talk of physical starters in combination with mental ones aquiring a rescue quality. Kipper (1986: 84) gives the example of someone pacing the room when faced with an unexpected or difficult question. Rather than being seen as nervousness it can be a 'positive manifestation which may indicate an appropriate behaviour. It signifies the process of getting ready to act.' It may be of more concern to a potential director if they experience little or no anxiety as it could be an indication that the rescue quality of their physical and mental starters are not operating for some reason.

Forming habits or rituals is often a useful way of preparing for the role. Some people have particular clothes, jewellery or shoes that make them feel more confident. Others will go through various tasks before directing, for example being able to prepare the room where the group is to meet. It is putting the anxiety into action, and can be a metaphor for clearing the mind – moving and arranging the chairs; checking the lighting; is it warm or cold in the room; which end to have the stage area, etc.

Imagining where the excess anxiety can be left before entering the room is another way some find helpful; being clear that any situation being encountered by the director in life that may hinder rather than enhance the role is left outside the group room; carrying on an internal conversation using the director's own 'good enough' parent. There are many different ways to enable oneself for the role, but what is most important is that the warm-up to this role of director fits the individual who is stepping into it.

Director's warm-up to the group prior to entering it

Here the focus is the director's relationship with the group, and will vary depending on the nature of the group. The following are some questions that it may be useful to ask oneself before engaging with the group.

In a *new group*: how many people are there? Who has done psychodrama before and who has not? What may their needs be in this moment? Do any of them know each other? What is the gender balance? Do you as director know any of them?

In an *on-going group*: what happened last week? Who played auxilary roles? Did those roles mirror personal issues? What came up for individuals in the sharing? Who has not worked recently? Who seems an isolate and who a star in the group? What are the relationships between members like at the moment? Who has put themselves forward and not been selected by the group and why may this be? What are the themes that have and have not been worked on? How is the director and/or co-director's relationship in the group? How is it with each other? What are the transference issues?

In a *one-off workshop*: similar questions as to the start of a group, but an important one to add here is whether people have chosen to be in the group, or have they been 'sent'? (This will be looked at in more detail later on.)

If working with a co-director it is useful to take time before the group to talk with them to re-connect as co-therapists, and establish areas that may need to be focused on in the group. Similarly, talking to other people involved with the clients' care if working within an institution or therapeutic community is important in terms of continuity of care and to facilitate good team work.

Warm-up to the group in situ

The director should have developed his/her own spontaneity sufficiently before entering the group, and be aware of any resistances or expectations of him/ herself or of the group. Part of this process will include having dealt with any fears or anxieties he/she may have.

In a new group, it is important that the director tries to communicate something of his/her style to the group. This can begin through an introductory talk by the director conveying a sense of authenticity and warmth to encourage trust within and between the group members, as well as increasing confidence in the abilities of the director. The group norms are beginning to be set during this process, including self-disclosure, spontaneity, humour, toleration of distance or reserve. Issues of confidentiality need to be clarified, what is and is not permissible, also the structure of the group during the time available – be that a day, a week-end, an on-going therapy group. Yalom placed the 'imparting of information' as very important: 'Most group therapists do not offer explicit didactic instruction in the interactional group therapy' (1985: 9).

Permission to go at one's own pace – 'The patient is permitted to be as unspontaneous or inexpressive as he/she is at this time' (Moreno and Moreno 1969: 236).

I would like to take a moment to explore the issue of confidentiality more fully. Although most people expect their sharing to be respected and to remain in the group, a consensus of what is actually meant by confidentiality is important. The generally accepted view point I have encountered is that it is permissible for a group member to share with someone outside of the group issues that have touched them, as long as it only involves their own personal material. It is not acceptable however, to identify the protagonist or other group members by name, or to disclose their life experiences shared in the group. If group members have some contact outside the group, it is important to encourage this to be brought into the group. Child protection issues need to be clarified, as do other areas that may have legal implications. A psychodramatist should always have a copy of their code of ethics available to the group members. If these points are adhered to, the group will feel a greater sense of trust and safety, and so enable each other to share very personal and traumatic areas of their lives.

During this introductory phase, the director must assess the group's response to him/her, e.g. does the group appreciate the humour? Is it an active group or not? Is there interaction between each other and the director, etc. From here the director can move into selecting and adapting warm-ups that are appropriate and 'fit' the group in the moment.

In an on-going group, re-connecting through some discussion about the previous weeks' work can focus the director and the group, and so pick up the process that had been developing and moving on with it. The dynamics between group members themselves and those with the director need to be kept in mind, and worked on as a group, which may involve spending a session focusing on this and not a psychodrama. This is important when there is conflict between group members that would interfere with the work and support of a protagonist, and so make the group an unsafe place to share.

Warm-up to the protagonist

There is often little time for this process, so again it is important that the director has been able to go through the previous three stages adequately. The initial discussion between the director and protagonist in terms of what the work is to focus on and how to start – the contract – allows time for the director and protagonist to warm-up to each other – mother and child need to warm-up to each other and the act of feeding to be able to complete the task adequately. It also gives the director time to assess whether or not physical contact is comfortable, e.g. does the protagonist move away or toward the director? Other questions to be aware of at this stage are: how anxious is the protagonist? How passive are they in terms of accepting whatever the director may say? Are they able to keep eye contact with the director and/or the group or do they avert their eyes or even have them closed? How high is the energy level – do they have a strong need for action? How verbal are they? By paying attention to these areas the director can have a stronger sense of how he/she needs to be in relation to the protagonist, which may then clarify any transferential issues on both sides. It also allows the director to gain some awareness as to how integrated the protagonist may be.

The warm-up process continues once the enactment begins through each scene the protagonist portrays, and as the work progresses from the original scene to the core of the issue.

GROUP PROCESS AND THE WARM-UP

Psychodrama is a method of group psychotherapy, and it is therefore important to be aware of and to follow the group process. Dalmiro Bustos once defined the group as the producer and the director the co-producer. His feeling was that the director should follow the group and facilitate where it is rather than impose a direction on it. This needs to be emphasised, as many directors come prepared with a list of warm-up exercises that they must put into effect, even if the group is following a different path. This is a sure way of creating resistance, a lack of trust, cohesion and spontaneity, even though to be prepared with ideas for warm-up exercises is comforting to the director. After all, he/she has to contain not only his/her uncertainty of what will occur, but that of the group too. To be able to adapt, change and even abandon these ideas and follow the group is not only more spontaneous, but also therapeutic. It is the needs of the group that are to be worked with, not the needs of the director.

If we can think of the concept of warming-up in relation to the group process, it may enable us to use the techniques of warm-up in a more appropriate and beneficial way. As well as the question 'Warm-up to what?' maybe we should also ask 'What and where is the group's warm-up?' This involves listening to the covert themes as well as the overt ones, in a similar way to defining the theme of a piece of jazz.

As we have learned from Moreno's idea of warm-up, we each have our own individual warming-up process, so in one sense the group members arrive already warmed up. The director needs to ascertain what issues are present in the group, for example a simple introduction and opportunity for individuals to share why they have come to this group can provide the information needed. The process has begun, and the director needs to listen to the themes and messages that are being given, and so create the warm-up exercise to facilitate these: 'Techniques without a context – group process – may violate people and groups' (Hollander and Hollander 1978).

REASONS FOR THE WARM-UP PHASE

There are some clear reasons for the warm-up phase of psychodrama. Antony Williams (1991) gives a list for the director to consider:

1   To set a framework for the group, such as how long it will last, what its general purposes are, and what kind of group it is.

2   To clarify the tasks of the group and to assist members to clarify their expectations of the group.
3   To establish and to model, where appropriate, norms for acceptability of action, spontaneity, and forceful expression.
4   To develop rapport and engagement with individual members and with the group as a system.
5   To develop group cohesion and a working basis of mutual trust between members.
6   To reassure the group of their expertise, their ability to warm up the group, and to manage safely what emerges as a result of the warm-up.
7   To accept reserved and shy behaviour; toleration of distance and difficulty indicates respect for members and reassures them that they are not expected to be 'group clones'.
8   To begin a process of information-exchange, whereby new meanings are able to be ascribed to present and past behaviour.

He particularly emphasises three factors:

• The need for the director to engender confidence that appropriate administrative and professional functions will be performed. This echoes Yalom's point.
• The director engages with each individual and with the group system as a whole, joining members at their level of meaning to find out what the problem – or training need – is.
• To pave the way for new meanings to be possible – a new response to a new situation – Moreno's definition of spontaneity.

Essentially, to provide a setting within which the group can survive difficult and even traumatic events that may be shared safely.

Leveton (1977) talks of the importance of alleviating the fears and anxieties that can be aroused from the thought of sharing parts of themselves and their lives that may otherwise have been kept 'secret'. Psychodrama is an action-based therapy where group members will be required to play roles, so the fears concerning acting or performing are also present. It is important for the director to find ways of alleviating these fears early on in a non-threatening and non-judgemental way.

A check list

Kellermann (1992) has a check list of questions to help in the processing of a director's work. The following points are under the warm-up section:

1   Was the director able to stimulate individual group members sufficiently and warm them up to action?

2   Was the director able to build sufficient cohesion and a constructive working climate in the group?
3   Was the type of warm-up exercise/s appropriately chosen?
4   Were the instructions to the warm-up exercise/s sufficiently clear?
5   Was there adequate follow up to the warm-up exercise/s?
6   Was the director able to help the group develop a specific theme upon which to focus?
7   Did the director consider group dynamic aspects and sociometry sufficiently at the beginning of the session?
8   Was the director sufficiently warmed-up to directing?

Let's take a look at these eight questions in more detail. The first two need to go hand in hand, in the sense that unless the director has found ways to alleviate anxieties and fears, and to build trust and so cohesion within the group, individual members' spontaneity will not have been mobilised and it will therefore be difficult for them to move into action. The director needs to be aware of how to aid the individual's warm-up to the group, and also to recognise the group as a system or organism that, in order to function at an optimum level, must feel safe and know the boundaries. Therefore another function of the warm-up is to create the group norms, which increases the level of cohesiveness. Yalom (1985) states that these group norms enable individuals to be accepted regardless of their past life, transgressions or perceived failings in their social universe.

Question number three refers to the appropriate selection of warm-up exercise/s. Again, this can be related to the issue of following the group process, and using the themes already present in the group to facilitate further exploration. Another way of looking at this would be to use the metaphor of 'following the emotional smoke' (M. Karp, personal communication) when working with a protagonist, that is to be alert to where their emotion is strongest. This can be applied to the group in the same way – where is the 'emotional smoke' of the group leading, and how is it best to encourage that?

Clear instructions – question four – are very important, as if the group members cannot hear what the director is saying, or receive confused information from him/her, they cannot follow the exercise and so the relationship between the director and group begins to break down. It can increase resistance within the group as well as ostracising members from each other and the director. The fifth question can be effective in this situation if the director becomes aware of the problem, in so much as he/she can suggest that members say how it felt not to understand what was going on. It is also useful to allow space for sharing in pairs, small groups or as a whole after each warm-up, as a potential protagonist can emerge at any time.

The sixth question links to the use of group process and the themes present at that time, and how the director helps individuals to focus on a particular issue that has emerged from the group, and its relationship to them personally.

Considering the group dynamics and sociometry – question seven – becomes more apparent as a group develops. Williams (1991: 98) comments: 'For leaders to refer to the "group dynamics" at this stage – a group's first session – is pointless, even sadistic.' He feels this to be important, along with the sociometry of a group as it matures over a period of time. However, simple sociometric exercises designed to make explicit connections between members can be extremely facilitative at the start of a group's life. For example, standing in a circle, initially the director calling out different situations that may be shared by group members – Who has a cat? Who hates cooking? etc. – and those who have a cat or hate cooking step into the centre. As the warm-up continues, other group members can offer situations. This can increase the connections in the group, as well as disclosing information about each other, and may also be an indication of what issues are present in the group by the topics the individuals call out.

Before continuing, I want to include Moreno's definition of sociometry which he thought of as a classificatory science which enquires 'into the evolution and organization of groups and the position of individuals within them' (Moreno 1953: 51).

It could also be described as a way of measuring people's connectedness – what choices do they make as regards each other? What is their position in the group? What role do they take in the group? It can reveal:

> hidden structures that give a group its form; the alliances, the hidden beliefs, the forbidden agendas, the ideological agreements, the 'stars' of the show, positive and negative. Sociometry focuses on the connections which exist between group members, and the reasons for those connections. But despite its concern with connections, it is not in itself necessarily an 'encounter'; it is a measure, an information-provider that stresses the social nature of everything we are and do. Our actions, beliefs and feelings come from and are maintained by the actions, beliefs and feelings of others.
>
> (Williams 1991: 127–128)

This description makes it very clear that the director should be aware of the links and choices between group members, and so an understanding of sociometry and how it relates and connects to the group process can only enhance the director's use of the warm-up and its continuing process throughout the group.

The final question regarding the director's warm-up has already been discussed, and can be measured by the level of the group's participation and interaction.

Optimum cohesion

Yalom (1985) summarised how a group can function if there is optimum cohesion, and as it is an aspect of a group that has frequently been mentioned in this chapter, it seems relevant to be clear about its importance.

1   The attraction members have for their group and for other members.
2   More acceptance, support and inclination to form meaningful relationships.
3   Group members are more inclined to express and explore themselves, become aware of and integrate hitherto unacceptable aspects of self, and relate more deeply to others.
4   Cohesive groups tend to be more stable with a better attendance and less turnover.
5   Although cohesive groups show greater acceptance, intimacy and under-standing, there is evidence that they also permit greater development and expression of hostility and conflict.

The therapeutic relationship

To conclude this section on the warm-up process, I would like to include Rogers's (1959) ideas on the therapeutic relationship. Although he was looking at individual therapeutic relationships, his description of an ideal therapist/client alliance applies to psychodrama in that it has the spirit of a 'client-centred' therapy (Blatner 1973). When the conditions of an ideal therapist/client – or director/group and director/protagonist – relationship exists, Rogers stated that a characteristic process was set in motion:

1   The patient is increasingly free in expressing his/her feelings.
2   He/she begins to test reality and to become more discriminatory in his/her feelings and perceptions of his/her environment, his/her self, other persons, and his/her experiences and concept of self.
3   He/she increasingly becomes aware of the incongruity between his/her experiences and his/her concept of self.
4   He/she becomes aware of feelings which have been previously denied or distorted in awareness.
5   His/her concept of self which now includes previously distorted or denied aspects becomes more congruent with his/her experience.
6   He/she becomes increasingly able to experience, without threat, the therapist's – director's/group's – unconditional positive regard and to feel an unconditional positive self-regard.
7   He/she increasingly experiences him/herself as the focus of evaluation of the nature and worth of an object or experience.
8   He/she reacts to experience less in terms of his/her perception of others' evaluation of him/her and more in terms of its effectiveness in enhancing his/her own development.

To my mind, the warm-up process should aim to achieve both Yalom's and Rogers's factors to enable effective therapy to occur.

CLASSIFICATION OF WARM-UP EXERCISES

This section will look at the different classifications of warm-up exercises, and their application in different settings with examples. These fall into four main groups: introductory, physical, intimacy, protagonist-centred.

Introductory – 'Getting to know you'

These are particularly used with a new group as a way to introduce the individual members to each other, and so begin the process of disclosure in a non-threatening way. The group members become more comfortable with each other and this will reduce the level of anxiety and so facilitate group cohesion.

Example: the director asks each member to consider their name and what it means to them, how it was chosen, who else in the family has/had it. A combination of these can be used, but it is best to keep it simple.

In a very large group of twenty or more – which generally happens with week-end workshops – the thought of trying to remember everyone's name can be inhibitive. The anxiety level may even rise, and it can be very freeing to give permission for everyone not to remember their names, and encourage members to ask each other if the need arises. A useful way of managing a large group is to divide it into small subgroups that can meet regularly throughout the life of the workshop. In these smaller groups, members can work at remembering names and feel they have a safer more intimate space to share in – similar to being in a family to cope with living in the world.

Physical – 'Let's get energised!'

This type of warm-up is designed to increase energy levels, introduce touch, allow the group to 'play' and reduce the level of anxiety. However, three points to bear in mind are:

1   Even though the director may feel this type of warm-up to be non-threatening, some group members may find them difficult or even feel unable to take part. This can be particularly so for people who have experienced physical or sexual abuse.
2   There is always a need to check whether anyone has some physical difficulty – bad back, hip, etc. The director should suggest the removal of glasses, long earrings, watches, etc. if there is to be a lot of physical interaction, and be sure there are no objects that may be a danger in the room. The group needs to feel physically safe as well as emotionally safe.
3   Be observant! A group member may be over-enthusiastic – exaggerating the movements, running when the instruction was to walk, in general, not paying attention to themselves or others.

Example: in hug tag someone is the chaser and has to catch another group member who then takes on the role. To avoid being caught, members have to hug each other in pairs for no more than five seconds and then find someone else to hug.

Intimacy – 'Getting to know you better'

Trust exercises are included in this category, as these warm-ups are designed to increase the trust amongst group members and to encourage intimacy in an appropriate and safe way, as well as to facilitate disclosure. Again, the director should not underestimate the power of these types of warm-up. He/she should let the group know he/she is aware of the power by being in a position in the room that gives the best view of the group. It is more usual for these warm-ups to be carried out in pairs or small groups. Many of these types of warm-up involve the group members being silent or closing their eyes.

Example: face massage – the director asks the group to divide up into pairs, and take it in turns to massage each other's face. Suggestions can be made to help facilitate group members in the warm-up, for example, take some time to mould the face into different emotions. The length of time for this warm-up would depend on how well members knew each other – 10 minutes for a new group and longer for a more established group. The director can then ask the members to share in their pairs.

Protagonist-centred – 'Who is ready to work?'

These are aimed at establishing a protagonist within the group by helping group members to get in touch with past, present or future conflicts, and to deepen the level of personal awareness and so evoke memories and emotions. As has already been stated, group members may have brought an issue to work on from outside the group, either by something that has happened to them, or by some seemingly minor incident that has produced a high level of emotion within them. For this reason, it may be sufficient to ask people to work in pairs or small groups and share what is with them in the moment, and whether or not they wish to work as a protagonist. Alternatively, it may be clear that a theme has emerged in the group, so applying this to a structured warm-up will facilitate the theme to emerge and connect it to group members.

Example: the theme may be death. The director can ask the group to share in pairs a loss that has been important to them and feels unfinished.

APPLYING THE WARM-UP IN DIFFERENT SITUATIONS

The following are four different situations that are usual for a psychodramatist to meet, with examples of the warming-up process for each.

Week-end workshop

The need to establish a safe environment for work to be carried out is important, and should be developed quickly as the group's life is short. Assuming the director has given him/herself good opportunity to go through their own warming-up process, the immediate consideration is how to begin to establish group cohesion and trust. One thing to facilitate at the start of any group is enabling members to speak, particularly as it may be that there are some who have never taken part in a group before. As we have noted, it is important to relate the structure of the workshop and any practical information. Clarification of confidentiality and the group boundaries can be achieved through the director's introduction, where the rapport between director and group begins. A copy of the psychodramatists' code of ethics should be available for group members to read.

When using structured warm-up techniques with a new group, it is helpful to begin the process in pairs, and gradually increase the numbers until the whole group is back together. This can reduce the anxiety of speaking in a large group, although an exception to this would be a simple name exercise. For example, if beginning the group by asking people to share in pairs, they can then be asked to join another pair, then a four, etc. This could then be developed by asking the groups of four to find a way of showing what they have been sharing about the workshop – e.g. their hopes, fears, how they want the group to be, etc. It is useful to introduce action and 'show me' as soon as possible. Psychodrama is concerned with enactment and not 'talking about', therefore the group needs to become accustomed to this early on.

Examples of warm-up to enactment

In the name game, each group member says their name and an association they have with it, or each shares their name, standing in a circle and throwing a small cushion to one another, first saying their own name and then the name of the person the cushion is being thrown to.

A more interesting introductory warm-up that introduces role reversal early on in the group is as follows. The director asks members to pair up and introduce themselves to their partner, and when 5 minutes is up, they are asked to repeat the process with the other introducing themselves. When another 5 minutes is up, they are asked to return to the group and introduce each other in role reversal, e.g. for Maggie and Susan – Susan will role reverse and speak as Maggie sharing what Maggie herself told Susan and vice versa. When each has finished, the director should check if there is anything the represented person wants to add or change. This is important so as to avoid the feeling of misrepresentation, or wrong information being given. The director should also suggest at the start of the warm-up, that the pairs check if there is any detail they would rather not be shared with the whole group at this time. It is important to give a description of the complete warm-up before commencing, and to emphasise that this is not a memory test or competition. This is a warm-up that can also be done in groups of three or four.

From this point, the warming-up process needs to develop the trust and sharing of the group. One of the things that is most difficult for members is the transition from audience to stage. A useful technique is to have two chairs on the stage area facing the group, one for the director and one for participants, the director then invites each member to make a statement to the group from the chair or to simply sit in it for a moment. An explanation of the reason for doing this should also be given: that by each person experiencing the stage area, it can decrease their anxiety towards it.

Another progression may be to use the empty chair technique and ask if anyone wishes to speak to the concept of the workshop, their anxiety, etc. From here, small pieces of work may be enacted and, in terms of time, this may take up to the lunch break.

An alternative to this would be to ask the group to pair up and think of what they have brought with them, and whether they want to address that now. This could then begin the process of establishing a protagonist and going into a psychodrama.

The transition from the introductory phase to the enactment is difficult, but it is often the case that the sooner the action occurs the quicker the group gels. One of the processes that helps cohesion and trust within a psychodrama group is the sharing at the end of a protagonist's enactment.

If the workshop has a theme, it is important to facilitate that, but there is still the need to check the individuals' warm-up to the workshop by simply asking why they have chosen to attend and what their expectations may be.

Always bear in mind that this group is only meeting for a short period of time, and although therapy may take place, it is not a therapy group.

One-day workshops

A similar format to the week-end workshop can be used. In my opinion, these are the most difficult workshops to run in terms of providing participants with an experience of psychodrama and balancing that against the brevity of the group. Using techniques that can demonstrate the method and be containing at the same time is important, and there are some warm-up exercises that can be used in a more complete way.

Example – photographs

1   Ask group members to pair up or be in small groups and share a photograph of themselves at any time in their life. It can be made more specific by adding a happy or sad time, an important moment, etc.
2   Inform the group as to the purpose of this exercise – members will be asked to show the group their photograph so that some of the techniques of psychodrama can be demonstrated.
3   Depending on time, let the group know how many of these photographs will be seen.
4   Set the scene of the photograph, who is in it, who took it, etc. Role reverse with the other people, objects, photographer, camera, etc. Ask the protagonist if they would want to change anything about it, if they want to make a statement to it or to a particular person involved, then suggest they go into the photograph and it be taken again.

An important consideration to bear in mind when asked to run a day's workshop on psychodrama by an organisation is this: does everyone want to be there, or have they been 'sent'? This can be checked out right at the beginning, e.g. through establishing a continuum line – one end for those who want to be there and the other for those who do not. The director may even want to consider giving participants permission to leave. Alternatively, use an empty chair for them to address either the group, psychodrama or whoever has 'sent' them. The group are into action and also addressing the split that could sabotage the experience for those who wish to be there. Working this way is following the group process – discovering what the warm-up is that has been brought to the group and using it.

On-going therapy groups

Here, the warming-up process to the group and the method can be taken at a more relaxed pace. The director will have had far more control over the construction of the group and the other practical issues, as he/she will have interviewed members before the start of the group, and so relationships and warm-up have begun. Providing a safe environment for members to come and share their experiences is paramount, and this can be done by building connections between the members, so that they feel less alone and 'different'. A group identity begins to be established, and in time becomes more defined than in a group with a short life span. The contract of the group is clear – therapy – which provides all the group members with a connection and identity from the start.

Even though the first and possibly second sessions can be taken up with establishing boundaries, encouraging the cohesion of the group, educating members into the method and techniques, it is still important to bring the group to action as soon as possible.

Once members have worked through their warm-up phase to the group itself, there is then the warm-up phase at the start of each session. This is where the warm-up and group process meet, and the director needs to bear in mind the themes that have occurred in the group; who has worked and who has not; dynamics between members. In the therapy groups I have run – and this seems to be common to most therapy groups I have heard about – structured warm-ups are very seldom used. A brief discussion of the previous week happens, then each member shares what is with them at that particular moment. It may even transpire that what is more important in the group is to tackle some of the issues present between members rather than going into an individual's psychodrama. If the group is not able to support an individual in their enactment, it can be damaging to continue without addressing what is happening between members.

A SUMMARY OF POINTS

To conclude this chapter, I would like to repeat some of the points made.

1   A warm-up to what? The director should warm up the group to a task and provide the facilities to carry that task through, e.g. the emergence of a protagonist.
2   Each person's level and speed of warm-up is different.
3   There should be enough opportunity to explore the issue brought forward by the protagonist – a common error is to spend too much time on warm-up and find there is little time left for enactment.
4   The director should be aware that a group member may become ready to take the protagonist's role at any time during the warming-up process.
5   Attention should be paid to physical difficulties group members have.
6   Attention should be given to the objects in the room – are they in the way, do they pose a danger, is there enough room, etc.
7   The director should never predict the response/outcome of a warm-up when deciding on what to do.
8   Always encourage sharing after any warm-up, particularly physical, intimate and protagonist-centred.
9   The director should not take part in the warm-up. The group needs to know that he/she is holding the boundaries; can act if a member becomes overly distressed; has some awareness of what is happening to the group; is available to work with the group's material and not be caught up in his/her own.
10   The director should give clear, firm instructions, and know how many people are in the group when suggesting working in pairs or threes, etc. – it can feel very uncomfortable if the director has asked the group to split into pairs and there is an uneven number.
11   A clear outline of the warm-up exercise should be given before the group is

asked to do it. This lessens the 'unknowness' and so anxiety, and prevents members feeling they have been tricked into something.

12   Always explain the 'why' of a warm-up. The director should share his/her thinking with the group; it is a group method.

13   'The patient – group member/protagonist – is permitted to be as unspontaneous or inexpressive as he/she is at this time' (Zerka Moreno 1969).

14   When working in a very large group, dividing into smaller groups to provide a safer more intimate space reduces the anxiety.

15   *The director should see the group as the producer and him/herself as the co-producer, there to facilitate whatever the group is with. The warm-up should enhance and reflect the group's process, not be imposed on it.*

Finally, it is important to see warm-up as a process rather than a technique. It is intended to aid individuals into encountering issues and emotions they bring to the group. More and more I feel it is an imposition to ask a group member to participate in a warm-up which does not reflect, incorporate and so facilitate what is already there.

BIBLIOGRAPHY

Blatner, H.A. (1973) *Acting-In: Practical Applications of Psychodramatic Methods*, New York: Springer.

Goldman, E.E. and Morrison, D.S. (1984) *Psychodrama: Experience and Process*, Dubuque, IA: Kendall Hunt.

Hollander, C.E. and Hollander, S.L. (1978) *The Warm-Up Box*, Denver, CO: Snow Lion Press.

Kellermann, P.F. (1992) *Focus on Psychodrama – The Therapeutic Aspects of Psychodrama*, London/Philadelphia: Jessica Kingsley.

Kipper, D.A. (1986) *Psychotherapy through Clinical Role Playing*, New York: Brunner/Mazel.

Leveton, E. (1977) *Psychodrama for the Timid Clinician*, New York: Springer.

Moreno, J.L. (1946) *Psychodrama, First Volume*, Beacon, NY: Beacon House.

Moreno, J.L. (1953) *Who Shall Survive? – Foundations of Sociometry, Group Psychotherapy and Sociodrama*, Beacon, NY: Beacon House.

Moreno, J.L. with Moreno, Z. (1969) *Psychodrama, Third Volume*, Beacon, NY: Beacon House.

Rogers, C.A. (1959) *Psychology: A Study of a Science, Vol. III*, New York: McGraw-Hill.

Williams, A. (1991) *Forbidden Agendas: Strategic Action in Groups*, London/New York: Tavistock/Routledge.

Yalom, I.D. (1985) *The Theory and Practice of Group Psychotherapy*, 3rd edn, New York: Basic Books.

The action – how is psychodrama done?

THE STAGE

The stage

The theatre of psychodrama

John Casson

ON STAGE

> You are in a theatre.
> The stage is empty.
> You step out into the space. How do you feel?
> (fear? excitement? lonely? a desire to be playful?)
> Some one has placed an empty chair on the stage. What do you do?
> (flee? sit on it? kick it over? speak to the person you imagine sitting
>   on it?)
> What is the audience reaction?

> I can take any empty space and call it a stage. A man walks across this empty
> space whilst someone else is watching him, and this is all that is needed for
> an act of theatre to be engaged.
>
> (Brook 1976: 11)

You are in a therapy group: the therapist places an empty chair in the space. She says, 'Who or what is in this chair for you? What do you need to communicate to that person?'

> Who/what do you imagine?
> How do you feel?
> What do you do?
> What is the audience reaction?

THE ORIGINAL PSYCHODRAMA STAGE

Psychodrama originated in the theatre. In Vienna from 1921–4 Moreno worked with actors creating spontaneous scenes (Moreno 1983: 39). From these early experiments he realised the therapeutic value of spontaneous enactment and created a form of psychotherapy that uses a stage as its place of healing. Moreno traced the origin of his form of the therapeutic stage back to his early experiences of story telling and dramatic play with children:

> One of my favorite pastimes was to sit at the foot of a large tree in the gardens of Vienna and let the children come and listen to a fairy tale. The most important part of the story was that I was sitting at the foot of the tree, like a being out of a fairy tale and that the children had been drawn to me as if by a magic flute and removed bodily from their drab surroundings into a fairy land. It was not so much what I told them, the tale itself, it was the act, the atmosphere of mystery, the paradox, the irreal become real. I was at the centre, often I moved up from the foot of the tree and sat higher, on a branch; the children formed a circle, a second circle behind the first, a third behind the second, many concentric circles. . . . The stimulus was not the stage of Shakespeare or the stage of the Greeks, I had taken the model from nature itself.
>
> (Moreno 1947: 4–5)

This design Moreno developed as the first modern theatre in the round.

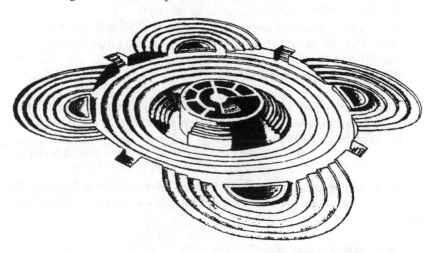

Vienna, 1924: based on the frontispiece of The Theatre of Spontaneity, Moreno, 1983

Writing whimsically of his discovery of the therapeutic stage Moreno acknowledged that the stage is born 'out of the seed in' the protagonist's mind: the stage is a place for mental projections, for dramatic, 'surplus' reality, infinite and playful.

The story of Johnny Psychodramatist

One day he had another inspiration . . . a seed fell from his mind to the ground. It made circles, one above the other. It was a stage upon which the moon shone its friendly light. He stepped upon it and acted the friendly neighbour, the strong courageous man and the bringer of luck. As he did this, he felt transformed, the stage underneath him grew bigger and bigger until it was as powerful and complete as any stage ever built. It had lights that simulated day and night. All the stage needed was a world to act upon it. From now on he initiated every man who came to him to be and act what he was in his fantasy. The story of Johnny who can build a stage for everyone out of the seed in their mind spread, and stages began to grow and blossom all over . . .

(Moreno 1956: in Fox 1987: 213–214)

This passage suggests the stage is a place of transformation, expansion, imagination, growth and light.

Theatre, since its shamanic origins in healing ritual, has been a place of the psyche; the theatrical space has always been psychological, spiritual and symbolic. Moreno reflected on the classical theatre of Greece and acknowledged the value of catharsis: a purging of emotions. In Sophocles' play *Antigone*, the Chorus sing a hymn to Dionysus invoking his 'swift healing', '*katharsios*' (Sophocles 1994: 39 and note 163). Aristotle in his *Poetics* recognised catharsis as an effect of tragedy (Fyfe 1967: 16).

Shakespeare also knew of the healing potential of drama. In *King Lear* there is a scene in which the king addresses an empty stool as his daughter Goneril in a 'psychodramatic' trial. Later in the play Edgar uses a guided fantasy and enactment to help his suicidal father (Gloucester). He states: 'Why I do trifle thus with his despair is done to cure it' (Act 4, scene 6, 33). In both these psychodramatic scenes other characters play auxiliary roles.

Moreno did refer to Shakespeare, Goethe and other theatrical antecedents of psychodrama in his writings (for example, quoting Goethe on the potential value of spontaneous theatre; Moreno and Diener 1972: 10) and, despite his disclaimer, Moreno's design for the psychodrama stage echoes that of the Elizabethan, and those more ancient stages, the classical Greek and shamanic theatres.

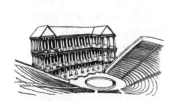

A Greek/Roman theatre
(reconstruction)

B Elizabethan theatre
(The Swan)

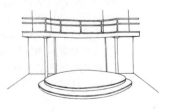

C Moreno's theatre
(Boughton, NY)

When Moreno built a theatre for psychodrama in 1936 he took from his first design the 'therapeutic principle of the circle' (Moreno 1985: 262) and translated this into three concentric circles at different levels. Zerka Moreno explains that the three levels were to be symbolic of the degree to which a person was ready to become a protagonist: as s/he warmed up to action s/he would step up first one and then another level until ready to work on the main stage (personal communication). To further develop the vertical dimension Moreno added a balcony above the stage.

> The design serves both theatrical and psychological functions. The levels may aid in the organisation of scenes or help clients and performers to start the action where they feel more comfortable; the gallery may be used to locate idealised or seemingly bigger than life figures.
>
> (Pendzik 1994: 30)

Describing Moreno's theatre at Beacon, New York, Umansky wrote:

> The theatre is approximately 70 feet long and 25 feet in width. It has a height of about 40 feet. Almost half of the theatre is taken up by the stage. There are three stage platforms in the form of concentric cirles. The largest one, about 16 feet in diameter, another platform two feet smaller in diameter and at the top, the main platform which has a diameter of 12 feet. The balcony, 9 feet above the stage, is as long as the width of the theatre, and beginning from the wall extends 3 feet to a line above the outer rim of the stage. It is supported by two posts which rise from the middle stage, and is railed in.

He describes the audience space and the coloured lights used to create different effects and then comments:

> Practically the design of the stage gives a large area for expressive move-ments. It facilitates scene setting and is of great suggestive utility. Theoretically the stages may symbolically represent terrestrial or celestial spheres of action. For instance, the balcony, which is really the fourth stage may be used in the case of a person who wishes to play Christ. He acts on the balcony, which represents Heaven, and the rest of the players act on the stage (Earth). Or, reversing the procedure if he wants to play Mephistopheles in Hell, the stage becomes his abode and the rest of the actors play upon the balcony (Earth). Again, in a case of feelings of inadequacy the top stage may represent perfection, and so, the actor may start on the lowest stage and gradually reach the top stage.
>
> (Umansky 1944 in Moreno 1985: 263)

Moreno's original theatre was moved from Beacon and reconstructed at Boughton Place, Highland, New York. It is a beautiful, harmonious, intimate space. The experience of going up on to the balcony is breathtaking: it is uplifting and provides a very different perspective on the scene below.

> The architectural design of the stage is made in accord with operational requirements. Its circular forms and levels of the stage, levels of aspiration, pointing out the vertical dimension, stimulate relief from tensions and permit mobility and flexibility of action.
>
> (Moreno 1993: 53–54)

WHY IS THE THEATRE OF PSYCHODRAMA EFFECTIVE?

1   Theatre stimulates spontaneity and creativity.
2   Theatre is a space where inner images can be externalised, embodied and concretised so that they can be worked with.
3   In the theatre anything is possible: surplus reality allows the protagonist to have what didn't happen in real life and to create new realities.
4   Theatre moves beyond language into action and emotion and provides the opportunity for the person to be both actor and audience (through the mirror technique) and so reflect on the experience, strengthening the observer ego.
5   Theatre stimulates the audience to make contact, through empathy and projective identification, with their own material.
6   By involving the protagonist in her/his sense of space and symbolism, theatre stimulates the right brain with its spatial awareness and emotional memory.

> Why a stage? It provides the actor with a living space which is multi-dimensional and flexible to the maximum. The living space of reality is often narrow and restraining, he may easily lose his equilibrium. On stage he may find it again due to its methodology of freedom – freedom from unbearable stress and freedom for experience and expression.
>
> (Moreno 1993: 53–54)

On the psychodrama stage a person can be anything they wish: psychodrama is *'the aesthetic demonstration of freedom'* (Moreno 1983: 82).

WARMING UP: SETTING THE SCENE

In theatre both actors and audience warm up to their roles: the audience by the many rituals of attending a play: buying tickets, having a drink, taking their seats; the actors by doing vocal and physical exercises. Moreno knew the value of warm-up in enabling people to be more spontaneous in their lives and regarded the first section of a psychodrama as a warm-up, enabling the group and protagonist to become more spontaneous and creative. Writing about the stage Moreno stresses the value of setting the scene for the protagonist's warm-up:

> The idea of a psychotherapy of space has been pioneered by psychodrama, which is action centred and comprehensively tries to integrate all the dimensions of living into itself. If a client steps into the therapeutic space, we insist on a description, delineation, and actualisation of the space in which the ensuing scene is to be portrayed – its horizontal and vertical dimensions, the objects in it, and their distance and relationship to one another.

> Here is an illustration of an actual case: the client is a teenage boy. He tells me, 'Doctor, I'm afraid to go home tonight.' I ask him, 'Why, what happened?' 'Well, this afternoon my mother and father had an argument and my father hit my mother and made her fall down the stairway. I saw her there, at the bottom of the stairs and became so furious at my father that I hit him. But then I got scared, took my bag of clothes, and ran away. Here I am, and I don't dare go home.'

> Now what do we do? How do we start psychodramatizing the incident? I ask the boy, 'Jack, where is the stairway? And where is your mother?' Jack moves about on the stage, points out the location of the stairway, places it in relation to the front door, the bedrooms, living room, etc., moving around in the space in which he experiences this episode, structuring it before our eyes.

> At this point we use a future technique. 'Jack, you go home now, but instead of really going to Brooklyn, where you live, you are going home right here in this room. Let's say you will be home in an hour from now. Set up all the spatial configurations as closely as possible. Who is home when you arrive and where are they located in space?' Jack explains and physically constructs the spatial arrangement: 'Well first of all I come in at the front door, here, into the living room. I expect my father to be over there, in his chair in the corner of the room, angry. My mother is in the bedroom upstairs, crying.' Now Jack proceeds to set up the rest of the space . . . (including) all things which he feels to be significant. He warms up more and more and gets increasingly involved in the situation. Soon he begins to see pictures on the walls; he notices that mother wears a certain dress, father smokes a cigar. . . . I cannot emphasise sufficiently that in our research the configurations of space as a part of the therapeutic process are of utmost importance. It warms up the protagonist to be and act himself in an environment which is modelled after that in which he lives.

> (Moreno and Moreno 1975: 13–14)

Role reversing with the scenery: embodying metaphors

It is useful in setting the scene for the protagonist to become aspects of that scene. These elements of the scenery, such as houses, rooms, cars, beds, mirrors can elucidate what the protagonist is containing, bottling up or holding within them; so for example it is useful to ask a protagonist role reversed into a family house, 'How does it feel to contain this family within you? What's the atmosphere like inside you?' These questions are to a house but they are also to the protagonist who, like a house, contains, within his mind, his family. Role reversing with objects can then be an owning of aspects of the self that have either been split off or are unconscious.

On becoming the fire

Joan contracts to work in an established therapy group on expressing her feelings towards her aunt and uncle. Uncle had sexually abused her as a child and aunt, a domineering, obsessional person, had colluded with the abuse and failed to protect Joan. The scene is set in the couple's lounge. Sensing the possibility of violence the director decides not to use members of the group as auxiliaries, simply to use empty chairs.

He invites Joan to speak to these chairs and confront them with her feelings. She freezes. The director half expected this from experience but wished to check out, diagnostically, how she is in relation to these people and to see if she is ready in her own role to express her feelings. Abused children, unable to fight or flee their abusers may freeze and dissociate from what is happening to them. Remembering that role reversal can increase the protagonist's energy, enabling her to get out of a stuck, powerless position the director invited her to role reverse out of her own frozen role into an object in the scene. This is a therapeutic dissociation: leaving the threatened and anxious person and entering into a solid object may seem at first an escape. Indeed, becoming a TV or a plaster duck on the wall might well be a lot safer in the house of an abuser than being a child. In as much as it allows the person to flee (which she was not able to do as a child) this technique empowers by giving freedom to move and moves with the resistance. There is also the likelihood that the object itself will be symbolic rather than a dead, objective item with no connection to the person. Often the director will invite the protagonist to identify a special object in the room and role reverse her with that object. When the protagonist identifies an object that comes to mind it is likely that it will have symbolic content otherwise it would not have come to mind. In this instance, the object chosen is the fire. In dramas of abuse fire, fireplaces, (gas or electric) cookers, provide important symbolic material. I will speculate why this is after describing what happens in this psychodrama.

The director immediately asks Joan to be the fire and interviews her as such.

Director What kind of fire are you?
Joan   A gas fire.
Director Are you on or off?
Joan   (as fire) I'm switched off.
Director Shall we turn you on?
Joan   No.
Director Why not?
Joan   She (referring to the aunt's chair) doesn't like the fumes.
Director Become the fumes (demonstrating). Move around the room as the fumes.

(The protagonist moves around the room waving her arms like clouds of fumes in a swimming motion. She has gone from frozen to free movement in 15 seconds.)

Director What do you want to do fumes?
Joan   I want to choke her (referring to aunt).

(The Director gets a large cushion and places it on aunt's empty chair.)

Director OK, go ahead, here she is, choke her.

(Joan puts her hands round aunt's (cushion) neck and strangles her.)

Joan   I feel like exploding.

   This last statement clearly comes from Joan as her self but seeing this metaphor of the fire as being a safe container for Joan the director decides to keep in the metaphor and replies,

Director OK, We'll have an explosion. Group, can you come round the gas fire. (The other members of the group surround Joan.) 5, 4, 3, 2, 1, BOOM! (The group explodes noisily outwards from Joan.)
Director Good heavens look at the mess, soot all over the wall, ornaments knocked over and broken, pictures fallen down, wall paper hanging off. (He is remembering that aunt was an obsessionally clean and tidy person: a hypocrite who hid the dirt and mess in her own home. Now the room is symbolically revealing the inner darkness and dirt in the relationships here. Having given Joan this brief guided fantasy the director checks to see if she has entered into it and to find out what is happening for her by questioning her.)
Director What do you see?
Joan   Well the explosion has knocked her over.
Director Do it.

(Joan pushes aunt's chair over backwards, the cushion falls on to the floor. Symbolically Joan has dethroned the domineering aunt. Only now can the psychodrama turn to the uncle as the feelings about aunt had previously stood in the way.)

Director   Where's uncle?
Joan   He's lying on the floor being pathetic, calling for her (aunt) to help him. (Joan laughs.) He's pathetic.

(Symbolically both these abusing adults are now powerless; only Joan is standing, they are both on the floor.)

Director   How do you feel now?
Joan   I feel like battering him.

(The Director places a cardboard box on uncle's chair and gives Joan a baton of rolled up newspaper reinforced by heavy duty tape.)

Director   OK, do it.

(Joan batters the box, flattening it and smashing it as she tells the uncle how angry she is about his abusive behaviour.)

From this example we can see how the role reversal into the object – the fire – warmed the protagonist up for action. The role was flexible, it shifted from fire to fumes to explosion and spontaneously back into the protagonist's own role as adult enabling her to move from frozen powerless child to active powerful adult.

THE SYMBOLISM OF FIRE

Theatre is not just the speaking of words on a stage but the exploring, concretisation and demonstration of images, symbols, relationships and actions that offer metaphors with multiple meanings to an audience, who then project their own feelings and fantasies onto the stage (Casson in Jennings 1997: 43–54). In this psychodrama what was the symbolism of the fire and what did it achieve? The symbolic associations of fire are extremely ancient and powerful. Fire is warmth and light. It is associated with love and lust. It can warm and cook (i.e. nurture and feed) and also burn and consume (i.e. hurt, devour, purify). The fireplace in the living room (prior to the age of TV and central heating) was the focus of the room. Indeed in ancient dwellings it was in the centre of the room. The word 'hearth' is directly related to the word 'heart', and so the hearth can be seen as a symbol of the heart and centre of the person: the seat of warmth, love, feelings. The symbolism of what kind of fire there is in the house of an abused person (or in the abuser's house) speaks of what kind of love there is therein. Is it real, artificial, dead and cold, burning or turned off? The fire can also represent a source of power and energy in the centre of the self and this was confirmed by other symbolic work which Joan had done some weeks previously when, drawing and then dramatising her image of the creation of the world, she had placed fire at the centre as the source of the creative energy. In this psychodrama the gas fire being turned off could represent the coldness in the aunt's and uncle's relationship and home. The poisonous fumes might symbolise the unexpressed, poisonous feelings that are kept repressed and it was clear that the explosion was a sudden release of the same. Joan had begun her drama feeling tense and with a headache. She ended relaxed, laughing and feeling lighter and better. Becoming the fire she had literally and symbolically 'warmed up', discovering her own internal fire, her ire, the burning rage that had previously consumed her in smouldering, black depression but could here burst out in open, blazing anger. The following week she reported that she felt much relieved and had realised that she had previously protected her aunt and uncle from her feelings. She also recognised that she had focused what feelings she was aware of on her aunt thus avoiding her violent feelings towards her abuser uncle. In her own role Joan had only the experience of being frozen, powerless and a victim. She was not conscious of her anger, violence and potential power. By role reversing her into a potent symbolic object that energy was released. Cox and Theilgaard (1994) in 'The Aeolian Mode: Mutative Metaphors in Psychotherapy', write of the energising power of elemental metaphors. This metaphor of the fire was to reappear weeks later when Joan, during a creative dramatherapy session, imagined herself as a free, playful and creative child quietly playing in the safe, nurturing presence of a loving grandmother by a warm, open fire.

THE PSYCHODRAMATIST AS THEATRE DIRECTOR ON STAGE

Kellermann (1992: 46), analysing the responsibilities of the psychodramatist, states that one of his/her roles is that of the producer: the theatre director responsible for staging and the aesthetic ideals of the psychodrama method. What then are the essential practical elements of psychodramatic stagecraft a director needs to know?

The stage manager's handbook hints

Safety

The prime responsibility of the psychodramatist is the safety of the protagonist and the group. Action techniques involve some risk and it is essential that the director pay attention to the basic safety of the space she/he is working in. Are there sharp edges – such as a mantle piece or head-height shelf? Are there objects which, if thrown, could cause damage?

Clearing the space

The director will prepare the room for psychodrama, clearing the space for safe action. As the stage must be able to become any place on earth or in the imagination it is important that it be free from specific associations: it is therefore best to have plain walls and a clear floor space. White walls reflect the colour of the lights.

The director on stage

Much of the time the director will be on stage supporting the protagonist. However it is important that the director does not take centre stage but moves in and out of the action as necessary and sometimes sits in the audience to see things from a distance. The director must not become so involved in the action that she/he loses sight of the group or becomes hypnotised by the transference or the drama. It is important that the director does not position him/herself between the protagonist and the audience in such a way as to block their view of the action or separate the protagonist from the group.

Use of space

As already stated, the spatial dimension is important: how much space does the protagonist want between herself and the other characters in the drama? Spatial awareness, being a right brain activity of personalised consciousness (see Sachs 1991), relates to symbolic processes and these can be concretised in the drama and represented through sculpting, which reveals the spatial dynamics of relationships.

Use of a platform

Moreno's design included a balcony for larger than life characters or 'heaven'. At the Holwell International Centre for Psychodrama and Sociodrama, North Devon, UK, there is a small platform, about 4 feet high. Psychodramatists may well have to work in rooms that have no such facilities. A table can be used though there will be concerns about safety. Even a small plinth, 1 foot high, can be remarkably useful. A protagonist so raised up can be empowered in relation to other figures and see things from a different perspective. It was Peter Slade, the founder of Dramatherapy in the UK, who first recommended the use of rostrum blocks (Slade 1995: 88).

The audience and the staging

The audience must be able to see the action otherwise they will lose touch and interest. Scenes can be literally turned round if they have been set up so that the protagonist's back is to the audience: the director can invite the group to imagine that the stage revolves and thus reset the scene. It is important to ensure the audience can hear: if a protagonist is speaking very quietly the director must repeat their words in a louder voice.

Changing scenes

Scenes can be dissolved instantly, though if furniture is used to represent significant material it may be necessary to check that items are de-roled before moving on (e.g. if a table had just been used as the slab in a morgue it might be difficult to sit down at it to eat dinner in the next scene).

Type and size of space for stage

It follows that some rooms are just too small for psychodrama. Blatner states the space 'should be at least approximately 12–15 feet in diameter' (Blatner 1973: 8). It is specifically stated in the British Psychodrama Association code of practice that: 'Psychodramatists will give attention to the physical environment in which they work with clients in order to provide a safe and secure space for therapy' (BPA 1994: 5).

Lighting

Moreno's stage design included coloured lights. Although these are not essential they do add much to the work. Colour symbolism is useful: red can signify hell or facilitate the expression of anger; blue may be used for dreams or deathbed scenes; green can denote a garden or woodland; yellow can be sunlight. Being able to dim the lights at moments of intimacy may facilitate catharsis and colours add atmosphere which in turn may help protagonists to get more in touch with feelings. The dimmer switches should be easily accessible to the director at the side of the stage or can be operated by a member of the group. The effects of the different colours can be used as a warm-up. In the absence of such equipment the lighting can still be varied: electric lights can be switched on/off. Clients have sometimes chosen to open the curtains to let light in: an action that is as much symbolic as actual. Ken Sprague gives a beautiful example of the use of natural sunlight in his chapter in *Psychodrama since Moreno* (Holmes *et al.* 1994: 29).

Equipment

Some psychodramatists would say they do not need any equipment. However some equipment can be useful.

- Chairs are essential for empty-chair work and can be used to symbolise many things.
- Batons (or batakas – 'encounter bats') for anger work: these can be made from rolled up newspaper covered in heavy duty tape or pipe insulating material reinforced by plastic pipe and covered in coloured tape. These are sometimes used on:
- pillows/cushions or

- cardboard boxes to help people express rage. As in the above example of Joan's psychodrama the protagonist may smash up a cardboard box.
- Some women prefer to kick cushions or rip sheets. (Hospital laundries have old sheets that can be torn up).
- A full-size dummy can also be useful for anger work.
- A few pieces of coloured cloth and/or a blanket.
- Some soft toys, a doll/teddy.
- A whiteboard, blackboard or flip chart can be used for drawing or writing up the contract for the session.
- 'A table can become a building top, a desk, a judge's seat, a breakfast-room table, or a cave in which to hide' (Blatner 1973: 7).
- Tissues and a waste bin.
- A bowl for being sick in (this is useful to reassure the client they won't make a mess and less likely to be actually used).

When *not* to use a stage

Richard does not want to use the stage: he feels it would be too empty, too exposed. He prefers to use the space in the centre of the circle of chairs where the group are sitting. He feels he needs the support of the circle of the group to face his feelings about his daughter's murder. He stands up and steps into the centre of the circle. To help him warm up to this scene Richard passes round the group the newspaper cuttings of his daughter's killing. The group sit in the circle surrounding him, witnessing his pain, containing and supporting him.

This is a pattern often witnessed in psychodrama: a circle and a centre. Such a ritual structure is an archetype of wholeness, of centering, of focusing, contacting the healing qualities of the self: relating the parts to the whole, the individual to the group: in effect a mandala. Moreno's own story of how his idea of the stage emerged from the concentric rings of children listening to his story telling in the Viennese park confirms that from the beginning his idea was a mandala. Even when we do not apparently use a 'stage' this archetype inherent in the actual stage is present in the circle of the group: Moreno's first design was a theatre in the round with the audience surrounding the action space. He did not want to use a space removed from the group by a proscenium.

Indeed it is not essential to use a separate stage area. Some psychodramatists prefer to work within the circle of the group rather than to move the protagonist out into another separate space. They are informed by group-analytic psychotherapy that emphasises the group as the container and locus of the therapy, or by person-centred philosophy that questions the need to theatricalise the therapeutic space. They are concerned to discourage a sense of a detached, 'observer' audience and encourage group involvement in a process. Both methods have valid reasons to use the space as they do, though something may be lost as well as gained. A visually impaired member of such a group told me that it was easier to visualise the psychodrama when it was set in a separate space than when it was played out in the middle of the group: then she could not get such a clear 'stage picture'. In the group space there may also be dangers from sudden movement, enacting scenes that might result in expressions of violent anger. The proximity of the group could be inhibiting. The opposite is also true: the proximity of the group could be experienced as supportive, containing and nurturing. The answer seems to be to ask the client what she wants: for some it is just too daunting to move into a larger separate space and the power to choose where the psychodrama is enacted seems rightly to belong to the protagonist. However, if the director senses that there is a possibility of safety being at risk, then it is wise to create distance between a protagonist and a figure with whom they are very angry.

Psychodramatists who work in school halls or theatres may well not use the raised stage (except as a higher platform for scenes that need to be raised up), preferring to work on the floor of the hall. Alternatively they may take the whole group up onto the stage area as not to do so would leave the audience too far below and removed from the main action, making it difficult for auxiliaries to move from their place in the audience up onto the stage and back. Intimacy may be lost and a separate stage space be too exposed and isolating for the protagonist.

SURPLUS REALITY: MAKING THE INVISIBLE VISIBLE

Richard steps into a space which is nowhere, a limbo: he reaches out to his murdered daughter. She is not there. He wants to ask her forgiveness for not having been able to protect her because he had not been there. He has lost her. Where is she? Gently the director asks him to role reverse with her and an auxiliary in his role asks the questions he had been asking. In the role of daughter he forgives himself and tells him she is not in pain and is free, and that she wants him also to be free from guilt. On returning to his own role and hearing these words spoken by an auxiliary Richard weeps. Later he feels a peace he has not experienced before.

This psychodrama took place within the circle of the group: the group being a container and a holding, witnessing audience.

Rosanne feels she needs to protect herself from the world. She feels she puts up a wall around herself. She demonstrates this castle, building it with the bodies of members of the group and then getting inside it. She feels safe but rather closed in, restricted. Yet she fears to leave its protective armour. She role reverses with the wall and speaks about her protective function, how strong she is, how old she is, when she had been most needed and whether she is still needed. By role reversing with the wall she is able to step out of her vulnerable, frightened self and own her strength, her ability to protect herself and inhabit the liminal space between inner and outer, from which she can look in at her vulnerable self and out at the world.

In this drama the group literally became the container which both concealed and revealed the protagonist's inner world. In other dramas the container may be a cage, a well, a box, a bottle; whatever symbolic object occurs in a dream, fantasy or figure of speech. Often protagonists speak of bottling things up, keeping the lid on, locking up the monster within, feeling trapped, constricted by body armour. In psychodrama such images are externalised, embodied and represented concretely so that the protagonist can explore and experience the release from such inner constriction, stuckness, rigidity and so flow, experience catharsis or unlock the secrets of such images.

Kellermann confirms this:

the psychodramatic stage offers an extraordinarily powerful vehicle for the externalisation of such internalised mental images; there, they are summoned to life and made to appear in a three-dimensional space.

(Kellermann 1992: 98)

Moreno writes in 'The Theatre of Spontaneity':

The stage space is an extension of life beyond the reality test of life itself. Reality and fantasy are not in conflict, but both are functions within a wider sphere – the psychodramatic world of objects, persons and events. In its logic the ghost of Hamlet's father is just as real and permitted to exist as Hamlet himself. Delusions and hallucinations are given flesh – embodiment on the stage – and an equality of status with normal sensory perceptions.

(Moreno 1993: 53–54)

Psychodramatic space is symbolic, poetic and plastic, rather than normal, prosaic, everyday space. Space in the theatre of psychodrama can be transformed in a moment from one place to another, from past to future, from large to small, inner to outer. The space is both real and surreal, actual and infinite, its boundaries limited only to our imagination. Indeed, theatrical and psychodramatic space is essentially psychological and symbolic. The space between two chairs can speak eloquently of the nature of the relationship between the two people in those chairs. The elasticity and symbolic nature of psychodramatic space can be illustrated as follows.

In a sociodramatic warm-up, group members are invited to place themselves as 'members' of a body, representing where they feel themselves to be in relation to the body of the group. (Who sees themselves as at the head or heart of the group, who is the listening ear, who the supportive leg?) The resulting arrangement reveals, in its spatial arrangement, something of the group dynamics. They are then invited to place themselves where they see themselves in relation to the body politic: the larger body of society and speak how they feel in that position. This reveals larger social/economic/cultural and political aspects of the group's life. Finally, they are invited to imagine that the whole room is their own personal body and to go inside to a place they need to visit for some healing. Thus the room has changed from macrocosm to microcosm, the same space expanding and contracting to enable exploration and play at different levels of reality.

A change of scenery: Marina's symbolic journey

A psychodramatist must be a master of such scene changing, following the protagonist wherever she wishes to go, even to another world.

Marina is a woman who needs to create her own space where she can be nurtured (she normally, as a mother, does all the nurturing of others and has her own space invaded by other people's demands). The psychodrama group members create a paradise island, the sea around it and the boat to reach it, and then become the islanders with their gifts of flowers, fruits, music, dance and wisdom. Almost the entire drama is spent in this relaxing, nurturing environment and when Marina returns home, bringing with her the islanders' gifts, she is able to rehearse telling her family she needs their help, support and also her own private space.

Such an imaginary drama creates the momentum for behavioural change but also harnesses the power of archetypal images – the sea journey, the water, the sun, the island, the wise woman, the ferryman, the fountain of youth (a cleansing, refreshing waterfall created by the group, showering gently, delicately using finger tips to massage and stroke her aura and body) to give Marina a healing, nurturing experience. In this psychodrama the protagonist role reverses with two positive images: the beautiful lily on the island and the wise woman. The role reversal into the lily triggers an association with the Biblical saying:

Consider the lilies of the field, how they grow; they toil not, neither do they
spin; and yet Solomon in all his glory was not arrayed like one of these.

Matthew 6, 28–29

In the role of lily Marina describs herself as beautiful (which she would not
have done in her own role through modesty) and accepts that she can just *be* without having to justify her existence with constant activity and caring for others. The
whole psychodrama is a nurturing experience, of her being and receiving rather
than doing and giving. As a mother and professional carer she has become
role-bound as a giver and these role reversals out of such a stuck role give her an
alternative experience of receiving and pleasing herself. The drama is gentle,
playful and joyous.

Psychodramas are not only about traumas but are also celebrations; not just
about harsh reality but also about creative, imaginative truth.

Kellermann, writing of the stagecraft skills of the psychodrama director,
states:

skilful stage-managers are able to turn the psychodramatic stage into a place
where anything, including the 'impossible', can happen. They are passion-
ately romantic and almost allergic to realism because realism ignores the
spirit of the person and does not provide access to the sacred, the ritualistic,
transcendental and cosmic dimensions of experience. Meshing fact and
fiction, they produce a kind of aesthetic truth in which the universals of time
and space are dissolved. Tricks that cheat death, instruments that tell the
future, devices that help remember the past, and magic shops are some of
the techniques psychodramatists use to produce dramatic art. Everybody
knows that sculptures do not talk, that God makes no bargains, that empty
chairs do not speak back and that walls between people are invisible. But
skilful psychodramatists are able to lead protagonists across the border that
separates the real outer world from the fantasy world of the imagination.
Before their natural suspicion is aroused, protagonists find themselves in
a boundless space where the experience of reality is expanded and, for a
short while, protagonists become more than mortal. When emphasising
the living spirit of inanimate objects in this way, psychodramatists produce
unpredictable moments of change which conventional theories cannot
sufficiently explain.

(Kellermann 1992: 50)

THE PHILOSOPHICAL FOUNDATIONS OF THE STAGE

Moreno developed his psychodramatic methods from his philosophy of the
Universals: Spontaneity/Creativity, Time, Space, Reality, Cosmos and the

Godhead. ('Cosmos' for Moreno signified the created, physical Universe; 'Godhead', the creator: whether human or divine. Moreno hoped to enable people to become co-creators of the Universe and creators of their lives.)

1   The stage is the place where spontaneity manifests in creative action in the here and now, yet also in 'dramatic time' (i.e. the drama can explore, through play, the past, present and future).
2   The stage is a space where two realities meet: everyday (consensus) reality and dramatic (surplus or inner, psychological, symbolic) reality.
3   The stage is also a microcosm of the Cosmos and shares qualities with the most ancient stages of shamanic and healing, sacred ritual. The stage can become anywhere in the world and be transformed in the twinkling of an eye from here to the Himalayas, to Heaven, to inside the human heart.
4   This theatre of therapeutic creativity also reaches transpersonal, archetypal depths and heights, and God is often present through role reversal in the action. S/He stands on the stage in the person of the protagonist as human creator of her/his own drama.

THE PSYCHOLOGICAL FOUNDATIONS OF THE STAGE

Above all, the stage is a space for creation. The space is open, cosmic, both empty and full of potential and personal:

> The heart of Kant's revolution in philosophy was his position that it is human consciousness, the nature of the human being's mental structures, that provides the external form of reality. Space itself, according to Kant, 'is not something objective and real but something subjective and ideal.'
>
> (Yalom 1980: 220)

Oliver Sachs confirms this:

> There is no representation of abstract 'space' in the brain – only of our own, individual, 'personal space' . . .
>
> (Sachs 1991: 188)

> Identity, memory and space . . . go together; they compose, they define, primary consciousness.
>
> (Sachs 1991: 186)

Sachs goes on to link body image and identity with the sense of spatial awareness: all functions of the right brain. The trance-like experiences of psychodrama protagonists may be due to a slight inhibition of the normal left brain dominance whilst right brain functions are stimulated. Emotions are processed in the right brain so the accessing of these through the engagement of right brain functions may be the reason why setting the scene warms up protagonists and can be sufficient to trigger catharsis. 'Everyday' reality may be the logical reality of the left brain and 'Dramatic' reality the personalised consciousness of the right brain: these two realities meet on the psychodrama stage. But the reality on stage is not just representational of inter- or intra-psychic states but a play space for free exploration of possibilities.

> Theatre and therapy are both concerned with potential space, the term which Winnicott (1980, 36) used to refer to an intermediate area of experience that lies between fantasy and reality. This space between symbol and symbolised, mediated by an interpreting self – an interpreting cast – is the space in which creativity becomes possible and in which we are alive as human beings, as opposed to being simply reflexive, reactive robots.
>
> (Cox 1994: 207)

The stage is the place where roles are played: Moreno stated that:

> Roles do not emerge from the self, but the self may emerge from roles.
>
> (Moreno 1993: 47)

Bill Radmall has suggested that the Self can be regarded as the stage: the space that expands as more roles are played upon it.

> The inner stage of a client may be equated with the concept of the self. It may be an appropriate metaphor for self, as self appears to be not so much a single entity but rather an arena wherein interaction between different components takes place.
>
> (Radmall 1995: 14)

Linda Winn also uses this metaphor for the intra-psychic world:

> If we recognise that in each of us there are a number of sub-personalities or different facets, then our inner world can be thought of as a stage on which various conflicts, arguments and dialogues are carried out . . .
>
> (Winn 1994: 85)

Moreno would agree with Shakespeare:

> All the world's a stage,
> And all the men and women merely players:
> They have their exits, and their entrances;
> And one man in his time plays many parts . . .
>
> (*As You Like It*, Act 2, Scene 7, 139–142)

ACKNOWLEDGEMENTS

The author would like to thank the following for their advice in the writing of this chapter: Anne Bannister, Clare Danielsson, Paul Holmes, Marcia Karp, Zerka Moreno. The illustrations for this chapter are by Andy Smith.

BIBLIOGRAPHY

Blatner, H.A. (1973) *Acting-In*, New York: Springer.
BPA (British Psychodrama Association) (1994) *Code of Practice*, available from the BPA Office, Heather Cottage, The Clachan, Roseneath, Dumbartonshire, G84 ORF.
Brook, P. (1976) *The Empty Space*, London: Pelican/Penguin.
Cox, M. and Theilgaard, A. (1994) *Mutative Metaphors in Psychotherapy*, London: Tavistock.
Fox, J. (ed.) (1987) *The Essential Moreno*, New York: Springer.
Fyfe, W.H. (1967) *Aristotle's Art of Poetry*, Oxford: Clarendon Press.
Holmes, P., Karp, M. and Watson, M. (eds) (1994) *Psychodrama since Moreno*, London: Routledge.
Jennings, S. (1997) *Dramatherapy Theory and Practice 3*, London: Routledge.
Kellermann, P.F. (1992) *Focus on Psychodrama*, London: Jessica Kingsley.
Moreno, J.L. (1947) *The Future of Man's Self*, Psychodrama Monographs No. 21, New York: Beacon House.
Moreno, J.L. (1983) *The Theatre of Spontaneity*, Ambler, PA: Beacon House.
Moreno, J.L. (1985) *Psychodrama, First Volume*, Ambler, PA: Beacon House.
Moreno, J.L. (1993) *Who Shall Survive?*, Student edition, Roanoke, VA: American Society of Group Psychotherapy and Psychodrama, Royal Publishing Co.
Moreno, J.L. and Diener, G. (1972) *Goethe and Psychodrama*, Psychodrama and Group Psychotherapy Monographs, No. 48, New York: Beacon House.
Moreno, J.L. and Moreno, Z. (1975) *Psychodrama, Third Volume*, New York: Beacon House.
Pendzik, S. (1994) 'The Theatre Stage and the Sacred Space: A Comparison', *Journal of the Arts in Psychotherapy*, Vol. 21, No. 1: 25–35 (Pergamon).
Radmall, B. (1995) 'The Use of Role Play in Dramatherapy', *Journal of the British Association for Dramatherapists*, Vol. 17, Nos 1–2.
Sachs, O. (1991) *A Leg to Stand On*, London: Picador.
Slade, P. (1995) *Child Play*, London: Jessica Kingsley.
Sophocles (1994) *Antigone, Oedipus the King, Electra*, trans. H.D.F. Kitto, Oxford: Oxford University Press.
Winn, L. (1994) *Post-Traumatic Stress Disorder and Dramatherapy*, London: Jessica Kingsley.
Yalom, I. (1980) *Existential Psychotherapy*, New York: Basic Books.

THE PROTAGONIST

Chapter 6

The protagonist

Kate Bradshaw Tauvon

[The protagonist] is asked to be himself on the stage, to portray his own private world. He is told to be himself, not an actor, as the actor is compelled to sacrifice his own private self to the role imposed upon him by a playwright . . . no one is as much of an authority on himself as himself.

(Moreno 1934/1993: 54)

WHAT IS A PROTAGONIST?

When Moreno describes the protagonist as an actor he intends it in the meaning of the one who enters into action. The word 'protagonist' when literally translated from the Greek means 'the first into action' or 'the first in the struggle'. According to Greek mythology the god Protagonos' name alluded to his being the first-born of all the gods. The protagonist in a psychodrama session is the person who is the main 'performer', the person who works on stage during the action phase of the group.

Initially in each session all group members are potential protagonists and sometimes during the warm-up phase, pair or small group exercises are used by the director giving everyone the experience of being protagonist at least for a short time. Each person has the opportunity then of presenting something of themselves and their lives. In moving from the warm-up phase into action, often one person is chosen to be the subject or protagonist of a group session. This person then goes forward as the group's representative to work in action, the 'first-born' on the stage. The protagonist works dramatically with the theme most relevant at that moment for the group, and is the person most warmed-up to work with that theme. Usually at this stage the protagonist is so involved in their own warm-up that they are unaware of the process links with the group. She may for example take up a situation at work where a colleague has recently left and a new colleague has joined the department. Another member of the group might be focusing on what happened to him when his brother left home. Maybe a group member has left the group and a new member has started. The theme could then be described as having to do with separation, abandonment, loss of an important person, adapting to an unsought change and sibling relationships.

It is my view that the theme of the psychodrama is always a reflection of the here-and-now situation in the group, in the protagonist's life and in the individual members' lives, even if the scene is set in the past or the future. Not all directors agree with this viewpoint. For example, some directors prefer when working with the group to do this only from a sociometric standpoint, based on ideas on tele, cognition and encounter. The concept of the group as an entity provoking transference responses is thus entirely irrelevant, as is the concept of transference in the protagonist's psychodramatic work. Other directors see the group only as a resource from which protagonists and auxiliaries can be drawn; to enable one person to work on their personal issues psychodramatically; and the source of sharing. The concept of the group as an entity provoking transference responses is equally irrelevant here. This model resembles the Gestalt approach, according to many psychodramatists a method developed from Morenean origins by Fritz Perls, among others – in my experience it is individual therapy in a group setting. It is not my aim here to define all models of psychodrama used in modern psychodrama practice, rather to emphasise that there are other paradigms than the one I describe in detail.

Directors do not always work with a single protagonist throughout one session. On occasions there may be enacted a series of 'vignettes', one-scene psychodramas, with a series of different protagonists. It may also be that during the drama the director may work with several protagonists simultaneously, a multiple-protagonist session. The latter practice requires a director with considerable experience.

The protagonist's position is privileged and not one into which a person should be coerced. The way a person enters the stage gives the director many clues, through body language and by what they say. The therapeutic alliance created at that point will influence the depth of the work. The protagonist must feel that it is they who are in control of what takes place, as they commence their work, and that they will be listened to and respected. Since it is the director who is trained in the method of psychodrama and is required to direct the drama, a working relationship needs to be developed. This necessitates the potential protagonist having a degree of trust in the director and often it is through the director that trust in the group and method develops. Consensus between the director, protagonist and group is essential for spontaneity to lead to creativity in the enactment. For the process to work well the group's warm-up is all-important. There is no such thing as a bad protagonist – only an insufficiently warmed-up group or director.

It may be that in an on-going group a person comes to the group already warmed-up to work with a specific issue. The director must be spontaneous enough to meet the situation. Individual members are strongly affected by each others' working material, consequently the warm-up may occur over a long period of time. Different members play out the group's story, questions and possible answers throughout the life of the group.

HOW IS A PROTAGONIST SELECTED?

Selection by the director – J. L. Moreno's method

J. L. Moreno often worked with psychotic clients and he would schedule psychodramas in advance. He would work with that client group using trained auxiliaries, as it was necessary with such clients to firmly structure the situation. Some directors today work in a similar way with a team of trained auxiliaries, often where the client group has experienced severe trauma, for example, victims of armed violence or incest, where it is advisable to limit what could be overwhelming dynamics.

The director may personally select the protagonist. I have seen Zerka Moreno do this, often in a very large group of 200–300 people, probably because the process of working towards a group choice would be prohibitive time-wise but her judgement is also founded on an astute capacity to gauge the group's needs. She has conveyed that she has an intrinsic belief in the group's capacity to warm up to supporting the protagonist's work. It is my view that this method of selection should be exceptional, as it is by far preferable, where time and group size allows, for the group to choose. The protagonist is then the group's sociometric choice and the work based on the group's process. As a psychodrama director there are many group pressures to demonstrate omnipotence which for everyone's health should be resisted. It takes great experience to know what forces are at large in a given moment and none of us is infallible. The experienced director may, however, select the protagonist from an assessment of the needs within the group. The choice is based on therapeutic experience. Such a choice may be made, for example, when a group member is unlikely to be chosen by a group because of undeveloped or unhealthy group dynamics or due to the protagonist's lack of capacity to express their need in a way that a group can appreciate.

Selection by the group

It is more usual to make use of the tele connections between members of a group than to pre-plan who will be the protagonist in a particular session. The group selects the protagonist by first listening to the alternative themes the potential protagonists express. There are many ways to indicate which theme or person the group supports. For example each person may place themselves behind the person who represents the theme they feel most closely connected to. Often I ask the group to *sense* where they will place themselves rather than to *think* it out. This facilitates each person's engagement in the drama. By placing themselves behind the protagonist a group member makes a personal commitment to work with that theme, even though it is someone else in the group who represents the theme on stage. It has many times been confirmed that it is the group which has infinite wisdom in choosing the protagonist, who will best represent the salient theme. They have knowledge that the director cannot always be aware of. If a creative working atmosphere has been facilitated, the wise director will trust the group's capacity to make the most informed decision.

Where there are several potential protagonists the director can ask them 'If it were not you who should work as protagonist now, which protagonist best represents the theme you would choose to work with?' The potential protagonists then decide between themselves who should work now. This method enables each person who has put themselves forward to be protagonist to make the sometimes difficult warm-up transition back from the role of potential protagonist to the role of audience member, who may be asked to play an auxiliary role. The group members outside the choice-making procedure, that is to say, those who had not opted to be the protagonist now, can sometimes feel excluded and the director needs to watch for this and take action if necessary.

Selection by individual members

Members of a group can be invited to express their wishes at the beginning of a working period, which could be a 3-hour session or could be a week-long workshop. An agenda is worked out which is then followed. This can be of value, for example, in a group with a high anxiety level, or in a training group. The group knows that new protagonists will not be chosen as the group process develops session by session and the warm-up occurs within that frame. This can be a very effective way to use the time as the group's energy is focused on the agreed work and not dissipated on other issues, which might have to do with competition, rivalry or fear of each other within the group.

Choice in advance

A variation on this method is that a protagonist can be selected for a session planned in advance even in a group where the norm is one of selection immediately prior to each protagonist-centred drama. Where a group member has great difficulty in spontaneously warming up to the role of protagonist a first step may be planning a session, whereby it is known in advance that that person will work on stage on a certain date. The group can begin directly with the drama after the director has established that the warm-up and focus in the session is adequate. The following example illustrates the intervention of a director which leads to a session planned in advance:

In the sharing phase of a particular session, one of the group members is totally silent. As her therapist I am aware that for the first time in the group, a situation almost identical to traumatic events which have occurred in her life has been represented on stage by another protagonist. Although she has not expressed anything verbally she is extremely tense and has almost stopped breathing. I mentally reverse roles with her and I know that she is deeply moved, frightened and is sitting with feelings she dare not take up, especially as we have reached the end of this group session. Attempts at encouraging her to share these feelings have been fruitless so I share what I experienced when I mentally reversed roles with her and suggest that in the next session she should be the protagonist. She bursts into tears and the group responds by supporting my suggestion. She agrees that she will work psychodramatically at the next session, with the material which is now so difficult to mention.

To ignore the physiological signals of this silent group member would be tantamount to re-traumatising her. As her therapist I know of the circumstances of her trauma and of course she knows that I know. As I understand it she told me because she wants to work through these events in the group and to do that somehow she has to be able to share the information in the context of the group. The group does not as yet have this information and they are therefore largely incapable of facilitating her sharing. An intervention of some sort by me is absolutely necessary if she is not to feel abandoned once again in the face of an overwhelming event. I assess that a week is too long a time for her alone to contain the anxiety resulting from the session and that by assisting her to commit herself to working the following week the anxiety can be held by the group as well until then. Knowing that she will have time then makes it more possible to come back, a feat which otherwise could be enormously difficult since she would be obliged to struggle in isolation with her ambivalence about naming the event. By saying what I experienced when I mentally reversed roles with her, I make overt that there is something to be shared with the group without breaching her trust and in that way assist her doing so. When the following week comes, she is of course not obliged to work if she is not ready but she has the option to work.

I will give you an example of another group member. I had considered discussing the idea of a choice in advance this time because this group member almost never opted to be the protagonist.

A man with a particularly high anxiety level has been a member of a group for four years and has only worked on a couple of occasions on stage in short vignettes (one-scene psychodramas). I have thought occasionally that he might need to know in advance that he is the chosen protagonist in order to gain the courage to try on the role but since he is clearly benefiting from the group I have withstood the temptation to push. I finally decide that the time has come to take up the issue with him and the group, when he spontaneously steps forward as a potential protagonist and is chosen. The theme of the drama is about being able to take action without intervention from authority figures. This example demonstrates something about tele but also about how different people's warming-up rates can be. I am convinced that allowing people to go at their own pace is a wise directorial strategy and a useful ground-rule which can be stated at the beginning of a group.

In this case the director and the group member were engaged in some kind of unspoken battle of wills. The group member had much earlier presented the problem in the group of not being able to take action without direct guidance from an authority figure but persisted through his behaviour in trying to gain the director's participation in his preferred pattern of relating. Naming the problem did not seem to facilitate moves towards the desired change. What I had earlier observed is the way in which he controls the steering wheel of his life, remaining in the known if uncomfortable role of 'child' or 'underdog', the risk of anything else being too anxiety-provoking. He has on other occasions taken the counter-role, namely that of 'top dog' or 'parent' demanding equally little risk of changing the equilibrium. As a director when confronting such a conflict it is hard to know what intervention to make and the timing of that intervention. At some point the group member has to try taking a new role, thereby confronting the anxiety and breaking the old mould which has formed earlier patterns of relating. For the change to be meaningful in his development, he needs to take this step without the intervention of an authority figure. The director must in these circumstances be able to resist being 'helpful' and instead be able to wait for the group member to initiate a new move. Then the director should be instantaneously ready to support him in his new initiative.

A TYPICAL SESSION

We begin with a warm-up which may be in the form of theatre games and/or a recounting of what each person has reflected over since the last session. Group members may relate anything of importance which they have experienced and which they would like the group to be aware of. This may take up to an hour of a 3-hour session. The group is then asked who feels warmed-up to work as the protagonist and to say a few words about what they would like the group's help in working with. Sometimes I get everyone to make a statement about what they need or want to work on, which puts some gentle pressure on the resistant and scared participants. They may be invited to express a feeling they experience just now and a scene or person they connect with that feeling, or give their work a title. When it is clear which members are potential protagonists the group members who have not put themselves forward are asked to select which theme they feel closest to and to demonstrate this by placing their hand on the shoulder of the person who has stated that they want to work with that theme.

Once the protagonist has been selected the director and protagonist go on to the designated stage area and the remainder of the group sit in a semi-circle at a little distance where they are able to watch the drama. Some directors prefer to work 'in the round' whereby the group sits in a circle and the drama is enacted in its midst. The protagonist is interviewed by the director to establish the working contract and may be asked to soliloquise, that is to walk around the stage speaking his thoughts aloud.

A first scene is established and the protagonist is asked to set the scene, using objects or people to represent the important aspects of the place. If it is a room in a house, the doors and windows are represented and any significant objects placed within the room. The protagonist may be asked to reverse roles with the house, the room or any of the objects in the room, to establish their significance and to help him warm up to what is to occur in that place. The time of the scene and the psychodramatic age of the protagonist is established. If other people are needed in the scene, group members are selected to represent them, warmed up to their roles and invited on to the stage. The protagonist may be invited to set the roles by role reversing with important figures or for example by giving three significant qualities in their character's relationship to them, in this scene. Once the protagonist has oriented the scene in terms of time, place and person the action can begin. If he is demonstrating something that happened in the past, the director is likely to ask him to reverse roles in order to demonstrate what happened. For the protagonist the act of showing a group of people what happened in his life, especially when it concerns an event where he felt totally unsupported or which was experienced as too awful or crazy to be true, can enable him to accept a grim moment in order to then let it go.

The protagonist may be directed to say or do what he would have liked to have done originally if circumstances had been more favourable and possibly to include others in the scene who ought to have been there. In dream scenes or enactments of fantasies the protagonist places his inner world on the stage, concretising the symbols to better understand them. The director needs to be aware of what is adequate in the scene, what is excessive, underdeveloped, conflicted or absent. Additional roles may need to be introduced to the scene if a component necessary to the protagonist's work is missing. Throughout the enactment, a dialogue is created between important figures in the protagonist's life, real or imagined and role reversals occur facilitating new insights. To see oneself from many new perspectives is a rich experience. This dialogue is both verbal and non-verbal and may include being held physically, hitting or kicking (directed in a way that no one is harmed), looking into another person's eyes, re-visiting a place dramatically which the protagonist may have dreaded or longed for, and experiencing the emotions connected to that place and events which may have occurred there or ought to have. Throughout the psychodrama the protagonist is as engaged as possible on all levels, physical, emotional, cognitive and spiritual. Laughing, crying, shaking with fear, shouting, relaxing, feeling safe, seeing and being seen, silently looking, saying what has been forbidden to say, are some oft-recurring experiences. Most importantly, through experiencing physically the emotional quality of an encounter, hearing and speaking the words and really seeing the other, in a defined context, reversing roles with the other and seeing oneself with the same intensity, enables the protagonist to unblock locked up painful memories, let go of the pain and pave the way for new possibilities. This process, where thoughts and feelings come together in the relevant context and in the presence of necessary others, is known as the catharsis of integration. The learning does not only take place during a psychodrama session but the process started there often continues weeks, months or even years afterwards. The pennies keep dropping in unexpected moments.

Where an historic scene has been enacted it is relevant to define the corollary in the protagonist's current life and to represent that dramatically. A scene in the future may be played out, in order to put into practice newly acquired skills or knowledge. When the drama is felt to be complete the protagonist is again oriented in time, place and person before sitting in the group circle to receive sharing.

During the sharing, the closure of a session, the protagonist remains largely silent and receives from the other group members whatever they want to share about the way the drama touched them and their lives. The sharing may be verbal or non-verbal. Hearing that others can connect with him in so many ways, that he is like so many others in so many ways, is often very moving for a protagonist and also has a healing effect. It may be hard for him to receive some comments, maybe he sees differences more than similarities. Sometimes a person sharing from his life experience connects with an aspect of the drama that he himself has been unaware of and has not yet registered could be an element worth considering. Not all sharing need necessarily be relevant to the protagonist. It can be hard work for him just to receive and to accept what is shared without blocking himself. If he is able to do this he can afterwards access, review and reflect on what his psychodrama has elicited in others and the learning can continue. Sometimes immediately after a session it is hard to recall what happened. The protagonist may be unclear what the steps through the drama have been and may need to discuss this with the group or the director at a later date. In an on-going group there is no hindrance to this but where the group will not meet again it is helpful for protagonists to know that they may contact the director. Such an agreement is confirming and respectful of the relationship the protagonist has with the group and the director and supports the work they have done together.

WHAT DOES A PROTAGONIST DO?

The protagonist, with the help of the director and the group, presents the issue to be explored in the group via their own drama. He or she takes the principal role in the enactment to be presented on stage. The protagonist can play roles other than their own and another group member can take the personal role of the protagonist, through the use of role reversal. The protagonist can also be taken out of the scene and observe the drama from a distance by using the mirror technique. Zerka Moreno has said that if you leave the protagonist in their own role, for example that of 'depressed person', what you will see will be diagnostically authentic.

> We try to take the person out of himself. If you leave him or her in the role of the depressed, the chances are that what you'll get is diagnostically valid, because you will see how the depression operates within the patient. But how are you going to pull the patient out of it? We find that the best solution is to take them away from their own identity, through having them enact the role of a significant person who is not depressed. It could be a child, or some other person who is loved by or loves the patient. It is remarkable how even a depressed person can be lifted out of a depression, at least momentarily. The patient can be made to feel what it is like not to be depressed, even for 5 or 10 minutes. That in itself is an eye-opener – the fact that they can warm up to a new emotional state.
>
> (Zerka T. Moreno 1975)

The main therapeutic technique which thaws a protagonist's frozen spontaneity and creativity is role reversal and it is principally this, which can effect change in a person's role repertoire.

Making a contract

Initially the director helps the protagonist focus on the area of conflict to be explored and a verbal contract is established. This is necessary to ensure that the protagonist shoulders the responsibility for what is taken up. It is of little use to produce a spectacular drama if the protagonist afterwards says that that was not what they wanted to work on. An agreed focus or focuses should be prioritised for the psychodramatic work to be done in this session. This should be a goal that is achievable in the time available. A person's life problems, dilemmas or questions cannot all be addressed in one single session and this can be stated.

> Over a period of time protagonists develop greater role-taking skills and are released from their old frozen attitudes and roles, becoming more authentic and open. It seems reasonable to assume that as protagonists experiment with new roles in the psychodramatic situation, they begin to change feeling

and thought in their new roles. Psychodrama presents an array of novel situations which require the total attention of the protagonist and group members for the production of adequate responses. The opportunity for the emergence of spontaneity is maximised in creating new behaviour.

(Karp 1994: 58)

Once having decided to work on stage, a contract might typically be worked out as follows:

Director   Do you have an idea of how you would like to begin your drama?
Protagonist   I have a pain in my stomach. I've been thinking about what happened at work yesterday and I don't know how I'm going to face going back. I am so angry about what my colleague has done.
Director   We could begin by having you reverse roles with your stomach and from that role express what you feel or we could set the scene of you place of work and you could show us what it was that happened yesterday that made you so angry. Which feels closest emotionally?
Protagonist   I keep playing over in my mind what happened so maybe it's best to start there.

Negotiating a contract is not always so straightforward. Sometimes the protagonist talks more than is needed, wanting to give a lot of details or cannot decide between several different problem areas. A useful ground-rule is to get the protagonist into action as soon as possible. This allows the director time to reflect and gives them the necessary distance to follow the emotional clues. It isn't unusual for the protagonist to want to delegate the decision and ask the director to decide what should happen. If you ask the protagonist to reverse roles with the director, they are likely to discover that each of us is the expert on our own life. No one else can know what one needs to do. Then the protagonist is more prepared to suggest a starting point.

The director can ask the protagonist what in their role or in this scene, is overdeveloped, adequate, underdeveloped, conflicted or absent. One can *stop and correct* what was happening in the scene by enacting what 'should' have happened, bring in someone one would have liked to be there or remove someone who 'should' not have been allowed to do what they did. A 'child' can receive the necessary support in order to grow rather than having to pretend to be strong. Often in such scenes we see the moment when the child decided to take to themselves a defence role such as 'becoming' a rock or 'becoming' invisible, a coping strategy which has got them through life but which hinders further development. By going to the scene the director can ask 'What would you need in order not to have to be a rock/be invisible?' and the protagonist can receive what is needed to be able to let go of what is no longer useful, by being able to take what they need, not only in the scene but in life from now on.

It is usual for the contract to be renewed throughout a drama in the face of new information. If we follow the example above, it may be that when we dramatise the scene the protagonist is reminded of something that has happened earlier in life. The colleague with whom the person is so angry may remind them of a brother and something that occurred between them when they were teenagers.

The contract renewal might go like this:

Director   You mentioned that you have felt like this before in relation to your brother. It could be useful to explore that, to see where this problem started. What do you think?
Protagonist OK.
Director   When did it occur?
Protagonist I was 14 and we were staying with relatives in the countryside.
Director   Set up the scene as you see it in your mind's eye.

This is followed by focusing questions, e.g. Where are we? Which room are we in? How big is the room? Who else is here? What is going on? Who speaks first?

A contract may be much more specific, for example:

Director   What would you like to have achieved by the end of this session?
Protagonist I would like to feel more confident about going back to work.
[and/or]   I would like to have tried to get rid of my stomach ache.
[and/or]   I would like to have better control of my anger.
[and/or]   I would like to understand why such a small thing has made me so angry and afraid.

At the end of the session, it would then be appropriate for the director to ask if the protagonist feels that the goals have been fulfilled and to take the necessary action if they have not.

Action

The protagonist may enact just one scene or several, which may take place in the past, present or future and which may or may not have occurred or be likely to occur in actuality. Since the basic work of the protagonist is to develop their spontaneity and creativity to be able to meet situations optimally, it is not always a requirement to go back in time to the origins of a behaviour or a response. Sometimes this is contra-indicated especially if an event has been particularly traumatic. A comparable spontaneity training situation can be improvised, in the realm of surplus reality instead. Working in a group be it as a protagonist, an auxiliary or a member of the audience often cannot function adequately until some bridge can be made between the inner and outer worlds. The transitional space can be the psychodrama theatre.

When working with the protagonist on stage the enactment is not a re-creation of reality, even when we go back to a scene in childhood, but the creation of a scene in surplus reality, something which is over and above reality. You might say that we are even creating a new reality. When joining a group each of us brings with us a world-view shaped by our life experiences to date. This is inevitable but expectations based on negative experiences can lead us in the role of 'director/producer' of our life play, to perpetuate a negative world-view, by casting our co-actors in life in old negatively loaded roles and re-producing our life play as a tragedy. We, simply expressed, replay an old script. This is the essence of transference and the instrument is 'projection'. We project the role we expect on to the other and if we persist, often through the process of projective identification, we get what we have demanded. In such a way a person who has been beaten as a child can precipitate a beating from a partner who never before has beaten anyone. In psychodrama we aim to leave old scripts and to constantly create new ones.

Derek

Derek had been given up to a children's home at the age of a few weeks old. Through the years he was passed from one institution to another (this occurred during a period when the authorities considered it unwise for children in such homes to become attached to any one particular member of staff). Every time he became attached to a member of staff he was moved to another institution. He had no positive memories of his life and had repressed much of his childhood. As an adult, not surprisingly, he had created no friendships and had never had a partner. He had begun training as a lawyer but gave it up when he became deeply depressed in the face of certain material which he was obliged to consider as a part of his training. He was anxious in joining the group and mistrusted us all although he still had a glimmer of hope in the therapists. 'The authorities know best' was the dictum which had steered his life, even if it was a reality which felt dire. Over a period of years in the group as well as grieving over the childhood he had not had, he enacted and built up a new childhood, with new memories. He experienced what it felt like to have parents, siblings and friends, who were represented by constant auxiliaries and who were, by the way, brought into almost every drama he presented as protagonist. He had the experience of playing such roles in others' dramas and finally was able to appreciate and internalise, that he was liked by others in the group and that he liked and trusted them. This led to the creation of friendships with others outside the group. He tried out some closer relationships and later I heard that he had a steady girlfriend and had taken up his studies again.

The protagonist in surplus reality scenes

Earlier I described a typical psychodrama session but the action need not have any apparent connection with a person's waking life, agreed reality or logic. The place of enactment could be on another planet, in another lifetime. The person might enact a relationship to another person who in factual terms does not exist. It is not at all unusual to work with a protagonist on a metaphoric level, in the sphere of surplus reality or on a fantasy level. Francis Batten, when discussing the role of the director as intermediary in such scenes, has cited the importance of the role of 'inter-reality' traveller:

> who has awareness and openness to different realities (e.g. scientific, consensus or mythic); to trances, transcendent or meditative states; to personal vision, dream, fantasy and the collective unconscious. The 'inter-reality travellers' do not lose their passports; i.e. as they cross frontiers, leaving and returning to consensus reality, they maintain a sense of Self.
>
> (Batten 1992: 62)

The role of inter-reality traveller is of course important for the protagonist too. The director meets the protagonist where they are. When working with a dream, a state of surplus reality supplied by nature, the protagonist presents the dream as they recall it. The content is not analysed or interpreted by the therapist but through role reversal with the different elements of the dream, the dreamer arrives at a new understanding of their meaning and may make links with events in their waking life. Throughout the enactment, the level of surplus reality is maintained. A similar way of working with a protagonist can be achieved by working through myths or fairy stories or even for example by enacting a whole drama in the role of another family member.

Mary Watkins, a Jungian analyst, has presented perspectives on imaginal dialogues which concur with Moreno's concept of surplus reality. She says:

> I shall place before you the view that imaginal dialogues do not merely reflect or distort reality, but create reality; that the real is not necessarily antithetical to the imaginal, but can be conceived of more broadly to include the imaginal; and that personifying is not an activity symptomatic of the primitivity of mind, but is expressive of its dramatic and poetic nature.
>
> (Watkins 1986/1990: 58)

An acceptance of the protagonist's experience of reality is the starting point of any psychodramatic work.

A group member, Caroline, had for some weeks talked about a woman, with whom she imagined her husband was having an affair. She had no concrete evidence that the relationship existed but the woman was affecting her marriage whether she existed in reality or not. She existed in Caroline's reality and was affecting her marriage, every living breathing moment of her own life and of her husband's. We worked with a scene in surplus reality on stage, whereby a meeting between the three of them was played out. By creating a relationship with the other woman, reversing roles with her, and creating a dialogue between herself, her husband and the other woman, Caroline was able to free herself from the paralysis which had prevented her from dealing with the marital problems and from making decisions about her own life.

An interesting footnote to Caroline's story was that despite earlier confrontations with her husband over a period of several months, where he had denied the existence of the other woman, it was later revealed that she did exist and that he had had a sexual relationship with her for several years. After that point they could talk about the truth of the situation. They almost separated but went on to fall in love all over again and make a new commitment to their own relationship. Her husband dared to have a different relationship with Caroline, being truer to himself.

The protagonist within systems

This might seem obvious but I will anyhow state that protagonists are not always best served by bringing into consciousness repressed pain which reveals itself in dreams or metaphoric description. There are many ways of working with transference. By working on a metaphoric level the necessary work can be done without re-traumatising a protagonist. Scientists have taught us that if something is changed on one level of functioning of a system then similar changes occur on all other levels within that system (the systems principle of isomorphy); for further reading see Agazarian and Peters *The Visible and Invisible Group* (1981/1989). If we think in terms of a person as a system with all their levels of functioning, physical, emotional, psychological, social, spiritual we can hypothesise that a change made anywhere within the person's being has effects on all other levels of their being. If we work psychodramatically for example with a nightmare to a point where the protagonist feels a sense of relief and is no longer afraid to sleep, it is likely that they will feel better in many ways. The events of life which precipitated the nightmare may not necessarily be mentioned but increased awareness on the cognitive level is a usual outcome, as is a reduction of psychosomatic symptoms. If we think of a group as a system the same can be said to be true, there are just a great many more levels. It is somewhat the same principle as three-dimensional chess.

Paul Holmes (1992: 18–29) reminds us that in a system 'the whole is greater than the sum of the parts'. He points out that a whole, working wristwatch (which is a system) is of more value than the same parts after having been run over by a bus. He compares this with a psychodrama group or a family group, both of which are systems, whereby 'the group is different and greater than a collection of individuals'. Holmes goes on to say that 'each part of a system has an effect on the other parts'. He describes the interactional systems a director might bear in mind when directing; the wheels within wheels; from the micro-cosmic – atomic, molecular, genetic levels, through the metaphoric 'inner world', to the individual, family, community, national and international levels. Changes within a person's nervous system will have an effect upon other bodily systems, which in their turn will have an effect on their emotional and cognitive systems. Someone with low blood sugar is likely to be irritable and a person is likely to experience physical symptoms if exposed to extreme or prolonged stress. 'In a psychotherapy group communication may be conscious, whether verbal or non-verbal interactions (e.g. body language, facial expressions). It may also involve unconscious processes' (Holmes 1992: 19). Systems can also be closed, that is to say that there is no communication link with other systems, or open. A closed system ceases to function when its energy runs out, as when a car battery becomes flat, or when a person isolates him/herself too much. To remain open, systems require a flow of energy back and forth, as is the case for the human body and a psychodrama group.

Multiple protagonists

In discussing what a protagonist does, it should be mentioned that on occasions dual or multiple protagonist sessions may be led. In this case two or more protagonists may enact scenes at the same time. To lead such sessions requires considerable experience so it does not fall within the remit of this chapter to expand on this way of working but it may be important to know that it is an alternative. Marcia Karp has described the procedure in detail, giving what for her have been increasingly clear indications when it is appropriate for more than one person to participate as protagonist in the same psychodrama and when it is not (Karp 1994: 45). Sometimes, she says, a person is warmed up to express themselves through seeing and participating in someone else's emotions. Their emotions and thoughts are ready and available to be expressed on the stage.

The protagonist gets 'stuck'

If it appears that the protagonist's energy becomes blocked and they are unable to find a way forward in the drama, there are many alternatives the director might choose prior to considering working with multiple protagonists. Remember that it is not at all unusual that just prior to catharsis a protagonist's energy level falters. The director may consider the following options, when the protagonist appears to be blocked:

- Make use of a double, who through the use of body clues and/or identification, may be able to set words on what the protagonist is thinking and feeling but not saying or may act simply as a support, which can enable the protagonist to return to a more spontaneous state.
- The protagonist can be directed to reverse roles with the block (concretisation) – what does it look like, say, do, who does it sound like? An auxiliary can then be chosen to represent the block, whom the protagonist then relates to.
- Use the mirror technique, whereby someone else takes the person's role in the scene and the protagonist can stand at a distance, thereby inviting another level of awareness and engagement in co-directing for a moment.
- Other group members may be directed to, one after the other, demonstrate what they might do in the scene – another form of mirroring (the protagonist steps out and looks on) or making use of floating doubling (the protagonist remains in the scene and one at a time group members come up and positioned immediately behind the shoulder of the protagonist put forward their response).
- Stop the scene there, since the protagonist is not duty-bound to produce a drama for the group. Sharing can lead to greater clarification.

What the director should *not* do is to start inventing scenes that have not originated with the protagonist!

THE PROTAGONIST IN THE SHARING PHASE

When the drama has reached the point of conclusion, the protagonist is usually asked to be silent and to receive the sharing of the group. The protagonist is returned from the somewhat emotionally naked position of being on stage, to the group, by listening to the way in which the other group members have identified with him/her. Often the sense of the protagonist is that through this process they are emotionally clothed again. Sometimes just eye-contact can convey a great deal and add to the healing of a session. Sometimes the protagonist's capacity to take in what others say or do is exhausted and the director may give the instruction to take in as much as they feel able to. Some directors prefer, on such occasions, to postpone the sharing until a later date, for example at the start of the following session. Since the sharing is designed not only for the benefit of the protagonist, but also to enable group members to place back into the group that which has been elicited in the group, rather than go away alone with it, it is generally speaking wiser to have the group share directly.

The protagonist should not be exposed to analysis or judgement at this point. It is often even the wrong time for feedback and the director must be vigilant in directing this phase of the session. Psychodrama has been likened to surgery and the sharing phase to post-operative care, during which the protagonist is often vulnerable and has a temporarily lowered defence system. The director should be aware of what the protagonist plans to do after the session and promote good 'aftercare'.

CONCLUSION

The protagonist is the 'first into action', the person who works on stage during the action phase of the group. They can be seen to be the group's representative working with the theme most relevant for the group at that time and are co-producer and co-director of their own drama. The protagonist may be selected by the director, the group or by individual group members within the group or in advance. After making a contract with the director they may enact scenes from the past, present or future, representing actual or imaginal events, in the sphere of surplus reality, creating a new reality and developing new scripts. Through the position of role reversal they throw new light on the situation both for themselves and for the group. They try on new roles, developing their role-taking skills, expanding their role-repertoire, raising their level of spontaneity and becoming more authentic and open. The protagonist often explores what is overdeveloped, adequate, underdeveloped, conflicted or absent in a role or scene, overtly or covertly. She works within systems – physiological, emotional, psychological, social and spiritual – which are her own and those with which her systems interact. Moreno described the protagonist's work on stage as loving and the sharing phase of the group as a 'love-back' rather an analysis or feedback. During the sharing phase of the group the protagonist's role is to remain silent, to hear and contain the connections others' lives have to their own and even during this phase to hold the connecting thread which runs throughout the group's life.

BIBLIOGRAPHY

Agazarian, Y. and Peters, R. (1981/1989) *The Visible and Invisible Group*, London: Routledge.

Batten, F. (1992) 'Magister Ludi, the Master of the Play – A Role Profile of the Playwright', thesis submitted as a partial requirement for ANZPA accreditation as a psychodrama director.

Holmes, P. (1992) *The Inner World Outside: Object Relations Theory and Psychodrama*, London: Routledge.

Karp, M. (1994) 'The River of Freedom', in P. Holmes, M. Karp and M. Watson (eds) *Innovations in Theory and Practice: Psychodrama since Moreno*, London: Routledge.

Moreno, J.L. (1934/1993) *Who Shall Survive?*, Student edn, Ambler, VA: American Society of Group Psychotherapy and Psychodrama.

Moreno, J.L. (1977) *Psychodrama, First Volume*, 4th edn, New York: Beacon House.

Moreno, Z.T. (1975) 'An Interview with Zerka T. Moreno. Dean of Training, the Moreno Institute, Beacon, NY', *Practical Psychology for Physicians*.

Watkins, M. (1986/1990) *Invisible Guests – The Development of Imaginal Dialogues*, Boston, MA: Sigo Press.

Chapter 7

The group

Anne Bannister

Picture the scene: a therapist gathers together a small number of people who are all in psychoanalysis. He sits each one on a 'regulation' analytic couch but *all in the same room*. He asks each person to 'free associate' in the same manner as they had been used to doing in their analytic sessions. Not surprisingly the result is chaos.

The therapist in this surreal drama was, of course, Dr Moreno (1977: xix) and the year was 1921. He concluded that a group assembled in this way had no common unconscious and that group tele had no opportunity to work because applying the strict rules for 'free association' prevented any group interaction.

Moreno was already working on his theories of sociometric choices. He understood that the interaction between two or more people, which he called tele, was very important in understanding the motivation of an individual. Some years earlier Freud had already explained his theories of transference and counter-transference in the relationship between therapist and patient. Transference is usually experienced as strong feelings towards a person which are inappropriate and are a displacement of feelings from someone in the patient or client's childhood. Countertransference is sometimes experienced by the therapist towards the client, for similar reasons.

Moreno realised though that tele was interaction which was not confined to the therapist and patient but it existed in schools, workplaces and within the home and it played an important part in determining how we make friends, how we learn better from some teachers rather than others, and how we choose life partners. He understood that by working with the forces of tele people could learn new ways and change their behaviour.

Much of Moreno's theory is based on his observations of children playing together in the parks of Vienna. Once a child feels comfortable in her own individual and separate existence, and once she feels secure in her relationship with her primary carer, she recognises the power of a group. Tele operates as children form liaisons with other children and they realise that a group of children can be as powerful as 'mother' or 'father' in protecting and promoting the needs of each individual child. In play children practise forming and reforming groups. Sometimes the groups are essentially task groups formed to build a 'den' or to attack another group. At other times the group exists for its own sake; roles are taken up and then dropped as a child energetically rehearses a new behaviour. If the rewards are not good for that child the new behaviour will be dropped for a while and a different interaction will occur.

This demonstrates how the group acts as an agent for change in individuals. The child learns to operate in a primary group, usually the family, then extends her field of operation to a peer group and so acquires a repertoire of roles. Adult role models are very important to adolescents (e.g. pop stars, sports personalities) but their influence is unlikely to be lasting unless the behaviour they suggest is acceptable within the young person's group situation.

A person is not simply a collection of roles, however. Indeed Moreno states (1993: 47): 'Roles do not emerge from the self, but the self may emerge from roles.' Roles belong largely in the realm of conscious behaviour whereas we all have an individual or personal unconscious which adds depth and spontaneity to our personalities.

UNCONSCIOUS INFLUENCES IN A THERAPEUTIC GROUP

The recognition of unconscious behaviour by group members, including the director, plays an important part in understanding fully the actions within the group. There are at least three levels of unconscious behaviour. Most psycho-therapists recognise that repressed material from the *personal unconscious* affects the behaviour of an individual. Most group therapists are also supremely aware that there is a *collective unconscious* in which archetypal images influence the whole group. Psychodramatists, who often use historical material when directing a protagonist, should also recognise the influence of the *co-unconscious* where our families, our ancestral roots and relationships within the group itself play their part in shaping our behaviour.

The personal unconscious

Freud hypothesised that the unconscious act was triggered by personal material which had been repressed. Jung agreed with this hypothesis and with the idea that true spontaneity was the unconscious mind acting autonomously, without conscious motivation. Psychodrama has been called, by Moreno, the Theatre for Spontaneity. It encourages the expression of the spontaneous act which is, in itself, the beginning of creativity. Creativity, of course, implies the growth of something new or different, at least to the creator, and that too is an agent for change.

Drama can be described as a spontaneous, creative act, a collaboration between the actors, without author or director. The actors may sometimes draw upon their personal experience to portray certain roles or actions, especially if their training was in 'method' acting (Stanislavski 1936), but often these actions produce spontaneous reactions in the other actors, and the audience, and these lead to a catharsis or a state where change and creativity is likely. Greek drama is a typical example of a creative act, sometimes initiated by the actors, in a theatre with no clear division between actors and audience, where the audience reacts spontaneously. This agent for change was used extensively within Greek culture.

Murray Cox has described a similar interaction in his description of Shakespearian performances in a secure psychiatric hospital (Cox 1992). Staged 'in the round', the depiction of rape and murder created awareness in the minds of the murderers and rapists in the audience. Spontaneously they reversed roles with that of their victim and became aware, perhaps for the first time, of the connection between the pain and fear of their victim, and their own pain and fear as they were victimised in childhood.

John Casson (1997) reminds us that Shakespeare understood this interaction perfectly. His frequent use of the 'play within a play' illustrates for a theatre audience the process whereby people can, through seeing their unconscious feelings projected into other actors, deal with personal material which is otherwise inaccessible.

To bring us up to date, Casson also reminds us that in 'Playback Theatre' (founded by Jonathan Fox and developed from Moreno's ideas) an audience member relates a personal experience and this is acted out spontaneously through a group of actors and a 'teller'. The catharsis and therapeutic experience of Playback Theatre can be similar to group experiences in psychodrama and dramatherapy.

Recently, on the 50th anniversary of the end of the Second World War, I had an experience of acting in a play about the war. The play had been written by an author who had listened to the personal stories of local people who had lived through that time. One story concerned a child who had been evacuated from the city to the country in 1939, when she was 4, to escape bombing, and who had then chosen to stay on with her foster mother after the war. Even as a young girl she could see that her future held more opportunities than in her deprived and overcrowded home. Whilst watching the scene, on stage, where the mother accepted the logic of the child's situation, the former child, now a woman of 60, experienced a cathartic reaction. Afterwards she told me that this was the first time that she had understood her mother's feelings and this had helped her to reconcile some unresolved guilt and pain concerning her own decision as a child.

It is important to remember that in the theatre the structure of the play provides the container for the catharsis. In a therapeutic group the protagonist (or central actor) will be nurtured and cared for by the group so that she may practise changes and make mistakes, without being punished. There is plenty of research evidence to show (see Kellermann 1992) that catharsis alone is not enough to bring about a psychotherapeutic cure. It can, however, remind a person of unconscious processes which may be the source of a difficulty. Many other factors, particularly in the group situation, contribute to the process of healing.

The collective unconscious

The collective unconscious is also a vital part of our personality and it is only in the interactions of the group that this can be developed. Carl Gustav Jung pioneered the idea of a part of the mind which was not conscious, yet was not repressed because it had not existed in the personal consciousness. It is the part of the mind which derives from archetypes, from heredity (Jung 1964). Sometimes this is described as instinct. Jung was not referring to cultural norms or taboos but to universal patterns and images which have existed cross-culturally for generations. Eternal symbols such as the cross, the serpent or dragon, the mandala, water as a life source, etc. appear in myth, legend, religion, fairy tales and paintings. In accepting the importance of this material Jung threw a light on dreams, delusions and hallucinations which gave form to our understanding of the processes of the mind.

This cross-cultural understanding is well illustrated in the stories told by dramatherapist, Alida Gersie (1992). She uses tales from Africa, North and South America, Australia, Asia and Europe to show the universal themes and ideas with which all peoples are familiar. Of particular interest are the ancient stories from traditions such as the Australian Aboriginal people, which cannot have been influenced by other cultures. She uses all the stories to stress the importance of our world eco-system and links together personal and group stories to show that they are all part of our universal story.

The co-unconscious

Moreno also discussed a form of the unconscious which was a shared link between people. He called it the co-unconscious (Moreno 1977: vii). It includes tele, but also has elements of the collective unconscious. Monica Zuretti (1994: 215) describes the 'cosmic matrix' which is a 'reservoir of those experiences which belong to the planetary existence of the human race'. She points out that this might be called spirit in some cultures. She states that the co-unconscious is the energy which sustains the group process.

Zuretti recognises the cosmic matrix, or co-unconscious, in memories of events which occurred prior to birth or conception. In a psychodrama group we frequently ask the protagonist to reverse roles with a parent or grandparent. Whilst in that role the protagonist may have memories or inexplicable feelings, belonging to the role, which provide some sort of explanation for her own current behaviour. These memories, of a distant past which could not have been directly experienced by the protagonist, are different from our personal repressed memories (the unconscious), and different also from the archetypal memories which can be studied in anthropology (the collective unconscious). The co-unconscious then is an extension of tele, it is the history of an individual, of a family, and of a group. This is the material with which we are working when we undertake the direction of a psychodrama group.

THE DIRECTOR

Before the group existed there was a void. Antony Williams (1991) says that psychodrama directors make a leap into the void and in so doing help to create a container where group members can let go of their past certainties. In my own work, with abused adults and children, the creation of a safe container is crucial. In order to do this it is essential to pay attention to structure and boundaries and also to be aware of the individual and group themes which develop as the group progresses.

Moreno provided a way in which both these matters can be attended to at the start of a group session. It is usually called warm-up. 'Warm-up', with its connotations of physical activity, is often misunderstood by beginners to psychodrama. It is clearly explained in Susie Taylor's chapter in this book. Here, however, I will focus on its purpose for the group, rather than for the individual.

To 'leap into the void' the director may tell a story, suggest a simple activity for the whole group, or request specific information from group members. In doing so she is preparing a framework for the group to decide on its culture, its norms, its identity. The focus is removed from the individual. Instead of 'Who am I?' the group member asks 'Who or what is this group?' Williams (1991: 89) points out that the demeanour of the director is cardinal. Although spontaneity may mean that 'anything can happen', it is important that the group trusts the competence of the director to handle it. The director, in turn, has to trust the group, and the method, as well as the individual, in order to encourage change.

A director who does not trust the group may be controlling and autocratic. The group will then react with subversion or repression, which will feed into the director's fear of trusting the group. It takes a powerful group to overcome this and some group members will withdraw from the struggle as it is too reminiscent of their own life struggle for survival.

Directors who do not trust the method, or their own competence in it, will not inspire confidence. Neither will they enjoy directing the group. They may project negativity or 'stuckness' in a way which is frightening for depressed or stuck group members. The group may feel confirmed in their own view that their position is hopeless. Sometimes, paradoxically, group members may find their own reservoir of hope and confidence, as a result, but this may be taking a clinically unacceptable risk with a group of depressive clients, for instance.

In order to trust the group, the director must believe that it contains within it all the ingredients, the seeds, for change. This means a belief that each individual has the power to heal him or herself. To access that power, however, the person must be in touch with his/her own unconscious needs, with the collective unconscious of humanity, and with the co-unconscious of the group. If the director is alert to these possibilities then the group itself becomes an instrument for healing as well as change.

During the warm-up then, the director and the group create the boundaries, which help to shape the container for the action. The shape of the container is further determined by the group themes which occur and recur during warm-up and also during the life of the group. A director may hold a simple 'check-in' warm-up where each person states how they are feeling at that moment. Often a feeling or state is fairly common in the group, or is triggered by a powerful event.

For instance, in a training group which lasts for four days, one member arrives a day late because she has to attend a family funeral. Because this is a new group it is important that I remind people that she is a potential group member and give the reason for her absence. We place a chair for her, in the group circle, and occasionally I ask a group member to reverse with the absent member so that her presence can be remembered. She says later that she feels it was easy to enter the group although she had been apprehensive about the missing day. I wonder if the theme of death might preoccupy the group (because of the family funeral) and for the first two days this is the case. On the third day however the theme changes slightly to one of grief for that which is lost and I realise that we often need to mourn past behaviours before we can bid them farewell. By the fourth day the mourning has been overtaken by a theme of renewal and an eagerness to practise new learning and new ways of living. The group have made the connection between their *personal* unconscious theme (family funerals), the *collective* unconscious theme of letting go of past behaviours (in order to learn the new ones proposed by the training) and the *co-unconscious* theme of group creativity.

ADVANTAGES AND DISADVANTAGES OF GROUP PSYCHOTHERAPY

The therapeutic group then, contains all the ingredients for therapeusis within its members and the director. Various schools of psychotherapy have disputed the relative importance of those ingredients. Group treatment evolved from individual psychotherapy and analysts, for instance, would stress the importance of the individual psychodynamics in a therapy group. As we saw in the introductory paragraph to this chapter, Moreno would probably not agree. Others, for instance Bion (1961), would emphasise the importance of the processes in the group itself. The middle way, accepting the individual and group processes, but concentrating on the value of the interpersonal relationships within the group, is more acceptable nowadays.

Ahead of his time, as always, Moreno was advocating this approach in his first volume on psychodrama, first published in 1946 (Moreno 1977). He explained that a psychodrama group contains all the elements of psychotherapy. The monologue or soliloquy (having elements of the Buddhist meditation) was present, as was the dialogue between two people, the basic component of all individual therapy. In addition, he felt that the group was much more accessible to people of all classes. The meditative approach was successful for only the chosen few, Moreno felt, and the dyadic approach was likely to be too expensive and unavailable for most people. The group method could be utilised by everyone.

This eclectic approach, far from being seen as 'less pure', is now accepted amongst group therapists from different schools, hence the successful alliances between group analysts and psychodramatists, person-centred therapists and psychodramatists, and dramatherapists and psychodramatists. Most of these, and other group workers would agree with Yalom's description of the advantages of group psychotherapy.

Yalom (1970) described the 'curative factors' of group psychotherapy as follows:

1 Imparting information
2 Instillation of hope
3 Universality
4 Altruism
5 The corrective recapitulation of the primary family group
6 Development of socialising techniques
7 Imitative behaviour
8 Interpersonal learning
9 Group cohesiveness
10 Catharsis

The first two factors and the last one, occur, of course, in individual therapy as well. In psychodrama groups, as we have already discussed, factor 3, universality, is particularly emphasised and factor 5, the re-creation of the family group is almost inevitable in a psychodramatic re-enactment. Factors 6 and 7 are deliberately encouraged by psychodramatic techniques such as 'mirroring' where group members re-enact a scene for a protagonist so that she may observe the action. Sometimes suggestions for different solutions are solicited from the group, especially if the protagonist seems 'stuck'. At this point interpersonal learning (factor 8) takes place. This can lead to altruism (factor 4) and group cohesiveness (factor 9).

However, it is my experience, and that of others, that group psychotherapy can sometimes be too threatening. In situations where there are many family secrets the issue of confidentiality can become overwhelmingly important. In childhood sexual abuse situations for instance, or where other issues of sexuality are involved, many people need the individual experience of 'an audience of one' who can witness their story and validate it, before they are ready to tell the story again to a wider group.

Although, nowadays, the issue of childhood sexual abuse is spoken of much more openly, the re-experiencing of a group situation for those who have been ritually sexually abused may be too distressing. This kind of abuse nearly always takes place in a group setting, often an extended family group, and it is therefore too distressing for many to enter group therapy. Similarly, institutional abuse, in school or children's home can create intense suspicion of any situation which appears to re-create these circumstances.

Recently I was working with a woman who was slowly coming to terms with the fact that her husband was a paedophile. Even though he had been to prison on more than one occasion for Schedule I offences (abuse of children) he had contrived to keep the secret from many members of his extended family. After some individual sessions with my client I suggest that she might like to join a group for women in similar circumstances. Her immediate reaction is horror, that she might meet someone she knows, but on further discussion she recognises that her over-reaction is a reflection of her former need to keep the 'family secret'. Gradually she realises that this is connected to her protection of her husband. Her motivation in coming to therapy is connected with her desire to protect her grandchildren and when she is reminded of this, she realises that the days of protecting her husband are over. She says that she has never spoken to another woman who may have suffered similarly to herself and she sees the advantages of the group.

Disadvantages in group therapy may also be apparent for those whose difficulties seem to be located immediately within the family, or in a 'couple' relationship. Tackling the issue head-on in family therapy sessions might be more appropriate although it is my experience that one member of a family, or one partner of a couple, is often much more motivated than the others or other. In group therapy, especially in psychodrama, it is usual to re-create the partnership or family within the group. Although group members know that they can only change their own behaviour, not that of others, they can see how their behaviour affects those closest to them. They are then in a better position to try out changed behaviour for themselves and to make decisions about their future.

GROUP NORMS AND GROUP CULTURE

Moreno used the term 'cultural conserve' to explain how a creative, spontaneous act can become a culture which can then be frozen in time and lose much of its original significance. Fox (1987) in his excellent distillation of Moreno's writing, gives us the theory and explains the importance of this idea. Ken Sprague (1994: 20) typically gives us a vibrant illustration of it. He describes himself reading Fox's book, *The Essential Moreno*, in a dentist's waiting room. He was exploring the 'cultural conserve' of the book. Moreno's original creative thought had become frozen, within the pages. A very young child, also in the waiting room, presented Ken Sprague with three toys for his consideration. Here was an act of spontaneity which could have become more creative if there had been opportunity for further interaction between the adult and the child. This in itself illustrates how spontaneity from one individual (the child in this case) made an opportunity for another individual (Sprague) to join in a creative action. In the event the action was stopped by the mother, who may have been anxious about the child's rather familiar behaviour, and by the dentist, who called Mr Sprague into his room.

Within a psychodrama group a spontaneous act, whether it is initiated by the director or another group member, can become an act of creation, which can then become part of the group culture. Each group will have its own culture, built partly from individual norms which people bring from their own family and social cultures, and partly from the cultural expectations which have grown around the practice of psychodrama.

It is important for the director to be aware of this interaction and to know when it is safe to challenge group norms if that would be therapeutic. Tuckman (1965) in a well-known paper, describes the stages of group interaction as 'forming, storming, norming and performing'. Most group facilitators would recognise these stages. Challenge can come after the forming has been at least expressed, if not completed, and it can come from the director or from other group members. Indeed, this explains the concept of 'storming' as group members decide to challenge group norms for themselves. Tuckman states that groups never get to the 'performing' stage but in psychodrama I believe that the open challenge offered in role reversal moves a group on towards more satisfactory 'performance'.

Moreno described role reversal as the engine which drives psychodrama. When someone reverses roles they see themselves through the eyes of the other but also they may experience a new way of looking at the world which is a revelation. Some years ago, when feminism was knocking on the door of male cultural conserves, a story was going the rounds about a surgeon who was asked to perform a dangerous, life-saving operation upon a child who had been brought to the casualty department after a road traffic accident. The surgeon refused saying, 'I cannot because this is my son.' The storyteller then stated that the surgeon was not the child's father and the listener, struggling with the cultural expectation that the surgeon was a male, had to state what was the relationship. A surprising number of people would suggest step-father, adoptive father, etc. before realising that the surgeon was a woman.

Such expectations of gender, race and class roles are increasingly being challenged in the public arena but a person's own cultural expectations may be harder to change. One exercise which I like to do in a psychodrama group particularly challenges these expectations. It is derived from sociodrama, which Moreno defined as a deep action method dealing with intergroup relations and collective ideologies. The way I present the exercise varies according to the composition of the group. For instance, I am sometimes asked to provide 'team-building' training for teams of teachers, social workers, or mixed teams of professionals from health and social services. The team may have been static for a long time but have suffered a recent loss or change of circumstance. Then the exercise will focus on the current culture of the group.

> One group I worked with had been operating for many years with a strict hierarchy which had worked well in that the young people for whom they were responsible had been well controlled. More recently, however, there had been a number of dangerous incidents where the young people had precipitated life-threatening situations; life-threatening both to children and staff. During the course of a morning I am told by some staff members that they 'want to get back on course', others say they are 'afraid of rocking the boat'. Some blame children for 'jumping overboard and causing panic'. I pick up the nautical metaphor which was part of the pervading group culture and ask them to set themselves out as a ship, sailing across the sea.
>
> They take the roles with which they feel most comfortable. There is no argument as the captain stands at the helm, his first lieutenant beside him, and everyone from the cook to the cabin boy (in this case a cabin girl) settle into place. The children, missing, of course, from this training day, are carried as cargo, 'below decks'. There are a number of revelations as people are asked to reverse roles with others. Sometimes they are asked to try out certain roles to gain insight. The small revolution of boat rockers becomes bolder, their oppressors become more confused as they realise how they have been tightening up their oppression in response to challenge. More importantly, perhaps, the team realise how the 'below deck cargo' of young people is reflecting or mirroring, in a subconscious way, the actions of those on deck.

In a newly formed team, or in a group where the metaphor was not apparent, I might pick a theme that I knew would resonate with their particular circumstances. A group of sexual abuse survivors are likely to have many concerns about their bodies. By recreating a 'body' in the group, with people choosing to stand as head, feet, heart, mouth, genitals, etc., members can explore, through role playing and role reversal, both their relationship with the group (I am the mouthpiece, etc.) and their personal feelings about bodies.

GROUP BOUNDARIES

I have already suggested that the group acts as a therapeutic container, especially for catharsis. The concept of a container implies boundaries and I believe these must be explicit and implicit. Moreno was specific about the use of the stage space and Casson, in Chapter 4 of this volume explains this clearly. The idea of the psychotherapy group as a circle, with the action contained within the space is used by Rogers and others as a safe structure.

Another explicit boundary is created by the agreement which many directors make with group members about group rules. These may or may not be written down but should always be explicit. Most groups are likely to want agreements about confidentiality, respecting feelings, respecting gender and culture and freedom to state a view which differs from the pervading opinion.

A third boundary is created by the conventions of psychodrama, which are not necessarily the same in different cultures. At international conferences the differences between the Australian school of psychodrama and the Scandinavian school or South American school for instance become very apparent. Those taking part in workshops led by directors of a different culture from their own should take account of this and build their own boundaries if they feel unsure. Visiting directors may be helped by ethical statements from those who are hosting the conference. Such statements can help a director working in an unfamiliar culture to keep within the norms of the host country.

In addition the director can help to create safety and boundaries by choosing psychodramatic techniques which are appropriate to the group. For instance, in a newly formed group exercises which stress interaction between two or three people will be preferable to anything which requires exposure in front of the whole group. Children and young people are likely to prefer working meta-phorically or symbolically. To act out an actual parent/child scene in a group for adolescents would be too threatening. To act out newspaper stories, inventions using 'soap opera' characters, or to work through the use of masks or puppets may be more acceptable. Most children have experienced bullying and they fear this if personal details are aired within the group.

Occasionally a director makes a creative leap and instigates an intervention for which the protagonist has not given permission. For instance a director may perceive that the protagonist, who is in the middle of re-enacting a difficult scene with her colleague, needs to talk to her father. The director may wish to move instantly to that scene and sometimes will do so without negotiation. This may be effective in that it bursts through a defence or block which the protagonist has erected. Occasionally pushing through this resistance can be justified with a particular protagonist, especially if the director knows him or her well and has worked with them before. However I believe that this technique can shatter the group safety and boundaries and the more anxious group members are likely to retreat even more heavily behind their own resistances. It is tempting for a director, who can thus achieve an almost 'magical' resolution but I believe it goes against group psychotherapy in the Morenian tradition. Although the worker in a psychodrama group is called a 'director' rather than a 'conductor' or a 'facilitator', I believe that the word refers to the theatrical origins of the method rather than to a power position.

Moreno's widow, Zerka, who has done so much to further the growth of psychodrama throughout the world, often uses her power as director in a responsible and caring fashion. A protagonist may be weeping as she remembers a painful scene with her mother. As director Zerka asks her to reverse roles. The protagonist struggles to change into the mother role. 'Are you crying now?' demands Zerka. 'No, of course not. Blow your nose then and be the mother.' Here the director facilitates the protagonist to action whilst still demonstrating, both to the protagonist and the group, that she is protective and caring. Once this has been established the group may cope with a more abrasive or creative intervention but the director should never concentrate on the tele between director and protagonist whilst ignoring the group tele. A director can only do this at her peril. She may find that she and the protagonist have moved forward, without the group, and this could be disastrous.

Jonathan Moreno (in Holmes *et al.* 1994: 106) uses the expression 'psycho-dramatic shock' to explain what occasionally happens when a director and protagonist have made a leap and the protagonist, for a short time, 'loses control'. He or she may speak in a mother tongue, previously 'forgotten', or revert to a babyish voice or actions. He points to the necessity of resolving such a 'shock' and suggests that the group be asked to provide a physically comforting and encircling 'womb' to cradle the protagonist. This illustrates that it is always important to keep the trust of the group, as well as the protagonist, in using psychodramatic techniques.

GROUP THEMES

In client groups where there is a shared similarity of personal history, as in groups for those who were sexually abused in childhood, certain themes arise regularly. Loss, intimacy, anger and guilt are all played out in the group arena. I have described elsewhere (Bannister 1992a) the dangers, for a director, of not recognising a group theme of control and power. This occurred in a therapy group which I ran for professional women who had been sexually abused in childhood. Perhaps it is worth repeating the key factors in this process, if only to illustrate the vital necessity for good supervision of, or consultancy for, the director.

The women in this group had coped with early abuse, and with later losses in relationships, by protecting their vulnerability at all costs. Naturally this continued in the group situation. Because I was anxious not to abuse the power of a director I tried to trade some of my vulnerability for a little of theirs. I did this by imparting more information about myself than I usually do in such situations. I soon found myself in a 'victim' role within the group, a role which could have encouraged the protective roles of the group members, but in fact succeeded in engaging some of their persecutory feelings. It must be remembered that, especially when sexual abuse occurs within the family, the potentially 'protective' role of mother is also seen, by the child, as vulnerable. Most of the group members had experienced their mothers as non-protective and weak. It was safer in this group, which must always recreate the family group to some extent, to identify with the abuser.

My supervisor pointed out the ways in which I was abdicating my power and responsibility and I was able to discuss what was happening, quite openly, with the group members. In this fairly short (six months) therapeutic group, a full resolution and a complete balance of power did not occur. The group did, however, help me to understand my own anxieties about abusing my power over those who have already been abused. More importantly perhaps the group members stated that by openly discussing the power dynamics they gained some insight into their own vulnerability and their own protective and abusive traits.

GROUP MYTHS AND STORIES

As we have seen, when we looked at group norms and group culture, patterns of behaviour soon form in groups as they do in families. Williams (1989) draws the parallels as he uses systems theory in psychodrama to understand why some people play defined roles (victim, rescuer, persecutor) in groups and in life. The myth is that the roles are exclusive and do not contain elements of each other. The group which I have just described, where the victims became somewhat persecutory, debunks the myth.

Myths about family patterns occur frequently in psychotherapy. Families often emphasise patterns which culture condones. For instance, in the British soap opera *Coronation Street*, a story with strong northern roots, many of the women are portrayed as strong, brave and very dominating. In contrast, many of the men are seen as weak characters, interested only in gambling and drinking. For some women, raised in this culture, there may be a dilemma between the apparent strengths of the women and the impotence and oppression they often experience as females in a patriarchal world.

Moreno stressed that spontaneity is the key to releasing myths inherent in family patterns. Marcia Karp (1994: 53) discusses spontaneity eloquently. She describes psychodrama as a 'production of small stories, drenched in the magnificent light of spontaneity, moving towards creative resolution'.

Spontaneity is not encouraged in most cultures. For example, the story told by Ken Sprague of the toddler who approached him with three toys included the mother effectively stopping the action. In the psychodrama group the action is always encouraged, spontaneity is applauded, creativity is esteemed. Marcia Karp's 'small stories' are the basic ingredients for the successful resolution. Story telling, then, should be brought into the group culture at the earliest opportunity.

It can start with the warm-up. The director tells a short story about events which occurred 'on the way to the group'. Perhaps the group members take this up with similar stories, or perhaps the director encourages improvisation of fantastic stories based on her original anecdote. This encourages the spontaneous recollection of family stories which are presented for re-enactment in psychodrama.

I feel it is important, however, for the development of group cohesion and for the encouragement of creativity, to bring in stories about the group itself, once its identity and culture is beginning to form. I do this by utilising techniques which are commonplace in work with children and adolescents, but I use them also with groups of adults. The group is asked to think of favourite fairy stories or other childhood tales and to share something of these with two or three others. Eventually a 'group favourite' emerges. Often this is an amalgamation of more than one story. It is a collaboration of half-remembered tales, of important childhood incidents or dreams, and the whole is acted out by the group. Of course, members choose roles, sometimes more than one person plays a role. Creativity is expanded when one person suggests that they should play the 'mischievous bit' of a character or the 'dark side' of a hero or heroine.

In encouraging such improvisation the group starts to build its own story, in which each person plays a part. Sometimes individual psychodramas emerge from the story, sometimes the group prefer to stay within the mythical structure. The end result is the same, deep feelings and themes are aroused within group members and some psychodramatic work will always ensue at a later date.

To further pursue the 'story' theme, I also like to use the group story as a means of closure when a group is coming to an end. This can be done by the director taking the group into a guided fantasy where the story of the group is told through a heroic journey. The story must contain the basic elements. These are:

- the central characters (in this case all the group members),
- the task (this can vary from 'finding the lost child' to 'meeting the wise person'),
- the journey (which will contain incidents from the group's life),
- the obstacles (again actual events will be brought to mind),
- the resolution (essentially how the group resolved problems),
- and, most important, hope for the future.

Alternatively, instead of guided fantasy, the director can use auxiliaries to encourage the group to re-play certain scenes. A longer exercise, taking perhaps a whole day or more, could be devised by the director merely giving the basic elements and leaving the group to devise the story in whatever way they wished.

GROUP CHARACTERISTICS

Each group will have its own unique character, just like individuals, but a knowledge of child development can often help a director to understand why a group is behaving in a certain way. I believe that this knowledge is vital for a psychotherapist and I suggest that all training courses should include child observation and discussions on child development. Peter Slade in *Child Play* (1995) explains that he developed dramatherapy from his observations of and interactions with children at play, mostly in educational settings. Moreno, of course, developed psychodrama from his observations of children at play and his own memories of playing as a child. I have developed the importance of play in my own work (Bannister 1992b).

Young children in a therapeutic group will spontaneously develop play, singly, in pairs or in small groups. Two or three therapists are necessary because some children prefer to interact with a known adult at first. In addition it is often important to a child to have a witness for their play. Some adults always want to interfere but a therapeutic adult will know whether she is required to intervene or whether she must merely respond. Slightly older children (6 to 10) will demand to be given tasks (as in school) in which they can co-operate to perform and complete. Again, two or three therapists are needed, mainly as resources for children to use as they require. Adolescents also need more than one therapist, sometimes as a resource, sometimes as a witness, and sometimes, especially, as a boundary maker.

In a chapter in *Dramatherapy with Children and Adolescents*, I give some examples of children's groups characterised by anger, antagonism, empathy or fear (Bannister 1995). In mixed gender groups, both of children and adults, gender conflict can be a major issue. The issues carried by the director have as much, if not more, influence upon the group as those issues which its members bring. It is a mistake, however, for the director to take total responsibility for the way a group is developing. Asking the group (including adolescent groups) to take more responsibility can be a strong, rather than a weak response to a difficult situation. The director shows trust in the group, the group responds, mutual 'blaming' is suspended, conflict is dropped in favour of constructive action.

Groups of young people and those of adults often regress in therapy to an earlier developmental level. If 'messy' materials (clay, finger paints) are available this regression can be encouraged. This early embodiment play has sometimes been curtailed or discouraged in childhood and a few sessions of 'enduring the mess' can be worthwhile. The group begins to 'grow up' as it moves from embodiment play to projective play with puppets, dolls and toy animals. Stories start here, fantastic interaction takes the play into the development of roles and psychodrama extends this infinitely. This developmental model of Embodiment – Projection – Role, is taken from Sue Jennings's work (Jennings *et al.* 1994).

If an adult group goes through one or more of these stages the director can understand how members have had a great need, an 'act hunger', as Moreno would term it, to fill in the missing parts of childhood development. A director who is aware would ensure that a group was not abandoned at a crucial stage. This might only replicate earlier abandonment by a parent and could cause further damage. Skilful steering of a group towards adulthood is part of the director's job.

Just as important is the director's protective role. With children's groups this may seem obvious. Bullying must be addressed and if it is brought into the open the group will probably find its own solution. The same applies to adult groups also. Recognising the vulnerability of group members to exposure of traumatic material from a protagonist is something I have touched on earlier when discussing 'psychodramatic shock'. It is particularly difficult in groups of survivors of abuse, especially if some of those survivors have taken on characteristics of their abusers, to protect themselves. I have found it useful to remember that suspending the action for a few moments seldom worries a protagonist who is eager to work but it is often worthwhile for a group member who is distressed. Noting the distress, asking what is required (someone to hold a hand or simply to sit beside) is helpful in itself. In the all-important sharing, at the end of the action, this earlier intervention may help a group member to vocalise their feelings. This sharing, from a person who is feeling victimised is often very helpful to a protagonist who is heavily into controlling roles.

SUMMARY

In this chapter we have looked at the components of a group, from each member's personal and collective unconscious to the co-unconscious of the group itself. We have seen how the role of the psychodrama director within the group plays its part in the character of a therapeutic group. In reminding ourselves of the advantages and disadvantages of group psychotherapy we have recognised the limitations of this method. The growth of the group, making its own rules and culture, setting its boundaries, developing its themes and stories has been outlined and this has been compared with the growth of the child and how this is expressed by the child in play. Just as a child develops unique characteristics, so does the group. We have seen how the director, through being aware, can help the group to 'fill in the gaps' from each member's own childhood and to experience, through the wholeness of the group experience, a different way of being.

REFERENCES

Bannister, A. (1992a) 'The Seductiveness of Power', *Changes*, Vol. 10, No. 4: 299–304.

Bannister, A. (1992b) *From Hearing to Healing*, Harlow: Longman.

Bannister, A. (1995) 'Images and Action', in S. Jennings (ed.) *Dramatherapy with Children and Adolescents*, London: Routledge.

Bion, W.R. (1961) *Experiences in Groups*, London: Tavistock.

Casson, J. (1997) 'The Therapeusis of the Audience', in S. Jennings (ed.) *Dramatherapy, Theory and Practice, 3*, London: Routledge.

Cox, M. (1992) *Shakespeare Comes to Broadmoor*, London: Jessica Kingsley.

Fox, J. (1987) *The Essential Moreno*, New York: Springer.

Gersie, A. (1992) *Earthtales: Storytelling in Times of Change*, London: Greenprint.

Jennings, S., Cattanach, A., Mitchell, S., Chesner, A. and Meldrum, B. (1994) *The Handbook of Dramatherapy*, London: Routledge.

Jung, C.G. (1964) *Man and his Symbols*, London: Aldus Books.

Karp, M. (1984) 'Psychodrama and Piccallilli', in P. Holmes, M. Karp and M. Watson (eds) *Psychodrama since Moreno*, London: Routledge.

Kellerman, P.F. (1992) *Focus on Psychodrama*, London: Jessica Kingsley.

Moreno, J.L. (1977) *Psychodrama, First Volume*, 5th edn, New York: Beacon House.

Moreno, J.L. (1993) *Who Shall Survive?* Student edition, Roanoke, VA: Royal Publishing.

Moreno, J.L. (1994) 'Psychodramatic Moral Philosophy and Ethics', in P. Holmes, M. Karp and M. Watson (eds) *Psychodrama since Moreno*, London: Routledge.

Slade, P. (1995) *Child Play*, London: Jessica Kingsley.

Stanislavski, C. (1936) *An Actor Prepares*, New York: Theatre Arts.

Sprague, K. (1994) 'Everybody's a Somebody', in P. Holmes, M. Karp and M. Watson (eds) *Psychodrama since Moreno*, London: Routledge.

Tuckman, B.W. (1965) 'Developmental Sequence in Small Groups', *Psychological Bulletin* 63: 384–399.

Williams, A. (1989) *'The Passionate Technique'*, London: Tavistock/Routledge.

Williams, A. (1991) *Forbidden Agendas*, London: Routledge.

Yalom, I.D. (1970) *The Theory and Practice of Group Psychotherapy*. New York: Basic Books.

Zuretti, M. (1994) 'The Co-Unconscious', in P. Holmes, M. Karp and M. Watson (eds) *Psychodrama Since Moreno*, London: Routledge.

THE AUXILIARY EGO

Chapter 8

The auxiliary ego

Paul Holmes

The story so far . . .

The protagonist selected by the group in this session is Mary who started the
meeting by complaining about the row she had had with her boss that day at work:

Mary He is so pushy, he always asks me to retype letters and tells me that I
could do better. But he's always out of the office at meetings. I get so
upset but I can't do anything about it.

Mary says she wishes to understand better why he gets her so upset. The
director agrees with Mary that her psychodrama should start in her office with a
member of the group playing her boss. The scene starts with Mary re-enacting
the incident at work. After a while the director asks her:

Director Have you ever felt like this before?
Mary Yes, when my father used to get so angry and upset when I did not do
my homework.

Mary and the director then agree that there is a need to go back to her childhood to explore this troubled relationship.

Director OK, Mary, who could play your father in this scene?
Mary John, would you be willing? (John nods his agreement).
Director Mary, reverse roles and be your father (she does this). . . . Now tell us
a little about yourself.
Mary (as 'father') Well, I was a very busy man, I had my shop to run . . .
money was always a worry. . . . I really hoped that Mary would get a
good job to help us out . . . but she just seemed to want to have a good
time.
Director Reverse back. Now John please take on the role of Mary's father.
Mary Why were you never at home?
John Well, if I didn't work so hard, there would have been no money to pay
all the bills.

INTRODUCTION

J. L. Moreno described auxiliary egos, the fourth of his essential instruments of psychodrama, as: 'the representation of absentees, individuals, delusions, symbols, ideals, animals and objects. They make the protagonist's world real, concrete and tangible' (Moreno 1969/1975: 17).

John, by agreeing to play, or 'hold the role' of Mary's father, became an *auxiliary ego* in this psychodrama. The idea that a person can actually take on the role of another person and *behave* as if they were this person in a psychotherapy session is a technique at the core of the practice of psychodrama. Indeed the concept of the auxiliary ego is unique and perhaps the most important of J. L. Moreno's therapeutic creations.

The process allows the protagonist's life (past, present and future) to be dramatically recreated on the psychodrama stage, others in the group taking on the roles of the various characters essential to the therapeutic drama. I will argue later in this chapter that these therapeutic techniques also allow for the protagonist's inner psychic world to be externalised, explored and changed.

Whilst in this chapter I usually use the term 'auxiliary ego' some contemporary psychodramatists, including Peter Felix Kellermann, argue that the addition of the word 'ego' is not helpful in this context as 'the auxiliary is an aid, not only to the "ego" but also to inner and outer "objects" and to the "symbolic inner world" at large' (Kellermann 1992: 106). This view certainly has some logic to it as, for many psychoanalysts, the term 'ego' refers specifically to only a part of an individual's mind or psyche (Laplanche and Pontalis 1967/1973).

However I still prefer to add the word 'ego' to the psychodramatic term as I believe its usage clearly stresses the fact that the role 'taken', 'held' or 'played' by another member of the group (the auxiliary ego) is an externalisation of aspects or roles in the protagonist's own inner world or psyche. This is a very different task from being simply an assistant to others (such as is the case with an auxiliary nurse or auxiliary fireman). Readers will however notice that, from time to time, I omit the word 'ego' in this chapter for brevity's sake.

In the early days of psychodrama (in the 1930s and 1940s) the role of the auxiliary egos were often taken on by psychiatric nurses, or social workers, trained by Moreno in his sanatorium to this task (Moreno and Moreno 1969/1975: 184; J. L. Moreno in Fox 1987: 68–80). In this respect the auxiliary egos resembled the team of professionals who surround a surgeon in an operating theatre, each has their own role and assists the surgeon in his task of helping his patient.

In modern psychodrama, however, it is more usual for all members of the group to become auxiliary egos for the protagonist as and when the drama of the sessions requires this. This changes the psychodramatic process from the treatment of an individual by a team to a fully fledged form of group psychotherapy (a term which Moreno himself coined).

The focus of this book is on protagonist-centred psychodrama, by this I mean it will be usual in a session for the issues of only one individual to be directly explored in dramatic action. The other members of the group will watch the drama or participate in a more active way as auxiliary egos. The selection and the role of the protagonist has been discussed in another chapter by Kate Bradshaw Tauvon.

The protagonist, selected by the group, becomes the focus of the group's issues and needs and their psychodrama will, in various ways, reflect the group's 'common concern'. Indeed the actual choice of which group members are selected by the protagonist to take on roles as auxiliary egos often reflects issues in the auxiliary as well as the protagonist and these individuals may also experience therapeutic benefit from the session. Such a complex therapeutic process can only succeed if there is close team work between the director, protagonist and all the other group members.

Auxiliary egos defined

Moreno explained that the auxiliary egos:

> are an extension of the director, exploring and guiding, but they are also extensions of the subject (protagonist), portraying the actual or imagined personae of his life drama. The functions of the auxiliary ego are threefold: to be an actor, portraying the roles required by the subject's world, to be a counsellor guiding the subject, and to be a special investigator.
>
> (Moreno 1946: 15)

Moreno appears to be describing in this paragraph the situation in which an auxiliary ego plays a named person in a psychodrama (as John did in Mary's session). However auxiliaries may also act as doubles to the protagonist (as described in Chapter 6) or be asked to play inanimate objects in the drama (as described by John Casson in Chapter 5).

Thus a group member may assist the protagonist in a number of different ways in a session. However, before I go on to describe in more detail how they may carry out these functions, I believe that there is a need to consider more fully the psychological significance for the protagonist of the tasks an auxiliary ego carries out in a session that makes psychodrama therapeutic.

A THEORETICAL DIGRESSION

The inner world outside

In my experience of psychodrama some directors give the impression that they are just following clinical intuition and appear not to feel the need for a clear theoretical framework or psychological theory of the mind to support their clinical practice. I would suggest, however, that without such a coherent theory, to provide a psychological 'guide' or 'map', the director may get lost in the session.

Different psychodramatists have used various theories (created by different therapists) to assist them in their therapeutic work. These include, amongst others, the ideas of Moreno himself, Carl Rogers and C.G. Jung.

I have personally found most useful those theories developed from the 1940s onwards by psychoanalysts who succeeded Freud in Britain and in the United States, including, amongst others, Melanie Klein, W.R.D. Fairbairn, Harry Guntrip and Otto Kernberg. I discuss their contribution to psychodrama in an earlier book *The Inner World Outside* (Holmes 1992).

These ideas, generally referred to as object relations theory, are complex, and the views of the different psychoanalytic authors are often confusingly contra-dictory on specific points. However the central concept is that the mind of an individual (what I will call *the psyche*) is the creation, over time from infancy onwards, of the internalisation of their relationships with other people.

The development of the psyche is obviously dependent on those in the external world with whom the child is in relationship (for example parents, siblings, teachers). It is however also influenced by factors present at birth such as that individual's own constitutional temperament and disposition.

In many ways the process of *internalisation* resembles that of *remembering* except that experiences influence the development of the child and become integral aspects of the personality rather than separate remembered events that can be recalled, that is to say, they become part of the self rather than becoming 'ego-dystonic' (i.e. experienced as different or separate from the self).

Otto Kernberg (1976: 26) describes how every interaction with the outside world (say a baby feeding from her mother) results in a 'memory trace' being laid down in the mind. This psychic record consists of an internalisation of aspects of the self in relationship with aspects of the other and is associated with a memory of the feeling or affect felt at that time. Each part of this dyad (self and other) have associated roles (for example a 'baby who takes' from a 'mother who gives'). In psychoanalytic terms these remembered aspects of the relation-ship become 'internal objects' within the mind (see Hinshelwood 1989: 366 for a discussion).

I have argued elsewhere (Holmes 1992) that the psychodramatic process can be seen as the externalisation on to the stage of the protagonist's inner object relationships from within their psyche world. In any scene the auxiliary ego may play either pole of such a dyadic relationship. In my example, the drama will involve a mother feeding her baby. Clearly the protagonist will be the 'baby' (i.e. herself as an infant) and the auxiliary will be asked to take on the role of the 'mother' in the session.

However, as I have indicated, the object relationship internalised in the psyche consists of *two* parts, *self* and *other*. When the protagonist is asked to role reverse by the director they change to play the other pole of the same relationship inter-nalised within their mind. Thus the auxiliary ego is enacting, in the psychodrama, both components of the protagonist's inner world, externalising self and other on to the psychodrama stage.

TECHNICAL CONSIDERATIONS

Before we move on to look at the functions of the auxiliary ego as described by Moreno let us now consider how some of the basic technical issues involved are resolved in the clinical practice of psychodrama.

The selection of auxiliary egos

So, how are group members selected to take on this role in a psychodrama? The action phase of the psychodrama will have started with the director and her protagonist talking together and deciding what their agreed therapeutic aim (or 'contract') will be in this particular drama. Mary, for example, discussed with her director her wish to become better at dealing with her difficult relationship with her boss at work.

Thereafter, this being psychodrama, the protagonist will be encouraged to move from a dialogue with the director into action. She will decide on a specific scene from her life (past, present or future) which she will set up on the stage. Mary's psychodrama started in her office at work. The director asked her to describe this room and to use simple props, such as chairs or cushions, to represent the furniture. Thus, in that space between reality and imagination, an important place from her external world is brought to life on the psychodrama stage.

This is the point in the therapeutic process where psychodrama diverges from almost all other forms of psychotherapy and other members of the group become involved in the action. Mary asked Charles to play her boss and together they re-enacted the scene from work.

Psychodrama has the potential to explore the historic roots of a problem by exploring scenes from the past (Goldman and Morrison 1984) and it became apparent that Mary now needed to explore her relationship with her father when she was an adolescent. The director will need to discover who is required in this scene:

Director OK, Mary, we have your father. Who else is there?
Mary My mother, of course, she was always so angry with my father.
Director Who in the group could play your mother?

The person who will become the auxiliary ego will usually be chosen by the protagonist. This allows the selection of someone who has the potential to 'take on', 'play' or 'hold' this role in a way which is satisfactory to the protagonist's needs in the drama.

Mary   Well, no one, she was such an awful person. . . . (Mary looks very
         worried). Well, if I have to choose, Jenny could. Will you Jenny?
Jenny   Yes of course.

The reasons for the selection of an auxiliary ego by the protagonist are
complex. A group member may be chosen for obvious reasons (such as being
the right age, gender or size for the role). The choice is made because the
protagonist knows that a particular member of the group has had a similar history
or experience to their own. Sometimes a group member gets known for being
good at playing 'bad fathers' or 'good mothers'.

However, often selection crosses these boundaries, group members being
asked to play a role because of less obvious and concrete features. The process
of tele is very important as the protagonist may just 'sense' that a certain person
will be good in the role regardless of their age or gender because of certain (often
unexpressed) aspects of their history and personality.

'Do I have to play this role?'

Although there is often the general expectation that a group member will agree
to take on a particular role for the protagonist, each person has the right to refuse
this task. This may happen, for example, when an individual is *always* asked to
play the same type of role (for example good mothers or abusive fathers) and
they get bored with this sort of 'type casting'.

Or a group member may feel the drama being enacted is too close to their own
emotional issues for their comfort. In such circumstances the director should ask
the protagonist to select someone else. It will, however, be appropriate for the
person who refused the role to share their reasons for doing this in the closing
phase of the session.

Sometimes a group member is simply too preoccupied with their own issues
and concerns at that point in time to be able to be an auxiliary. In such situations
the group must be tolerant and understanding of the needs of the individual.

Getting an auxiliary ego into role

Once an auxiliary is selected the next task is to assist them to take on the assigned
role as fully as possible. Their task is to play the role as closely as possible to
the protagonist's expectations, for clearly the only person who has any real
knowledge of this role is the group member at the centre of the drama. To assist
in this process the director may ask the protagonist to role reverse and become
this other person in their life.

Director   (to Mary) Mary, reverse roles and be your father.

Mary is asked to take a couple of steps sideways on the stage. This establishes
that each person in the drama has a different physical position in space.

Director   Thank you. Well, it is nice to meet you (the director may offer his hand in greeting).

The director may notice that the protagonist still has her own body posture.

Director   OK father, show how you normally stand.

Suddenly Mary braces her back, hand on hips and adopts her father's physical stance. The very act of starting to use her father's body language helps the protagonist enter the role of her father (which of course is a well established 'internal object' in her psyche).

Director   So, father, tell us a little about yourself.

The protagonist may start speaking easily in this role, indeed some individuals seem to find it easier to talk in another role than when they are in their own role. However they might need support and encouragement from the director who may ask some questions to facilitate the process.

Director   So, how old are you? What work do you do? What do you think of your daughter Mary?

The director of course waits for an answer to each question and decides on the next question on the basis of their previous response. Through this process a clear impression of the father emerges. Or, to be more psychologically correct, that version of her father that has been remembered and internalised by Mary in her mind.

After a while the director will ask the protagonist to reverse back into their own role, the auxiliary ego taking on the role of Mary's father.

When speed in the drama is of the essence, the director may role-in an auxiliary by just asking the protagonist to say three things about that person. Such brief comments are usually sufficient for the group member at least to start taking on this role in the psychodrama.

Sometimes, but in my clinical practice rarely, the director herself will choose an auxiliary. This may be the case when the protagonist is so deeply involved in the drama that to ask them to make this choice would totally disrupt the flow of the session or because the auxiliary is going to be asked to play a role rather peripheral to the protagonist.

Director   OK Mary, we will go to a scene in the future. Where will you confront your father?
Mary   In his favourite restaurant. That would shock him.
Director   Jim, could you be a waiter please?

Just as in life, the protagonist may build up quite a cast of characters around them in a psychodrama: mother, father, brothers and sisters, neighbours, abusive school teachers, even sometimes God and the Devil. Group members will need to be carefully directed to take on these important roles in the psychodrama so that their work as auxiliary egos is in the interests of the protagonist.

THE THERAPEUTIC FUNCTIONS OF THE AUXILIARY EGO

Now that we have the auxiliary egos in role we will consider in more detail their tasks in the developing psychodrama. Moreno's existential philosophy stresses that we all meet as equals in encounters in the here-and-now, indeed the director must accept that she too enters the group as the equal of all the other members but with added responsibilities. That is not to say that each person in the group occupies the same roles. Indeed in a psychodrama session each member will participate in the life of the group by taking on a number of different roles (at different times), such as 'supporter', 'confidant', 'group provocateur' and, when required, the role of an auxiliary ego.

Many of these roles are of course shared with the director as psychodrama is the result of a process of co-creation in which the creative and spontaneous contributions of director, protagonist and the group members combine to produce a drama that has emotional significance for the protagonist (and the rest of the group) thus allowing the possibility of therapeutic movement.

That is not to say every one in the group has the same role and responsibilities as the director who, in the role of psychotherapist and group leader, has the particular and important job of assisting all the group members in their therapeutic journeys.

Group members may even direct psychodramas. This sharing of roles is clearly an important feature of training groups; however, sometimes in therapeutic groups it is also appropriate for group members (other than the designated group leader) to take on the role of 'psychodrama director'. However this step needs both careful consideration and supervision by the group leader.

The relationship between a psychodrama director and the members of her group is complex and many-layered. In some sessions the role of 'director' may be clear, in other meetings the roles of 'father' or 'mother' may become predominant in the group's mind in a way which psychoanalysts would describe as the 'transference'. There is no simple solution to how the director might deal with the situation when transference, as opposed to 'here and now' reality, begins to dominate their relationship with a group member.

The roles of the auxiliary egos

Peter Felix Kellermann attributes four principal roles to the psychodrama director: producer, therapist, analyst and group leader (1992: 46). Two of these roles (analyst and therapist) are of course carried out by all psychotherapists (whether they work in one-to-one therapy or in groups). Group therapists (of any school) add a third role, that of group leader, to their repertoire of roles. Psychodramatists add a fourth crucial task, that of dramatic producer, to the list. In every session the director must attempt to juggle all four roles, a requirement that, in my opinion, makes psychodrama one of the most difficult forms of psychotherapy for the therapist.

In psychodrama the director is assisted in the complex task of creating a psychodrama by the other group members. It is clear that the first three of the roles described to the psychodrama director by Kellermann correspond to the tasks that Moreno saw as being those of the auxiliary ego:

The roles of an auxiliary ego (Moreno 1946: 15)	*The roles of the director* (Kellermann 1992: 46)
counsellor	therapist (an agent of change, influencing people and healing)
special investigator	analyst (someone who empathises and has understanding)
actor	producer (who acts as a theatre director, involved with staging and with aesthetic considerations)

Kellermann's fourth task is that of group leader. I would argue that all those in the group have some responsibility for the group's survival (i.e. everyone has some involvement in the process of the group's leadership) even though they are not the formal leader (or director) of the group.

It is thus clear that in psychodrama the whole group share, to varying degrees, the various roles that make the process therapeutic. Indeed the level of activity, creativity and spontaneity in all the group members is crucially related to the final quality and success of a session. This situation may be contrasted to that of the medical or psychoanalytic model in which there is a clear distinction between the doctor (or psychoanalyst) and their patient. The former has to be active (and powerful) whilst the latter is the (often passive) recipient of their doctor's (or analyst's) care and treatment.

Let us now consider the auxiliary ego's tasks from two other perspectives; that of an extension of the director and as an extension of the protagonist.

The auxiliary ego as an extension of the director

It is generally accepted that only one individual (unless the sessions are run by two co-therapists) takes on the role of 'director' in a group, a role that is given to this person through the contact that brings the group together for an agreed therapeutic task. However, as I have indicated, different aspects of their directorial task may be 'shared' with the auxiliary egos.

To be a special investigator

The process of psychodrama allows the protagonist, the group and the director to explore the inner worlds of all the members of the group. The unique techniques of psychodrama allow each person in the group the role of 'psychic' investigator. The director, as a trained psychotherapist, may develop a clear understanding of the psychological ways in which the protagonist functions in life. In psychoanalytic therapy these ideas are fed back to the patient through the use of interpretations.

In psychodrama an auxiliary ego, using their empathic role as 'special investigator' or 'analyst' will also gain an understanding of the protagonist. Moreover an auxiliary ego will gain information about the person they are playing through the process of taking on the role, they may adopt body positions, develop feelings and thoughts and even say things that are only possible because they are *in role* as that person.

Mary	Why do you always put so much pressure on me?
'Father'	You know I wanted to do better in my life, but I didn't have the opportunities you have. You have to succeed for me!
Mary	You know, that is just what I thought my father felt about me, but he never ever said it to me when I was a child.

To be a counsellor guiding the subject

Once in the role as an auxiliary ego, the group member may be encouraged to ad lib, that is to develop the script of their role beyond the text that was initially given by the protagonist in a role reversal with that character. It is through the freedom given by this process that the auxiliary may influence the course of the psychodrama (and thus the therapy of the protagonist). The auxiliary will develop a level of knowledge of the protagonist (using tele and empathy) and use this understanding, without further instructions from the director or protagonist, to further the action thus assisting the protagonist in their therapeutic journey.

The creative potentials of an auxiliary ego must be exercised with care as on occasions a protagonist (with fragile ego boundaries) might be very disturbed by the auxiliary's efforts. In such a situation the director will need to pick up their confusion and distress and then insist that the auxiliary follows, as far as is possible, the exact words of the protagonist.

However, the auxiliary's actions often do not follow the instructions of the director, but are spontaneous responses to the drama, assisting it to unfold and develop and often allowing the protagonist to access previously forgotten or repressed parts of their life drama. They are thus then in the role of 'counsellor' or 'therapist' when they actually speak these words in a session. For example, an auxiliary (acting as the protagonist's double) can support or influence the therapeutic process by stating things the protagonist may never have dared say, or even perhaps dared to think. In this way the protagonist may gain understanding and insight into their relationships with themselves and with the world, without the psychotherapist/director making an analytic interpretation.

John	(as 'father') You know I never really wanted a child. We only had you to please your mother.
Director	(to Mary) Is that right? Has your father said the right thing?
Mary	(to director) Yes, but I have never thought of it before, I guess that it was always too painful.
Mary	(to 'father') How could you! And how could she! I thought you really loved me!
Director	(to Mary) Role reverse, be your father.
Mary	(as her 'father') I did love you. But it was always so hard to show you.

It must be stressed, however, that the director keeps the final responsibility to monitor, stage manage and if necessary control the spontaneous contributions of an auxiliary. On occasions a group member may, out of undue enthusiasm or confusion with their own issues, no longer contribute to the psychodrama in the best interests of the protagonist, but be placing their own needs first.

In these situations the director may check the auxiliary's contributions out with the protagonist.

John (as 'father') But you were always my special girl, my little favourite.

Mary looks rather worried. The auxiliary's comments have taken her by surprise. The director checks out the situation with her:

Director	So, would your father say that?
Mary	No.
Director	Then role reverse and show us what he might have said in this situation.
Mary	(as 'father') I did love you but you never lived up to my expectations of you. Now, your brother, I could always see that he was going to be a success in life.

To be an actor

It may seem a very obvious statement, but it must not be forgotten that psychodrama is an active, dramatic form of psychotherapy. To this end the director must co-create (with the protagonist and with the group) a theatrical momentum within which the magical therapeutic process can develop.

Once an auxiliary ego is in role they have the task, at least from their own position, of maintaining the dramatic flow of the session (under the guidance of the director). They are encouraged to develop their role from the basic substrate given to them by the protagonist. They may take risks in what they say or do (as long as such developments are attuned to the protagonist's needs and personal drama). It is the director's responsibility to check out with the protagonist that such developments feel right.

The auxiliary egos, through their involvement in the theatrical aspects of the psychodrama will also have a powerful influence on the dramatic shape and style of the session. For example the group member playing the waiter in the scene in the restaurant will set the tone for Mary's rather tense meeting with her father.

Thus the auxiliary's role allows them to be analyst, counsellor and creative actor in the protagonist's drama. However, it is worth repeating that it is the director's responsibility to ensure that the psychodrama progresses in the best interests of the protagonist.

The auxiliary ego as an extension of the protagonist

So, just as the auxiliary egos share certain tasks with the director, they are also (at one and the same time) active psychological extensions of the protagonist. They may do this in a role in the drama or they may carry out this task as a double for the protagonist.

The auxiliary's function is to bring the inner object from the protagonist's life into an external reality in the session. They must *become* for the duration of the psychodramatic action the protagonist's mother or father, brother or sister. Their task is to portray (to use Moreno's words again) 'the actual or imagined personae of his life drama'. As I have indicated in my theoretical digression the characters they play are in fact aspects of the protagonist's psyche (even if normally considered as 'other' rather than as part of 'self').

Once selected for the task of taking on the roles of these other people in the protagonist's life the auxiliary's responsibility is to assist in the psychodramatic process. To this end they must subsume, as far as they are able, their own overt emotional needs to those of the protagonist. They must try to follow the lead they have been given by the protagonist when she indicated the key features of this part. It is essential that they act and speak in a way that is congruent to the protagonist's needs. I have already described what the director may do when the auxiliary diverges, for whatever reason, from this task.

To those who have never experienced a psychodrama session it may seem that an auxiliary ego requires Oscar-winning skills to allow a protagonist to 'believe' that they are talking to their mother. How can any ordinary member of a psychotherapy group have this ability? How indeed can an over-weight middle-aged man become the young and handsome boyfriend the protagonist has not seen for thirty years? Or how can the bright young group member be taken seriously as an ageing grandparent?

Truth to tell, with great ease, for the ability for almost any auxiliary to achieve this goal is perhaps one of the most surprising aspects of psychodrama. The process may almost seem magical and what is perhaps so remarkable is the ease and regularity with which this occurs in almost every session, regardless of whom is in the group. To an extraordinary degree an auxiliary can access this role and play it in the psychodrama through the use of the information given to them by the protagonist and through their use of tele and empathy.

I believe the mechanism may be best understood by considering that the protagonist *and* (but to a lesser degree) the auxiliary ego enter a state of light trance or reverie induced by the process of psychodrama. At one time I thought of hypnosis as being synonymous with the deep trances I associate with the theatre and light entertainment on television. More recently I have become aware that trance states may vary from the deepest: 'You will forget all this when I click my fingers', to a subtle alteration in the state of consciousness. It is in the latter state that psychodrama works. The protagonist hovers between being fully awake, oriented and in touch with the here-and-now reality of working in a psychodrama group and a state of light trance. In the former they remain in a working collaboration with the director, in the latter the drama feels to them 'as if' it were totally real.

However, the trance states are light and reality is always close to hand. It is crucial the process continues in the playful state of 'as if'. Moreno described psychodrama 'as a way to change the world in the here and now using the fundamental rules of imagination without falling into the abyss of illusion, hallucination, or delusion' (see Moreno 1969/1975 for a fuller discussion).

What is perhaps even more remarkable is that the auxiliary ego may join the protagonist in this magical world. Together they create the scene that meets the protagonist's therapeutic needs in the session. At first the auxiliary will follow the 'text' as laid down in the early stages of the psychodrama, often using the same words as those used by the protagonist when reversed into this person's role. However the auxiliary has often been selected for this role as the protagonist has a sense that the auxiliary will be able to continue in it and indeed develop it without constant prompting. In this way they become an extension of the protagonist's inner world, allowing internalised roles to be externalised and dramatised on the psychodramatic stage.

The drama at this stage is likely to be based more-or-less in reality; however as the action continues the auxiliary must increasingly use their own sense (based on tele, intuition and empathy) to co-create with protagonist and director a scene which differs from the starting point of the drama.

The issue of touch in psychodrama

Psychodrama is an active and physical form of therapy so the issues of touch and movement require special attention.

> ... in the psychodramatic approach to human relations we are interested in following the model of life, itself, and within limits making use of the bodily contact technique (which) is obviously contra-indicated if used to gratify the therapist.
>
> (Moreno 1969/1975: 17)

The same rules clearly apply to the other members of the group. As auxiliary egos, in role, they may touch and hug a protagonist say as their mother. Such contact may be heartfelt and experienced with the process of the psychodrama as coming from the 'mother'. However, boundaries must be drawn and group members must not over-step what is appropriate in a therapeutic group. For example the director would need to intervene if two members began to actually kiss in role during a session.

Physical contact is not always affectionate and may be violent or abusive. The director might feel that the exploration of such an episode in the protagonist's life is central to the therapeutic task. However clear instructions will need to be given to protect all the group members from inappropriate physical contact (be this too intimate or too violent). It is essential that the magical 'as if' aspect of the dramatic process remains in place. Cushions (held by other members of the group) can be used to protect an auxiliary from an angry assault by the protagonist, or cushions alone can be thumped in the physical component of catharsis. It is however important to add that, in psychodrama, these cushions will usually be seen as representing *somebody* or *some thing* rather than being the anonymous recipient of the protagonist's rage and energy.

What does the auxiliary ego gain from the psychodrama?

So far in this chapter the focus has been on the psychodramatic process meeting the needs of the protagonist, auxiliary egos being asked to take on or hold roles to further this individual's therapeutic journey.

However there can be no doubt that, in various ways, the group member acting as an auxiliary ego may also gain great benefit. As I have described above these auxiliaries are often selected for a particular role because of some overt or covert personal characteristic. The very step of taking on a role so similar to some internal aspect of their own personality can be stressful, but it can also be deeply rewarding. The sharing, the last phase of a psychodrama session, gives the auxiliary ego an opportunity to explore their links with the protagonist and the drama within which they have played a crucial role. Indeed this process may well warm the auxiliary up to undertake their own psychodrama on this shared theme in a subsequent session.

The auxiliary ego may also benefit from the act of playing a role apparently distant from their repertoire of roles in everyday life. I can, for example, remember the enthusiasm (and indeed pleasure) with which a very kindly and non-assertive man in a therapy group took on the roles of very aggressive and abusive men. It was clear that through doing this (in the aid of the protagonists' psychodramas) he was able to experience a more assertive and direct aspect of his own personality. This, of course, does not mean he then had permission to go and be abusive in his own life. However, it did raise issues for him about his own style of relating to other people that he was able to explore later in his own psychodramas.

The auxiliary leaves a role

Auxiliary egos, as I have described, are asked to take on roles for a number of reasons, some of which may have as much to do with their own personality as with the protagonist's dramatic needs. Therefore the manner in which a member of the group leaves a role is as important as the way in which they at first adopt it.

As the drama moves on, often through a number of different scenes, the need for a particular auxiliary will change. The director may thus just thank them and ask them to leave the stage area and to sit down. This action alone has the effect of allowing them, to a degree, to leave the role they have been playing and to become themselves.

However this step is often not, in itself, sufficient and the auxiliary may continue to feel *as if* they were still the bad father or dead mother. This tendency to cling to a role may just reflect the dramatic intensity with which they occupied this role for the protagonist. However, as I have noted earlier, it may also relate to some identification with the role taken. This may be obvious and direct (for example John is a father and had a father himself). Sometimes the link may be less clear and relate to some deeper identification.

Whatever the nature of these associations, it is very important that the auxiliary leaves these roles behind when they leave the session. The process of *de-roling* in psychodrama occurs in the last phase of the session, sharing. It is normally sufficient for each group member to share both from the role they have taken and then as themselves. The director must however watch to ensure that all auxiliaries have shared and, as far as is possible, returned to their own sense of self. This important subject is covered in more depth in the chapter written by Gillie Ruscombe-King (Chapter 10).

REFERENCES

Fox, J. (ed.) (1987) *The Essential Moreno. Writings on Psychodrama, Group Method and Spontaneity by J.L. Moreno MD*, New York: Springer.

Goldman, E.E. and Morrison, D.S. (1984) *Psychodrama: Experience and Process*, Dubuque, IA: Kendall Hunt.

Hinshelwood, R.D. (1989) *A Dictionary of Kleinian Thought*, London: Free Association Books.

Holmes, P. (1992) *The Inner World Outside. Object Relations Theory and Psychodrama*, London: Routledge.

Kellermann, P.F. (1992) *Focus on Psychodrama: The Therapeutic Aspects of Psychodrama*, London: Jessica Kingsley.

Kernberg, O.F. (1976) *Object-Relations Theory and Clinical Psychoanalysis*, New York: Jason Aronson.

Laplanche, J. and Pontalis, J. B. (1967/1973) *The Language of Psychoanalysis*, London: Hogarth Press.

Moreno, J.L. (1946) *Psychodrama, First Volume*, Beacon, NY: Beacon House.

Moreno, J.L. and Moreno, Z. T. (1969/1975) *Psychodrama, Third Volume*, Beacon, NY: Beacon House.

THE DIRECTOR

Chapter 9

The director

Cognition in action

Marcia Karp

I feel safe inside me, Mum. I'll break my leg and that stuff, but I think I'll always be safe. I'm like a giant tube. Everything that has ever been known and everything that will be known passes through me. I just receive it and pass it along.

(Poppy Sprague, age 8, 1985)

PHILOSOPHY: COGNITION TAKES PLACE WHEN YOU ACT ON WHAT YOU KNOW

Perhaps an essential core of being is to know, and to know that you know.

Cognition is a complex process which incorporates the sum total of life experience. It takes place when you trust everything you know. In that moment of fusion, a heightened state of awareness occurs and you activate all your experience.

The quality of listening equals the ability to be immersed in the moment and vice versa; the quality of being immersed in the moment equals the quality of listening. A friend of mine, Midge, said 'I listen very well and then I say things that surprise myself'.

Cognition is defined as the action or faculty of knowing, perceiving and conceiving. It is the opposite to an emotion or a volition. Cognition is a perception, a sensation, or a notion or an intuition.

This fusion of knowing and acting is not acknowledged as part of the way we live our lives; therefore it is hard for us to name it and to trust it.

Because we do not know how to name it we call it intuition or a hunch. *Cognition is our deepest and most spontaneous form of knowing*. It can provide the essence and fullness of our existence. Perhaps we need a new language to describe living 'moment to moment' (J. Krishnamurti 1991). Spiritual teachers tell us we should consistently live our lives in moment to momentness.

A woman, for example, may know when she is about to be hit by her partner. She can read the subtext which informs her knowing. She has cognition of what is about to happen. She can choose to act on what she knows or not.

A phone rings and the listener knows before speaking, who is on the other end.

A director in psychodrama may know that an issue for the protagonist is a lack of self-esteem. The director may see it, sense it and hear it. The director may choose to follow what is 'known'. Doubt can be a friend of the director. It is easy to check out what is doubtful for example. 'I notice you have difficulty looking at me when you speak. Are you afraid of what I may think of you?' In this kind of naive enquiry, confirmation occurs when doubt meets knowing.

This chapter will look at the role of the director in psychodrama and at how the skills and intuition of the director are part of a larger process of cognition.

To begin the subject of directing, I offer an excerpt from a discussion occurring at the end of this chapter. Anne Ancelin Schützenberger is talking to me.

Anne   Psychodrama is an existential psychotherapy. It has to be in the here and now, free floating with the protagonist. Sometimes you are with the subject and sometimes you are back into yourself, able to cut it, change it, produce something new, something in the future, something different.

Marcia   Sessions that are too pre-planned or pre-thought don't work. The concept of the here and now is simply that it is *here* and it is *now*. It is not *there* and *then*. Probably that is the saving grace of a group. Something new is produced every second, and it is the director's role to catch that new thing.

A STORY ABOUT KNOWING

As the chapter on directing unfolds I am struck by a comment made to me by a taxi driver the morning after the Dunblane tragedy in Scotland, 1996, where sixteen 5-year-olds were shot dead in their physical education class by a suspicious loner obsessed with guns and young boys. During the twenty-four hours after the event, neighbours, parents and a Member of Parliament were making statements about the murderer, Thomas Hamilton. 'Hamilton made your flesh crawl', said one. Another said: 'He was a man who carried a grudge, he believed there was a huge conspiracy against him.' 'He just crept along the hedge', 'He was quite disturbing', said a neighbour. Prior to the school killings, several parents had taken their sons out of a youth club Hamilton was running. A parent reported, 'The last time I spoke to the police about him, they told me that they were sure he was doing something wrong, but they couldn't prove it.' The policeman's parting words were 'One of these days he'll overstep the mark, and that's when we'll catch him.' It was too late. The murderer shot himself along with the sixteen children. Hamilton's mother was shocked at hearing her son had been responsible for the massacre, 'I have never known him to get angry', she said. The mother was a woman Hamilton believed to be his older sister. He was raised by elderly grandparents whom he believed to be his parents. It was only later in life that he learned the truth of these relationships.

The taxi driver and I were speechless at the radio news of the massacre. 'I bet there's a lot of people who wished they'd listened to their instincts and acted on a gut reaction', he said. How difficult is the eternal struggle, to know something and to act on what you know. Sophisticated learning, rules and instruction chip away at our more basic wisdom and soon, we become like the centipede who can't walk because he's confused about which foot to use first.

Cognition and emotion are like siblings. The galloping panic to make a respectable decision can often trample the parent (cognition). Cognition is ever patient, waiting to be heard in its wisdom. If neighbours, police and parents had acted on their gut feelings and persisted with their creative wisdom there might now be a teacher and her children still alive. Ironically, months before the tragedy, it was Hamilton who hit back at the campaign against himself and delivered 7,000 leaflets to prospective parents of the youth club he ran in Dunblane to clear his name. His persistence to clear his name was the very persistence that was needed to name him before the tragedy occurred.

TRUSTING COGNITION ALLOWS THE DIRECTOR SPONTANEITY

The crucial relevance of this story to directing psychodrama is in trusting cognition. *Trusting cognition is what allows* one to be spontaneous. Spontaneity gives the skills authenticity. Though authenticity is one of the foundation stones of good directing, it is difficult to teach directors to trust their hunches, to trust their intuition and their cognition. To whittle down thinking, observing and knowing into simple action is difficult; the timing is nearly impossible. Yet timing, as in the Dunblane tragedy, is of utmost importance. Each role reversal in directing, each scene change, each auxiliary ego choice is somewhat of a calm emergency. If the role reversal is late, it loses its meaning; if too early it can be ineffective or disrespectful. If the scene changes too soon, the inappropriate timing casts dust over the brilliantly exposed gems. If an auxiliary is chosen too late, the story may have already been told; the impact of the drama lost and the need for enactment gone.

WHAT IS THE ROLE OF THE DIRECTOR?

The director is a co-producer of the drama taking clues from the person seeking help. In most therapies, this is the therapist, facilitator or group leader. In psychodrama, the director is a trained person to help guide the action. 'I have nothing to work with and therefore the production is one that I structure gradually' (Moreno 1942).

The major role of the director is to stimulate spontaneity, to prompt, to guide and to structure the psychodrama from apparently nothing into something real for the person enacting the drama and for the group watching the drama. Each moment should live as if it is happening in the here and now. The protagonist holds the key to the inner and outer world. The director holds the door which opens and closes and the group provides the frame.

WHAT DOES THE DIRECTOR DO?

Directing the group

The chief concern of the director is the immediate behaviour of the group in front of her. In the beginning of the group she may notice two people sitting together but avoiding any contact, or one or two physically isolated from the others.

As the director observes the dynamics of the immediate group, non-verbal body language may indicate who of the group is ready to represent an aspect of life in front of the others. The tool to measure group dynamics is called sociometry. A sociogram or map of those dynamics invented by J.L. Moreno indicates the choices and rejections made by group members based on specific criteria. For example, who would you most like to sit next to? Who would you least like to sit next to? Eventually, a protagonist or subject is selected by the group, by the director or self-selected and supported by the others. The group assist the protagonist and provide a world that is absolutely real.

In psychodrama, the director takes the person into her own space on the group stage and follows the lead. Together they set up a situation that represents the protagonist's life. 'The scene is created by the subject. The director encourages the person to act out their problems naturally and spontaneously. The protagonists direct their own therapy, stopping when they feel the need' (Moreno and Moreno 1977). The director has many functions: producer, therapist, action analyst and group leader are among the main ones.

> As producer he has to be on the alert to turn every clue which the subject offers into dramatic action to make the line of production one with the life line of the subject, and never to lose rapport with the audience. At times the director may become indirect and passive and for all practical purposes, the session seems to be run by the subject. As analyst he may complement his own interpretation by responses coming from an informant in the audience.
>
> (Moreno 1953: 83)

Though one particular story is enacted, psychodrama is a group process. Each person is a therapeutic agent of the other and group members often gain as much from the session as the protagonist. As therapist, the director makes therapeutic choices, informs and educates the protagonist. When appropriate, the protagonist and the director work in tandem. At other times one is led by the other.

Directing the story and scenes

The director takes a story from a group member and through action separates the text from the subtext. Directing is a parallel activity. A story is enacted and parallel to that a trained evaluation of what is happening is on-going. The director intercepts, breaks and dramatically re-orders the scenes as the clues come from the protagonist.

In directing the scenes, the emphasis is not on the dramatic effect, but on how true to life the scene feels. Good theatre is breathless production with authenticity as the aim. Detailed presentation is important. If the director is naively inquisitive and is a good social and environmental investigator, the protagonist will follow with spontaneous presentation of particular details in their living and working space. For example:

Director   Show us your mother's hospital room.
Protagonist   (Sets up room.)
Director   Be your mother in bed. Are you lying down or sitting?
Protagonist   I'm lying down and staring at the ceiling.
Director   Are you in pain?
Protagonist   No, not physically. I just don't want to live. I want to join my husband who died in the accident.
Director   The accident? What happened?

This is a naive question that a 5-year-old might ask. If the timing is right, even a naive question is acceptable to the protagonist, often invited. The subject of an 'accident' was brought by the protagonist. Many directors are afraid to be bold and economic in their questioning. Some directors confuse simplicity with intrusion; however, if you follow the contextual lead of the protagonist you, as director, can follow what has already been given. The protagonist is worried about her baby who is agitated. She assumes the role of her own mother.

Protagonist   (as mother) My husband crashed the car in a fog. I don't know how he could do that to me. He left me alone and now I don't know how to live without him. He did everything.
Director   You sound angry.
Protagonist   I never got angry at him; only about him to others.
Director   Who to? To your daughter here, for example?
Protagonist   Yes, I tell her about him all the time.
Director   Can you show us what you say to her? Choose someone to be your mother now so you can be yourself.
Protagonist   (She chooses a plump, kind-faced member of the group to play the role. She observes her mother lying on the hospital bed and begins to cry.)

Director	Tell your mother what makes you cry.
Protagonist	(facing mother) I want you to be happy about my baby. I am 5 months pregnant. I'm sad and you're sad and my father will never see my baby.
Director	What do you miss most about your father?
Protagonist	The way he held me. He loved me. I wanted my baby to feel his love too but she never will. I used to sit on his lap when I was little. (She smiles.)
Director	You'd like your child to sit on his lap?
Protagonist	Yes, it would be my dream.
Director	Shall we do it now?
Protagonist	How can we? (looking sad but interested) She's not even born yet.
Director	Let's give you a chance to be a 5-month-old unborn baby. Would you like to feel what that would be like?
Protagonist	Yes. Now that my baby is 6 months old in real life, she is both happy and agitated. I think it began here, at this time. I also feel happy and agitated in the hospital room.

Supporting, enhancing and following go hand in hand with intercepting, changing and adding to the scene. The protagonist becomes her unborn baby. In the next scene she watches her future child sitting in the lap of her dead father. She then assumes the role of herself sitting with father, saying what she was never able to say to her father when she herself was a child.

Directing the protagonist

What becomes produced in the structure of dramatic scenes is generally what the protagonist cannot produce alone, namely insight into patterns of behaviour.

The protagonist in the above example had originally presented the problem of having a 6-month-old child who was both agitated and happy. During the time of her parents' accident she was herself 'agitated and happy'; which was a partial repetition of her childhood.

The protagonist said after the session: 'I was aware of those events but I never connected them to the mothering I had and the parenting of my daughter. It's like I found a part of myself that was there but unconstructed. It's as if I've woken up.' Psychodrama gives opportunities for enactment that life doesn't offer. The director helps to shape the enactment. The protagonist, in the above example, was involved in an unconscious maternal repetition.

It is interesting to note here that the original aims of Moreno's spontaneity training, which was the precursor to psychodrama, were:

1   better integration of emotional mechanisms in the acting personality;
2   the integration of knowledge in the acting personality;

3   and better adjustment of the acting personality to other persons in the immediate environment.

(Moreno 1942)

The better adjustment of the acting personality to other persons in the immediate environment meant that the unconscious behaviour of the protagonist must be made conscious. Conscious behaviour has a better chance of not being repeated.

It gives the protagonist a chance to make the choice of continuing or ending the behaviour.

Directing unconscious content

It is important for the director to respect the survival process thus far contained within the protagonist. Information is repressed, in the mind, for a reason. What Moreno said about spontaneity training is also true of psychodrama. 'The detailed presentation of things that are usually omitted may therefore be just the point' (Moreno 1942).

This omission may sometimes be misinterpreted as a conscious resistance. The very nature of resistance is that it is often an unknown process to the resister.

One of the greatest contributions of Freud, after he stopped utilising massage and hypnosis to create suggestibility, was his discovery of unconscious resistance. Before, by making a patient relaxed and therefore suggestible, he had bypassed the very process he wanted to explore. He began to interpret the resistance and the patient spoke about material that they would otherwise forget and resist (Jacobs 1996).

Directing auxiliary egos

Auxiliary ego direction is well covered in Chapter 7 by Paul Holmes. In it he discusses the term ego stressing the fact that the role taken by a group member is held or played and is 'an extension of aspects or roles in the protagonist's own inner world or psyche'.

It is quite daring for a stranger to attempt to play a role well known to the protagonist. The greatest fear of group members, when beginning to play an auxiliary role, is their fear of getting it wrong. This is quite a natural fear and one that the director should be aware of and take into consideration. The auxiliary ego, as well as the protagonist, needs acknowledgement and encouragement to continue such a daring task. To present personal intimacy (the protagonist's task) and to represent the intimacy of an unknown role (the auxiliary ego's task) may seem quite usual for the director, but it is often unusual both for protagonist and the auxiliary ego.

Directing with encouragement and neutrality

The director guides, reflects, encourages, enhances and tries to see the human story revealed from the protagonist's point of view. It is rare in life to be in trouble and to have someone in our corner throughout the duration of that troubled time. Essentially the director is a found advocate, a witness for the story teller. The protagonist may be vulnerable, suggestive and needy. The therapist attempts to stay in an objective, unbiased and neutral place while handling the subjectivity, bias and strong opinions of the protagonist. All is to be considered, heard and worked through.

The director's neutrality is often a calm blank canvas on which the protagonist can finally paint her real colours. As an artist's assistant, the director makes the palette available, from which the protagonist can select colours to paint.

An extraordinary story, illustrative of the colour analogy, was told to me by Anne Schützenberger. She was working with the Dalai Lama in North America. A chronic patient was brought to them. The woman had been hospitalised for years, having no function in her arms or legs. Anne asked the woman why her legs and arms were black. The woman responded by telling her that her extremities were black ever since her sister died forty years earlier.

'What happened then?' asked Anne.

The protagonist played out a scene after her sister died. The dead child, aged 2, was too big for the prepared coffin. The protagonist was 4. In front of her eyes, the funeral directors broke the arms and legs of the still body in order to fit the child into the coffin. At the time, the protagonist could only watch, horrified and in silence. Forty years later, the little child now entered the situation again, with the guidance of a psychodramatist.

'What are you feeling that you cannot say?' asked the director.

As the protagonist began to weep for her sister, scream at the men who broke the little body of her sister and rage at her parents for allowing it, the black skin of the protagonist began to turn pink. Her own arms and legs began to come back to their natural colour, a colour which had been absent for forty years. When the dead child's arms and legs were broken, the protagonist had had a sympathetic reaction which was locked in her limbs. Hidden family loyalty is a subject that Schützenberger writes about and works with often (Schützenberger 1996).

WHAT MAKES A GOOD DIRECTOR?

Directing: skill and personality

In psychotherapy it is extremely difficult if not impossible to separate the skill from the personality of the therapist. Skill and personality are, at least in the act of performance, inseparably one.

The tension between personality and skill influence the four major roles of the director: group leader, therapist, action analyst and producer.

Remember that the director meets a group first in the role of group leader. Equality of status should be established, that is every member of the group is equal. Each presents themselves according to what he or she is, and with whatever life warm-up has occurred. The director is at the beginning of creation, naive, fresh, discovering and being co-responsible for each new moment. Here is where spontaneity begets spontaneity. If the director is free and easy then the sense of anything can happen, anything is possible is communicated. The group feels free to create moments together rather than passively attending a play.

For many years I have pondered the question, what makes a good director? As a trainer of psychodrama directors, it is interesting to see the parallel of skill and personality develop in the trainee. As the personality improves and clarifies through personal therapy, work as a protagonist, examination and change in sociometric status, through supervision, acceptance and ease with the authority of the trainer, so then do the skills improve.

In January 1996 at breakfast in Myrtle Beach, South Carolina four of us sat pondering the question. We devised the following list of qualities for a good director and a not-so-good director.

A list of qualities for a good director, by Zerka Moreno, Marcia Karp, Poppy Sprague and Deborah Smith

- Courage
- Emotional energy
- Fearlessness
- A no-holds-barred approach
- Imagination
- Outrageousness
- Listening with the third ear (hearing what is not being said)
- Ability to stop the protagonist from talking and knowing when to go back into action
- Being in the protagonist's corner and leaping out of it when necessary
- Knowing when to end with graceful closure (so many directors know where to start but not where to end)
- Integration in how the director dresses and presents him or herself
- Patience and curiosity (a trainee said to Zerka: 'I can't get them to ask the kind of questions you ask.' In response Zerka said: 'Ask naive questions. Don't know too much but know in conjunction with the feelings.'
- Jolt the protagonist out of their over-preparation
- Compassion and a sense of timing
- Being able to admit: 'I'm not sure I understand what you said, can you say it again?'
- Honesty
- To be an absolute advocate for the protagonist

- Respect for the protagonist's space
- Discard and dispense with critical judgement
- Enthusiasm for what could happen
- Interview the protagonist and auxiliary naively to create a bigger view
- Sense of humour
- Flexibility and humility

As we ended the discussion Zerka said, 'Personally, I don't think there's anything more valuable than knowing who you are and what your limitations are. The me/not me area gives the director distance to be able to survey the situation. It is important to be present without obstructing or getting in the way.'

What makes a not-so-good director?

- Being judgemental and impatient
- When the patient is brighter than the therapist
- When the director lacks the confidence to admit what she does not know
- Mixing the subjective/objective axis and not knowing whether the psychodrama belongs to the protagonist or the director (me/not me area)
- Being seduced by the protagonist's 'talking gymnastics'. Eventually the protagonist will criticise the director for 'wandering'. Clear focus and structure are needed for the wandering protagonist.
- Using skill without heart. If compassion and love are not transferred, the protagonist feels that unsuccessful techniques have been used and it increases the protagonist's feelings of helplessness. When the director is stuck she should say so and together they may work out where to go. Many protagonists have already been over-parented so the last thing they need is preconceived ideas of what they should do and say.
- Nervousness and anxiety are easily felt by a group and the group produces mirrored responses such as lack of co-operation, hesitancy and people leaving.
- Fear is a killer to a director. An ill patient once said to Zerka: 'I was helped because you didn't run away from my psychosis.'
- As a trainer, I don't like to watch a director who does not want to be there. My advice to the director who does not want to be there is 'Don't.'
- Sentimentalising the end of a psychodrama

Stereotyping is a trap directors may fall into. When the preconceived stereotype is latched on to by the director, she stops listening and begins to steer the action to where the director assumes it has to go, based on her prior decisions. The feeling that the session can go anywhere, at any time, including stopping altogether, should be held in mind. This freedom of gymnastic footwork is exhilarating if the anything-can-happen atmosphere exists. Then it helps to shape the *sui generis*, one-of-a-kind session, in which people feel privileged to participate.

REACTIONS TO THE DIRECTOR

The transference of Freud and Moreno

It is important to remember that often reactions to the group leader do not originate in the present moment. Individuals in the group come ready to repeat behaviour that has happened to them before in life.

The group member may come prepared to resist authority, to feel burdened and exploited and expects that no one thing can help. Resistance can be acknowledged and utilised. Moreno suggests that the therapist occasionally also may have transference towards the patient.

> Mental processes in his own mind, related to the patient, have a definite effect upon his conduct during the psychodramatic work. The suggestions he makes to the patient, the role in which he acts, the analytical interpretation he gives, influence the outcome of treatment. Transference develops on both poles.
>
> (Moreno and Moreno 1977: 227)

Moreno points out that though transference may be worked through with one's own therapist prior to group work it does not mean he has become free from transference in regard to any new individual he may meet in future. He would have to gain the armour of a saint.

> His armour may crack at any time a new patient marches in, and the kind of complexes the patient throws at him may make a great difference in his conduct. Every new patient produces a spontaneous relationship with the therapist and no analysis can preview or check the emotional difficulties emerging on the spur of the moment.
>
> (Moreno and Moreno 1977: 227)

Although Gillie Ruscombe-King discusses transference in Chapter 9 (Sharing) I would like to discuss Moreno's concept of transference related to the director.

Like the current guidelines of the United Kingdom Council for Psychotherapists, Moreno recommended in 1950 that the therapist is in her own therapy during the treatment of others. Specifically, we know that the director guides the initial group warm-up, helps a representative voice move through action scenes toward problem solving and after sufficient closure, helps group members to identify with the work done by sharing similar life experiences.

Directors look for adequacy and consistency in their work while utilising two parallel processes of transference

In order to be adequate and consistent the directors constantly need to monitor their own behaviour.

When a director begins a group, she forms a positive alliance with group members. She provides a good-enough parent model, at times remains neutral and at times takes the side of the protagonist, aiming to remain authentic and appropriately stabilised throughout.

There are two parallel processes occurring. The patient's response to the director and the director's response to the protagonist. Moreno thought this was not 'counter-' transference, but two parallel processes of transference, that have the possibility of being productive or unproductive. It is the director's task to make them productive (Hare and Hare 1997).

Often when I have a protagonist damaged by parental misuse of power, I consciously transfer my optimism, hope, encouragement, faith and esteem towards that person, and during their work. This positive flow, for a short time may re-parent the protagonist during the psychodramatic process. Often they find themselves liberated from the I-can't, I-won't, I-can-never type of prison so common in low self-esteem and parental misuse of power.

TOTAL INVOLVEMENT AND MORENO'S CONCEPT OF THE GODHEAD

> I visualised a healer as a spontaneous-creative protagonist in the midst of a group. A healer without theories and methods is like a painter without arms.
>
> (Moreno 1955: 19)

It may be helpful here to look at what ideas underpin the role of director. Is she a therapist with simply a set of skills for enactment or is there an overall philosophy in the democratic application of action-centred groupwork?

The concept of the Godhead is one of Moreno's core ideas and yet it is often overlooked. It may be because people confuse it with egotism, with being better than others, with being God-like and therefore too far from real people. Nothing could be further from the truth. Moreno's concept of the Godhead has been largely misunderstood and under used. It is about ordinary people taking responsibility for ordinary living.

He said that a creative definition of God-playing is total involvement – to put everything of the unborn into the first moment of being. Moreno wanted each of us to be fully inside civilisation and not outside it.

All my inspiration for my methods and techniques have come directly from my idea of the Godhead and from the principle of the genesis.

(Moreno 1955: 8)

I think Moreno focused on the Godhead to help us more fully participate in all aspects of life – both personal and professional. To just be – as if we were at the beginning of creation, naive, fresh, discovering and being responsible for each new moment created. When pondering what God was like on the first day of creation, Moreno thought he was:

knowing and wise with the ability to penetrate the abyss of the universe. Hovering over the first day's chaos, he was there to create, not to analyse or to just take part. God was first a creator, an actor. He had to create the world before he had time to analyse it. He would put every part of the chaos into the melting pot. All events have equal merit, hate and stupidity are just as close to his heart as love and wisdom.

(Moreno 1955: 8)

Key ideas of the Godhead

1 To each according to what he or she is.
2 If God assigned spontaneity and creativity to each individual he created innumerable oppositions. God is dependent on everyone.
3 God-playing is maximum involvement and having faith in human intention.
4 Spontaneity and creativity is a propelling force in human progress.
5 The nearer people are to you (in spatial proximity) the more attention and acceptance is spent and needed. The nearer people are to you, in time, the more time is spent. The here and now comes first.
6 Moreno was interested in human beings sharing the responsibility of creating their existence so it did not fall on the shoulders of one but it was shared. 'If God ever comes back, he'll come back as a group' (Moreno 1955: 12).
7 The creator is only interested in the creations, not in the possessions. This is in opposition to the concept of 'the father' who may be possessive, and protective.
8 Anonymity is the natural form in which to operate collectively and autonomously. Moreno wrote the book, *The Words of the Father* (1941), in which he role-reversed as God. He produced it anonymously.
9 The 'act' is the *atmosphere* of a creation, not the content or result.
10 Share the responsibility for all living things.
11 Be an ambassador of the universe and acknowledge that each of us is the same in our right to 'ambassadorship'. Play the role well, with care, diligence, caution and alertness.
12 The power of godliness is in each of us. We each have that potential.

A DISCUSSION ON DIRECTING BETWEEN ANNE ANCELIN SCHÜTZENBERGER AND MARCIA KARP, APRIL 1996

In preparing for this chapter I had a discussion with Moreno's original student, Anne Schützenberger. At the time of writing she was 78 years old and a wise scholar and practitioner.

Anne   I think that the director of psychodrama is like a captain of a ship, master of the ship, doing what she pleases – *maitre bon après Dieu* – and I think what is very important for a director is to feel that anything is possible. The director should be free, to invent any new technique. For me a session of psychodrama is a mixture of art, science, creativity, psychotherapy and training, so it has to be a unique creation, very beautiful in itself.

Marcia I like the kind of group that feels, this group only happened with us. There could not have been another group like this, completely *sui generis*: our creation, one of a kind.

Anne   For me, the main inventions of the genius of Moreno are first, role reversal: see the world as the other sees it. Second is the projection into the future or surplus reality: to give the protagonist things that life has not given, and to open him for the future. The third and, for me, maybe the most important, Moreno discovered the co-unconscious of the group. I will remind you that if Freud discovered the individual unconscious; Jung the collective unconscious; Moreno discovered the group unconscious and the co-unconscious of the group. When the director is directing he is tuned into the group feelings and the sociometry of the group and can understand what is happening under the surface of group communication.

Marcia How do you warm yourself up as a director?

Anne   Usually, I sit quietly and watch. I listen to the group and I look at the group. I look very much at the non-verbal communication. I look if people . . . sometimes people sit by colours: all the blue blouses and blue shirts will be together. Sometimes all the men are together and all the women are together. I mean there is something about how a group sits and speaks and starts to talk that warms me up very much to the work.

Marcia My warm-up is to find a place where I can empty myself. It might be going for a walk; it might be from nature or silence. I used to over-prepare sessions. Now my warm-up is more about me that it is about my interaction with the group. If I am prepared to receive, then the interaction is clear. There has been an unfortunate pattern of warm-ups where the group has music, or action-oriented games. I don't remember Moreno using these.

Anne   Never. That reminds me that I saw Moreno drop the protagonist more often than is done now. He would decide if the person was ready to work or not ready to work. He was feeling free: he was never committed to the session. This is one of the main lessons I learned from him. I am not committed to running psychodrama. . . . I am committed to be fair to myself, the protagonist, the group, and to be there.

Marcia   Or if there was something false in what was being presented. Moreno was very good at picking that up.

Anne   There is a chemistry working between the director, the protagonist and the group. If it is not there, everything is false. It becomes bad theatre.

Marcia   One of the things that makes a good director is involvement, curiosity, a kind of nose for where the energy lies, where the energy is coming from.

Anne   That is it exactly. Someone who will carry the energy of the group, and very often it is better picked up by the director than elected or selected by the group. They may be so much in need that they don't feel it. I think having small nothings is a very good warm-up for the group. One of the definitions of psychodrama given by Moreno is to play one's life on the stage but another less well-known definition is that it is a physical battle and a mind battle between the director and the resistance of the protagonist. So one of the ways to make a good psychodrama is to catch the protagonist unaware, not let him build a defence. Small nothings and vignettes are ways to have the protagonist open up and not be defensive. People are sometimes afraid to make a full psychodrama but few will refuse to make a small vignette.

Marcia   Yes, I think it is true that the undefended place is important. . . . I am thinking of people who direct sessions with too much of a formulaic idea of what it is to direct, so they may ask the protagonist to be the auxiliary, then the auxiliary comes up and is the role, then they do the next one, and the next one, and so on, and it gets rather boring. As Merlyn Pitzele once said, I have never seen a boring psychodrama but I have seen boring psychodramatists. Sometimes people try to remember the techniques and forget what they are for. One of the original reasons for devising psychodrama was to train spontaneity. The director needs to remember, when rushing towards the end of a resolution, that she is also training spontaneity both in the protagonist and in the people who play the different roles; also in the director, keeping the director fresh. So everybody in the group is training in spontaneity.

Anne   There are other things which have to be said about directing. You are not obliged to make one scene extend for one hour. An interesting way to work is to achieve a catharsis and then stop. Another way to work is to have, let's say, twenty minutes warming up of the group, have a twenty-minute psychodrama and have a good forty minutes sharing, putting many vignettes in the sharing. The catharsis of the audience is very important. For me there is no difference in being a protagonist or being a member of the audience having a catharsis, being able to speak about it, cry about it or share it with the group. You can do many things in an hour.

Marcia So, when we talk about protagonist-centred psychodrama, in fact the protagonist is always changing every moment. The spotlight of the protagonist can move, once the action and the energy has changed or shifted. The director has to be very flexible to see the spotlight change from one part of the room to another.

Anne I have two examples that come to mind. I once did a psychodrama in surplus reality – about the death of a father. The protagonist could not attend the death of his father because he could not get a plane ticket. He arrived the next day and his father was dead. We did surplus reality and he talked to his dead father as if he was there when he died. There was lots of emotion; there was a big catharsis. During the sharing, because part of the group was crying, we had seven or eight vignettes with the dying father, or the dead father, dead mother, dead grandmother, dead cat, dead neighbour. They were moved by the psychodrama and they each quite naturally took about one, two or three minutes to have their own vignette from the audience. So, as you said, the spotlight moved but it was at the same time different, important, very short and a very good sharing for the protagonist. Another thing came to me as you were speaking. I think it was at the Congress in Copenhagen. We had a strong psychodrama, then we had a sharing with vignettes. Much later, in Buenos Aires, a lady came to me asking, 'did I remember Copenhagen?' I said, 'Yes, but what do you mean?' She said, 'You did a vignette with me in the audience, in the sharing, and it was about me having stopped my university studies. You worked with me for a few minutes and after that I went to university again. I finished. I am now a fully fledged psychologist and a psychotherapist, and all that change came from the sharing vignette.' It is crucial to know that many important things happen in the audience.

Marcia It is a real affirmation about timing which is something that we don't talk enough about in directing psychodrama . . . timing. When a person comes to us with a problem, it is important to ask the question, why now? Why have you brought this particular problem to me now? The person begins to think, well, what is happening in my life that makes it so crucial now? What happens in the small vignettes during the sharing is that the person's timing has come to a crescendo. Cognitively and emotionally things come together, forming a combustion which ignites into a truth that cannot be held back. I think the director has to have gymnastic shoes on to catch the energy of the group. Many people have said to me, 'If you hadn't seen me or encouraged me at that time I would never have been able to say that', or 'I would never have been able to do that.' Maybe, as directors, we have to be prepared to see that when the focus changes, it is also to do with internal timing which has shifted from 'I could never say that', 'I could never do that', to 'I can do that now', 'I am thinking that now', and 'Now is the time'. Einstein used to say: 'Imagination is more important than knowledge.' When a person imagines, while watching others playing roles, that they see themselves, for example, talking to a dead mother that they never had a chance to talk to, then now is the time.

Anne   They see themselves in their mind's eye doing that.

Marcia   ... and they have almost visualised it before it happens and because they are ripe for that enactment of their own visualisation, their hope is highest at that point. In order for anybody to change in life, they have to have hope and motivation to change, otherwise they won't change.

Anne   I would like to come back to something you said before. My late friend, Eduardo Cortisa, used to say that a group therapist should have eyes revolving around like a ...

Marcia   A lighthouse beacon?

Anne   Yes, going around the group. Then you see whose breathing pattern changes, who becomes pale, who becomes red, who has tears in their eyes, who starts to move to the edge of their chair, who starts to open their mouth as if they want to say something.

Marcia   Anne, you and I often say, that to be a director you have to be a little bit of a witch and I think that witchery, in a way, is this kind of open reality where ... you have eyes and ears more open than normal and you are picking up clues. I am thinking of a woman I was working with from Argentina. She was a very small woman, and I said to her, 'Were you a premature baby?' She said 'Yes, I was.' Well, that didn't seem to me very strange because she was small, so she may have been a small baby. Then I said to her, 'Were you born in the Andes?' She said 'Yes, how do you know the Andes?' I said, 'I don't know, you were talking about seeing mountains or hills or something like that.' Then I asked her a third question: 'Were you the eldest child?' She said 'Yes, I was.' Now, in asking those three questions, it seemed to me very obvious. However, other people thought that I was some sort of witch. I know it happens to you a lot. I think it is simply being in tune visually, listening to verbal and non-verbal clues. When the observational qualities are high for the director, then information is coming in and being absorbed. The director can naively ask questions, like a little kid does, 'Oh aren't you small. Were you a small as a baby?'

Anne   I think the co-unconscious of Moreno is stronger than Jung's collective unconscious. It is more complicated. I think you can be open-minded in this way only when you have been on the stage long enough, if you have run groups long enough. You don't have to think about it; it comes naturally to you ...

Marcia And if you have nothing to prove. Often young directors are trying
to prove something. Probably one of the great healing qualities of
therapists is that they are, simply, with the person who needs healing,
proving nothing, just being. This 'being with' is profound because
when the co-unconscious is working together, trust is building between
them, love is flowing between them, caring is flowing between them
and the 'being-together-aspect' contains and holds the creativity of the
healing process. What happens with young directors is that they start
the opposite way. They start with the creativity thinking that it will
produce trust and co-unconsciousness. Maybe it works from the other
way, that the creativity is an invention built between people who trust
each other and who want to create together.

Anne When you know your theory and your techniques enough, then you are
free to be centred on the client.

Marcia I become the person I am working with, then I can see from inside their
own needs. My skills are only there to facilitate the needs in the client
or the patient or the protagonist.

Anne Psychodrama is an existential psychotherapy. You move, free floating
in the here and now with the protagonist.

Marcia Sessions that are pre-planned or pre-thought don't work. The concept
of the here and now is simply that it is *here* and it is *now* and it is not
there and *then*. Probably that is the saving grace of a group because
something new is produced every second, and it's the director's role to
catch that new thing. We are holding hands with the person's readiness.
A good director stays with the protagonist through productive and non-
productive moments. The director is a midwife in bringing forth what
is needed and what is unborn.

CLOSURE OF THE DIRECTOR: COGNITION IN ACTION

*The director needs to use her eyes and ears to courageously observe and act on
the hidden, the unspoken and the non-verbal clues given by the members of the
group and by the protagonist.*

In training thousands of directors over thirty years, a statement often made
by the trainee comes to mind: 'I was just going to do that. I knew that was the
next thing to do. I was thinking about it just when you said it.'

Because so many of us have been damaged by criticism and judgement
we have unfortunately internalised a massive critic which destabilises our
confidence and makes us hesitate in doing the things we know we can do. We
need to get rid of the critic and do.

There is a wonderful story about procrastination. An old couple, 93 and 96, were visited by the police and a social worker at 3:00 a.m., because they were causing such a commotion and woke all the neighbours.

> 'I hate her, I want a divorce', said the husband.
> 'I can't live with him any longer', said the 93-year-old wife.
> 'Why now? Why have you waited so long for this to happen?' said the social worker.
> 'We thought we would wait until all the children were dead.'

To use timing, to act on what you know, to utilise conviction about one's own gut reaction, to trust intuition, to let intuition inform skills, to incorporate the sum total of life experience in the moment of cognition and then to act on it, that is the task of the director in psychodrama. I wish you courage, inspiration, skill; enjoyment and good luck.

BIBLIOGRAPHY

Hare, P. and Hare, J. (1997) *Biography of J.L. Moreno*, London: Sage.

Holmes, P. (1998) This volume.

Jacobs, L. (1996) *Freud*, London: Sage.

Krishnamurti, J. (1991) *Commentaries on Living*, 3rd series, ed. D. Rajagopal, London: Gollancz.

Moreno, J.L. (1941) *The Words of the Father*, New York: Beacon House.

Moreno, J.L. (1942) *Introduction to Psychodrama*, produced 1997 by René Marineau, Université du Québec à Trois-Rivières.

Moreno, J.L. (1953) *Who Shall Survive?*, New York: Beacon House.

Moreno, J.L. (1955) *Preludes to my Autobiography*, New York: Beacon House.

Moreno, J.L. and Moreno, Z. (1977) *Psychodrama, First Volume*, New York: Beacon House.

Schützenberger, A.A. (1996) *Aïe, mes Aïeux, liens transgénérationnels, secrets de famille, génosociogrames (Ouch, My Ancestors)*, Paris: DDB.

Chapter 10

The sharing

Gillie Ruscombe-King

Give truth and receive truth; give love to the group and it will return love to you; give spontaneity and spontaneity will return.

(Moreno 1953: 114)

The process of sharing in the method of psychodrama is an essential component of its task. This chapter will explore how the process of sharing occurs, what form sharing may take and the director's response to that process.

Classically, a psychodramatic enactment has three stages – the warm-up, the action and the sharing, with the appropriate intensity of work attached to each phase. So it is not surprising to find the chapter on sharing at the latter end of the book. After the psychodramatic enactment, the participants are invited by the director to 'share', verbally and non-verbally, feelings, thoughts and associations to the enactment that has just taken place. It can be done in a number of ways. Most commonly, the action or scene setting is disbanded; any props, e.g. cushions, toys, that have been used in the scene for significant objects (for example, my first teddy or a bag of anger) are de-roled – that is they are clearly described as what they actually are; the group reassembles in a circle, as it began, to recreate the 'action' of the group process. The protagonist and all auxiliaries are included in the circle as a way of reinstating each individual as a group member. Sharing takes place face to face across the circle. Should the group be very large and unable to make a workable round, the protagonist may remain on stage next to the director. Members of the group are invited to come up on to the stage with their sharing. If this is the method adopted, it is important that the protagonist is then re-established within the group as a group member and reasserts his or her own identity. The essential part of the sharing process is to facilitate a single protagonist-centred enactment into a process of group psychotherapy.

HOW AND WHY DOES SHARING TAKE PLACE?

The director returns the protagonist to the group

There is a need to reorient the protagonist into the present – in time, space and context. The protagonist, for example, may have found the hurt 3-year-old child within herself. The purpose of the group is to help her experience that aspect of herself and integrate it with the mature married woman with two teenage sons. She needs reclothing with all aspects of herself. After intense psychodramatic work, there is often a sense of being dazed, even disoriented and the director needs to facilitate time and space for the integration of the work to take place. Elaine Goldman, an American psychodramatist, says that the director, in essence, returns the protagonist to the group. For example:

> After witnessing Helen's work, Mary said: 'It was so wonderful to see you cradle your own son in that way. My mother, like yours, never had time for me and I have struggled so hard with my own children.'

Sharing helps the protagonist feel acceptable

Powerful identifications in other group members will have been stimulated. Sharing these identifications is crucial to the therapeutic work of the group. It enables the protagonist to feel less isolated, less alone. Goldman (1984: 15) describes the importance of 'linking the protagonist with his environment rather than alienating him from it'. Irvin Yalom's work, when describing the curative factors in group psychotherapy cites 'universality' as important. Many clients, he believes, come to therapy with a sense that:

> they are unique in their pain and they alone have frightening or unaccept-able problems, impulses, thoughts and fantasies. After hearing other mem-bers disclose distress similar to their own, clients report that 'the disconfirmation of their feelings of uniqueness is a powerful source of relief', and that they feel 'more in touch with the world'.
>
> (Yalom 1975: 7–8)

> James describes his agony when surrounded by domestic violence. Joseph begins to sob, not wholly because of what James has described but mainly at the sense of relief that someone else knows how it has been for him in his home.

Catharsis

Yalom also cites 'catharsis' as another important curative factor in group therapy. While acknowledging that, classically, catharsis in psychodrama belongs to the action phase, group members can become very emotionally laden, through identification with the protagonist, and need to communicate their feelings (Yalom 1975: 83).

> Jonathan, in his sharing, simply says: 'I feel very moved by your work, Jo. I, too, know what it feels like to be lost in a crowd.'

The power of sharing from group members

The emotional response to the 'staged' enactment can be more intense than that expressed by the protagonist, to the point where a group member is warmed up to work. For example:

> After Anne describes the death of her grandmother, Lucy begins to sob uncontrollably and is unable to speak.

Such is the power of identification. The director's management of this scenario will be discussed later in the chapter. The task of the sharing is the making of what is internal external, of what is private public and what feels alienating and paralysing into connections that are universal and liberating. That is the purpose of sharing in a group.

Intellectual catharsis

Intellectual catharsis is as important as emotional discharge. The intellectual understanding of or insight into a persistent pattern of behaviour or emotional response can create a sense of relief. To cite Yalom again, self understanding has a major influence in personal growth and change. 'Learning why I think and feel the way I do (i.e. learning some of the causes and sources of problems) can induce enormous relief of conflict' (Yalom 1975: 84).

> Joan, in her sharing with Roger, says: 'I could never understand why my mother was so beastly to my sister and to me. Her own mother rejected her when she was 3.'

The purpose of the sharing is to enable what has been unconscious to become conscious and to create a time for group members to articulate any or all aspects of this recognition if they are able.

WHAT IS THE DIRECTOR'S TASK IN THE SHARING?

Staging

In classical psychodrama, the 'sharing' phase takes place at the end of the group, with participants seated where each person can be seen and heard. The staging and physical management of the sharing needs attention, to encourage intimacy and to facilitate sometimes difficult disclosure. The stage becomes everyone's place of work. However, the geographical positioning of each member is, in itself, a non verbal sharing and needs to be recognised as such.

> Jane, after witnessing Veronica's psychodrama about lack of confidence, refuses to join the circle and sits head in hands. The director leaves a space, suggesting to Jane that she join the group when she is able and adds that perhaps she is telling us something important about how Veronica's work has touched her.

Staging for the sharing is as important as the staging for the action and has to reflect the needs of the group and not those of the director.

Analysis vs. sharing

Sharing is a time for relating personal experiences and associations related to the enactment and the whole-group experience. There may be something important to share from the warm up, from a personal interaction, from an auxiliary role or with an auxiliary. It is time for self-reflection. It is not the time for analysis of the action, of what the protagonist did or did not do or say, nor indeed what the director or auxiliaries did or did not do or say. This is the province of processing (in a training context) or supervision and will be addressed in the next chapter. If analysis of the process begins, it is vital for the director to intervene by educating or reminding group members of the task of sharing – reclothing the protagonist, sharing of identifications and promoting group interaction and process.

Helen   (to protagonist Paul) Why did you put so much coal on the fire all the time?

Director (to Helen) I am wondering how you might identify with that particular part of the action? Let's remember we are not here to analyse what we have witnessed.

It is equally important that the director makes this intervention with clarity and sensitivity, with no judgement. When analysis is occurring, it can be a defensive manoeuvre against the pain of the association aroused, creating a psychological resistance to exploring that pain. The defence may be a projective mechanism. Projection may be defined as seeing, feeling or responding to some aspect of another's behaviour, attitude or emotional position but not being able to see it in oneself. It is an unconscious process and will remain unconscious as a defence against the difficulty of assigning the identified behaviour to oneself; e.g. that man is really boring. The task of the therapy is to enable the individual to acknowledge that aspect of themselves, i.e. 'I think I am perhaps a boring person' to allow them the opportunity to change things in themselves.

To continue the above example:

Helen (to Director) Yes, I know that but it is a ridiculous waste of coal.

Helen is perhaps telling us about an anxiety she has surrounding the image of 'putting on too much coal and therefore wasting it' but feels that the anxiety or fear is momentarily too great to embrace. She therefore defends herself from this fear by placing herself in a parental role, although at some level, the identification still lies with the protagonist. The director needs to visualise, momentarily, Helen's own psychodrama around this issue to enable her to disentangle the defence.

Director (to Helen) I am wondering if you have been given the message that you are wasting coal?

Depending on Helen's capacity to re-own her projection, she may say: 'I sound just like my mother! She was always on at us for wasting the coal. We had no money, you see.' Or she may have to work at this for longer and may say: 'I don't know, never really thought about it. But it is true what I am saying, isn't it? He is using too much coal.'

She is now looking for recognition from the director.

Director (to Helen) We can hear what you say and maybe we need more time to think this one over.

Not all projections are so easy to manage. Hostile, even angry outbursts at the protagonist, auxiliaries or director are not uncommon.

Jo (shouting to John) How dare you treat your wife like that? (and then to director) and you (pointing), you should have stopped him!

Clearly, a scene with projections of such ferocity needs careful unpicking. Time is needed for some ventilation as angry feelings in sharing are as valid as tears although they may be less welcome. Time is needed for understanding. It could be said that another protagonist has emerged and a vignette is now happening involving projective and transferential issues. It is not acceptable for the protagonist to be mercilessly attacked. Therefore the director needs to ask him/herself: 'What is Jo really saying?'

By mentally doubling Jo, he may be saying/thinking : 'Christ! Have I really done something like that?!' and towards the director: 'Why didn't you protect/ help me with this?' (fear, insecurity and lack of safety) as if to a mother/father (transference). It is here that the director's analytic antennae may be helpful to clarify the process within the sharing.

Director   (to Jo) I am wondering if something has frightened you?

Depending on Jo's response to this intervention, and his capacity to drop his highly aroused defence, the scene could go in many ways.

Jo   (to Director) You are a fine one to talk!

Director – thinking to him/herself that the focus has shifted to the director and therefore the protagonist is not being attacked, what is Jo really saying?

Director   (to Jo) I am wondering if you feel you have lost trust in me. . . . (Jo may find this very difficult and the director needs to remember that the group is an important tool for containment and identification) . . . and I am wondering if other people here have lost trust in important people?

Other group members give some experiences and then John speaks to Jo.

John   But Jo, that is why I was such a bastard to her. She let me down from day one and I couldn't bear it.

Jo may be able to struggle with some identification, he may not. He may need to go away from the group and think. But essentially, the director has followed the task of disentangling the projection from the protagonist, facilitated identification and provided Jo with a forum to translate fearful conflict into consciousness from where he has a choice to work.

Non-verbal sharing

Sometimes, words are difficult. Useful expression can happen non-verbally – through a glance, squeezing the protagonist's hand or by an embrace. This action may help the words to come and facilitate the process of verbal sharing. Sometimes, just holding a group member who has been profoundly moved can give him/her a sense of containment, perhaps hitherto not experienced. Containment and holding is a primary task of the group process and can provide the necessary phase of integration of inner strength before further exploration. Non verbal sharing can feel comforting, welcoming and warm.

Projection and identification

The director has to be alert to the fact that with any act of sharing, there may be an element of projection rather than identification. Projection, as previously suggested, may be defined as seeing, feeling or responding to some aspect of another's behaviour, attitude or emotional position but not being able to see it in oneself. It is therefore the director's task to identify this process and help the individual work with it.

> After an enactment involving some conflict with mother, Joan became rather overpowering in her comforting of the protagonist. Her actions indicated to the director that something was not quite right and through frank discussion with the protagonist and Joan, it seemed that Joan had observed her own guilt as a mother and could only identify her pain through seeing the protagonist as her daughter.

All interactions will enable further work and it is the task of the director to ensure that all group members own their own projections from the protagonist (and auxiliaries) and that projections are translated into identifications. All responses to the enactment are important, creating a group matrix where profound intrapersonal and interpersonal learning can take place. Monica Zuretti describes the sharing as 'a space in which maturity can emerge' (Zuretti 1994: 213).

SHARING FROM THE AUXILIARY ROLE

In all methods of group psychotherapy, members of the group are wittingly or unwittingly assigned roles. 'You speak just like my sister' or 'Why are you so rigid?' In psychodrama, roles are assigned purposefully and directly in the action phase. 'I would like you to play my father.' Moreno would argue that the concept 'of 'tele' – a mutuality of experience either known or unknown – is a potent force in auxiliary selection. Personal understanding can be gained from playing an auxiliary both for the auxiliary, for the protagonist and for the group as a whole.

Rachel   (speaking to Chris) As your sister, I felt so helpless, I just did not know what to say. I too feel helpless sometimes when confronted with anger in this group.

Sharing from auxiliary role can enable the group process to be exposed and used constructively. It is therefore the director's task to ask for feedback and experience of the role before de-roling of the auxiliary takes place.

Jane   (to Protagonist) As your mother, I felt so frightened for you. I felt such a strong urge to protect you.
John   (protagonist) Well, as you saw, I often seek women to protect me.
Jane   (de-roled, as herself) I have just realised that I am always having to protect Michael, my 'little' brother. He is 29 now!! And that is because my wretched parents were never there to look after him.

From this sharing the director may need to remain mindful of the transference towards him/her in this situation. Here we have an enactment of Jane playing mother again. Perhaps unconsciously she slips into this role all too easily – and what of her feelings towards the director who stands by and lets this happen?

Should someone be assigned a 'bad' role – 'I could not possibly ask anyone to play HIM!' – sensitive sharing from this role could be vital to help change perceptions.

James   (to Joshua) As your stepfather, I felt that I got so angry with you because I felt so inadequate/insecure/overwhelmed.
Joshua   I never thought he had any feelings other than anger!

But again, the director needs to watch closely for projection from auxiliary role.

Andrea   (to protagonist) You were such an irritating little boy.
Director   Are you speaking as Joshua's mother or as Andrea?
Andrea   As Joshua's mother, I mean, look at him, he was such a . . .
Director   Does this have a parallel in your own life?

Depending on the strength of the defence to that identification, Andrea may come to see that she too was a very clingy child, or that she had found her own children unbearably clingy. If she is unable to make that shift, the director may have to be firm about clarifying the projection. It may be held in the group until such time as it can be worked with. It may be useful for Joshua's learning to see that he chose an auxiliary that 'cannot let go'.

De-roling auxiliaries

De-roling auxiliaries is a fundamental part of sharing. Clarifying and stating how the person playing the role is different to that role is vital to re-establish personal identity and clarification of self to the group. This can be done after the person playing the role shares what feelings and thoughts they have had in the role.

Director OK Jane, you have identified that you have been protective towards your brother. In what ways are you different to John's mother?
Jane John's mother did not have anyone to support her. I have Peter, my partner. And I do not like budgies!

Clarification of personal identity in the group enables each individual to retain his/her integrity in the presence of the 'whole' and therefore limits the risk of the group repeatedly assigning roles – i.e. choosing Jane as 'the protective one'. It can happen that 'Heather' is always picked as, for example, the little sister. If the sharing and de-roling has been satisfactorily completed, then the director can see that this is a dynamic issue between 'Heather' and the group rather than the result of an incomplete process.

SHARING THROUGH FEEDBACK

In Yalom's list of curative factors in group psychotherapy, he highlights the importance of interpersonal learning. Within this he includes:

- Other members honestly telling me what they think of me.
- Group members pointing out some of my habits or mannerisms that annoy other people.
- Feeling more trustful of groups and of other people.
- The group giving me an opportunity to approach others.

(Yalom 1975: 79)

All interpersonal behaviour will create dynamics that can enhance learning.
To return once again to the example of John and Jane sharing the 'protective-ness':

John I have always felt rather irritated by you and perhaps that explains why.
Jane (roars with laughter) Peter is always saying that I fuss.

This example has an obvious dynamic element and informs Jane as to how she comes across. More straightforward examples may be observations that a group member is always early, or sits in the same place or scratches his nose before he speaks. More emotive feedback may include statements like: 'I can't understand a word you say.'

SHARING THROUGHOUT THE GROUP

Interactions such as these may happen at any time in the group and may not be confined to the closing stages of the group.

Individual response to Group Context

Margaret walks into the group room and says; 'Oh my goodness, it is cold in here!' – a simple remark and probably based on some reality. However, after some dialogue with Janet who says: 'You are always complaining of feeling cold!' – Margaret realises that 'being cold' is something she has struggled with for many years and is related to cold unloving parents.

The response to the action 'of the moment', i.e. 'the cold', triggers an association. By declaring the association and sharing it with the group, it becomes conscious to her, to the group and therefore becomes available for work. The group can remain warm and receptive in response to the issue of her 'coldness' and in spite of it. In the sharing of the 'coldness', and through its reception, there may be a realisation that this is a transference phenomenon to the group – i.e. she perceives the group 'as if' it were cold. Should she begin to experience the group as warm and friendly, her perception may dissolve and she would be working at feeling received.

> The reality of the therapeutic setting is that by exposing needs it is unable to satisfy, it returns individuals to the ambivalent uncertainty or isolation of childhood or traumatic experience, but this time round with the possibility of coming to terms with those needs through the supporting presence and awareness of other group members. . . . There is an awareness to the truth that all those things which harm or destroy the self arise from within, for we grow our own worlds and carry them with us always. As one gets nearer to the crowd the less it appears as a solid threatening mass, rather the crowd becomes a loosely arranged bunch of people with whom one can communicate on many levels.
>
> (Marie Stride n.d.: 37)

Identifying group process

What is said by individuals can inform the director of some aspect of the group process that needs to be addressed.

Amanda comes into the group very annoyed. Someone cut in front of her at the roundabout on her way home from work and she is feeling cross. The director needs to consider why she chooses to bring to the group this apparently small incident. With some facilitation from the director or group member – 'I am wondering if you are describing some issue in this group?' – it transpires that she is feeling very competitive with other group members who she perceives as always 'getting in first'. Her contribution opens up significant work for her and the whole group on issues of sibling rivalry and competition.

S.H. Foulkes, in his important work describing group-analytic psychotherapy, talks of the possibility of seeing the processes in a group on the basis of figure–ground relationship: one can focus on an individual or individuals as the foreground with the group as the background; or vice versa, on the group-as-a-whole as foreground, as figure, and see the individuals' reactions as ground. This becomes important both theoretically and practically when we have to deal with the relationship of the individual to the group, or vice versa. He believes that it is most useful to put the processes of 'communication' and the commonly held ground, the 'communion', into the centre of one's consideration (Foulkes and Anthony 1973: 20).

The group, within a discussion about shops, may be discussing who is getting 'a good deal' from the group. From this arises a contribution from Jacob that he never gets a good deal from anything and that he got a very 'bad deal' from his father.

The group is thus telling the director what is ripe for work and what as a group they could be interested in exploring.

Identifying transference issues

Peter has a tyrannical father and an inadequate mother. He is tense and preoccupied, and although he can play an auxiliary role, he is unable to ask for anything for himself: 'I'm alright, let someone else

> have a go.' With cautious doubling, and warm group sharing, it becomes clear that he is really saying: 'I'm not alright as I have never been able to express myself. I can't do it here.'

It may take someone a long time to tease out this transference issue. Patient and careful observation of the 'here and now' enactment towards the director (or other group members) will enable the work to happen.

Transference phenomena may emerge very fast.

> It is the first group that Tom has attended. The group is anxious and talkative. To focus the group on more personal interchange, the director requests the group to throw a cushion to each member. . . . After a few exchanges, the cushion is again thrown to Tom, whereupon he slumps into a corner, holding the cushion, quivering and speechless. He pushes away all offers of help, and when the director goes forward, he shouts: 'Go away, I hate this stupid exercise. Is this meant to help me? You're just like my stepmother, she used to hit me with a stick!'
>
> (adapted from Ruscombe-King 1991: 163)

The director needs to help Tom and the group to work carefully and cautiously with this powerful sharing. A psychodramatic enactment is occurring 'in the present'.

> The director suggests that the group makes a circle around Tom and sitting with the group says: 'I think I remind you of those in the past that have been cruel and unpredictable. Perhaps we can share those experiences together, which may help Tom to tell us more about the pain that he is feeling now.' With some tentative sharing about difficult parents, Tom becomes more relaxed and is able to offload some of the very painful memories he had been carrying for years. He begins to feel safer in himself and therefore the slow work of experiencing authority differently has begun.

Finding a sense of self and therefore a separateness from the director can provide a real sense of liberation.

> Sam is 20, still living with dominating parents. After some six months in a group, he is late for the group. His previous response would have

been high anxiety and huge guilt. On this occasion, the bus has broken down and events are entirely out of his hands. For the first time he is able to see the reality of the situation – he apologises, asserts his position and steps into the group with more appropriate adjustment.

Closing and completing the transference at termination of the group is important.

To return to the example of Tom, by the end of his stay in the group, albeit a limited and time boundaried period in a residential setting, Tom becomes much less hostile to the director, is able to receive warmth, encouragement and help from the group. He is able to identify in his life those who are there to nurture and protect him. Thus he is able to reclaim the powerful negative projections and identify within himself some nurturing and positive experiences or 'roles' within himself.

SHARING BY THE DIRECTOR

There are different styles and approaches to this often thorny issue. Some psychodrama directors choose to share very openly in response to whatever arises. Some directors will choose situations from their past that are not too 'emotionally loaded' while maintaining a 'non-client' role. Some directors relinquish the role of director and take the protagonist's role. Others maintain a distance and do not offer anything of their own life experiences.

Many will say that, depending on the context of work, their contribution to the sharing process will differ, i.e. in a clinical setting, they might not share in the same way as in say a training setting. Perhaps there is no 'right or wrong'. However, what is crucial to sound psychotherapeutic practice is:

1   whatever action is taken by the director, the conscious motivation is clearly recognised and the consequences of that action are worked with accordingly;
2   that the unconscious motivation is put under careful scrutiny in supervision;
3   that the director is consistent in terms of his/her interventions.

Lucinda has completed an awkward and at times difficult enactment. The sharing is subdued and sticky. The director turns to Lucinda and says 'I have felt awkward at times.' On reflection, it becomes clear that this comment is motivated by the director's own anxiety to 'rescue' the awkward situation – a countertransferential remark. Perhaps the director's own skills feel at stake here and there is an unconscious need to 'rescue' a sense of esteem. It might be more helpful to recognise the sense of awkwardness in the group and enable the other group members to express it. 'My sense is that you are not alone with your awkwardness, Lucinda.'

The above example would not be so potent if the director had made a professional and considered decision to share with the protagonist after every session. 'I sometimes feel awkward when I go for an interview.' The director then has to consider how that information has been received. The power of the director's role can never be underestimated and the director's sharing can often be given undue weight in terms of its content. In some cases, depending on the relationship with the director, such sharing cannot be absorbed and is frankly disbelieved.

Looking at this from the point of view of role theory, sharing from the director's role can be seen as relinquishing and de-roling from the directorial role to becoming 'a real person'. This thinking may be valuable and provides an interesting model. However, to provide total clarity, a statement such as 'Speaking as Gillie' leaves the group members in no doubt about their own responsibility to their perceptions of the role. Fudging the boundaries is not good practice. Some might argue that directorial sharing provides a good role model. Again, the consequences of that view need to be borne in mind. It may promote inadequacy, envy, mistrust, heightened admiration. From a training point of view, directorial sharing needs careful discussion and scrutiny to promote a clear model of practice. The purpose of sharing is to enhance identification. 'Penetration of boundaries is a unilateral action, transcendence of barriers a mutual one' (Stride n.d.: 31).

CLOSURE

Time together in the group has passed, concentration is disappearing, participants may be feeling 'full up'. Closing the group, enabling members to feel safe enough to leave is a very important directorial task. Such a task may be very simple; it may be very complicated; it will vary according to the context or place in which the group is taking place. In principle, the ending of every session needs to leave members feeling 'safe enough' to pick up their lives in an appropriate way.

Psychodrama is a directive method and powerful forces of omnipotence and control are at the disposal of the director and 'handed' to the director throughout the group. These forces need to be 'handed back' to all group members in order that they are able to reclaim that part of them that has been temporarily projected. Reintegration may be quite straightforward as people complete their sharing.

John After hearing what you said, Duncan, I feel much freer to go and talk to my wife.

Or it may be far more complex and sticky:

Jane I am feeling very confused by what you said, Graham.

A simple direction may be needed to clarify the 'I' or ego strength:

Director Can you identify one thing that is not confusing for you before you leave, Jane?

Transference issues will undoubtedly complicate and indeed inform the process of closure and will take a longer period of time to clarify. Depending on the way group members can reclaim or reintegrate, the director can be informed of the nature of the transference issues left unresolved.

Jo I don't want to go home. You are the only person that can help me (idealisation in the transference).

or

Jane I haven't got anything to offer this group even when we share (unresolved rejection in relation to the group and perhaps the director).

The reader may be asking the question: 'How can I tell when the sharing is "safe enough?"' Working towards appropriate closure can contribute significantly to completing the group. Time boundaries around a group or session are important. Time is used in our society as a means to prepare for an event. In all psychotherapeutic methods, the length of sessions is clearly identified in order for the client to be prepared for the end of the session and for separation from the therapist. The client can prepare for the reinstatement of defences that are needed to handle 'the outside world' and that are necessarily lowered in a therapeutic setting. All psychodrama sessions need to have time boundaries so that the closure process can be honoured.

The context of the psychodrama session may dictate the time available. Out-patient groups usually have to vacate premises; groups in residential settings – hospitals, clinics – may have specific times for lunch, etc. In some residential settings, there may be no such constraints and the sessions may last until the session is completed. While supporting the notion of flexibility and freedom to create empowerment, this way of working can ride across the important notion of reclaiming power and reinstating defences. Furthermore, some of the training for psychodramatists is conducted in settings where flexibility is at hand. It is even more important to address, in training, the notion of closure and the importance of time boundaries in order to inform good practice. Perhaps, in settings where there is flexibility, new time boundaries need to be clearly negotiated, with agreement between the director and the group members rather than a quick decision taken by the director. Every psychotherapist will tell you that important material often comes at the end of a session – because of the safety of the imposition of a time boundary. Psychodrama is no different. It is important that every director recognises this phenomenon.

Complications in closure

What if powerful material presents in the sharing? The task of sharing is to translate projection into identification. Sometimes that identification can be overwhelming. Classically, the feelings are spoken, fears are shared, embraces offered. If feelings are overwhelming and 'unspeakable', this can feel awkward, difficult and anxiety-provoking. I would argue that group safety is created by the group boundary.

Director   James, I can see that you are struggling with something very difficult. We have 10 minutes to help you with this.

A time-limited space has been clarified. To some it may feel that a sense of restriction has been imposed. This response might point to an issue of transference – an issue that needs time and patience to untease. Or an issue of countertransference may arise – the director unwittingly seeing an aspect of self in the client. By keeping to the clarity of the boundary, James is given a choice, handed the power to act, from which further work can emerge.

James   I have just realised how much I *hate* my sister.

It has been spoken. There is some release.

It may be tempting for the director to think: 'Ah! Perhaps we can help James with this.' It could be that James is invited to look at this issue. Indeed it can tumble into an entire new psychodrama. While this is at one level laudable, the psychodramatist is at risk of becoming omnipotent – fixing all, saving all, working it all out – and needing, through personal anxiety, to make things safe. The capacity to direct can be over-used – perhaps unconsciously – to impress, to establish esteem or to overcome a dynamic or unconscious anxiety. All directors are exposed to such forces. He/she may step into a countertransference phenomenon where he/she is responding to the client as if he/she was the client. The client may represent an aspect of the director that is unclear or indeed unknown. In the example with James, the director may unconsciously identify with him as 'the helpless child' or 'the deserted brother' and prepare to direct as a result of that dynamic rather than for James's expressed need.

It may be that it was because the group was ending and separation was imminent that James was able to get in touch with this issue that moved him so deeply. Perhaps the group and/or director represented the sister that did constantly desert him. This is where quiet, reflective clarification through sharing and talking can promote self-understanding within the boundaries of self-empowerment. It may be helpful for James to make a statement of intent – to acknowledge work to be done as well as a closure of the work in the here and now.

James   I feel very angry and I need to understand why I react to my sister in this way.

The director must therefore always monitor in him/herself a personal response to the sharing process and needs to be able to discuss it in a supervisory setting.

What if James has no release and is still struggling after 10 minutes? Although it may be tempting to extend the time boundaries 'to help', it is important for the director to think through this scenario in order to be 'prepared'. There are several possible options:

- negotiate a time extension with the group
- spend time with James individually after the group
- ask group members to spend time with him after the session
- ask James to take responsibility for his distress and return to the group to explore his difficulties.

Of course, the context in which the session has taken place may point to the best course of action for the director. In a residential setting, this situation will feel more manageable as the group can sit with him, providing support as needed. Things are very different when this happens, say, at the end of a public workshop where the director has been working without the continuity of further contact. Whatever the context it helps to embrace basic psychotherapeutic principles:

- always remain mindful of time
- closure for each session is important work
- the director needs to keep to the boundaries negotiated in order to help the group members reclothe
- the director puts in place safety nets for the safety of group members and to reduce anxiety for the director.

Psychodramatists, as a matter of professional conduct, need to make it their responsibility to have access to contact points for the group participants outside the psychodrama session – next of kin, sister, friend, general practitioner, to promote and if necessary provide a safety net for the interface between the psychodrama session and the outside world. Sound, safe practice will reduce the director's anxieties which in turn will produce more creative and professional thinking.

So, in James's case, what is safe sensible professional practice? Depending on the context in which we meet him, there are points to consider:

- In a residential, hospital setting or clinic, consult with other staff involved in his care, to provide a team approach.
- In a residential, psychodrama setting, ensure plenty of time for closure. A whole day is never too long to say goodbye. Intense feelings of bonding and sharing develop over such times, with emotional regression and a relinquishment of outside responsibilities. Reclamation of personal integrity and power through the course of saying goodbye is a very important process needing time and sensitivity. James would need that time.
- During a weekend workshop, it is tempting to pack in too much, to meet everybody's needs. Have closure in mind from the beginning of the last day for the reasons stated above.
- In an out-patient group remind him that the group is available the following week and that he is in the throes of important work.
- assess whether consultation with others is appropriate.

These decisions may raise all sorts of difficult and uncomfortable feelings which need extensive work and discussion in supervision. For the purpose of this chapter, the director needs to make the sharing safe enough and extend their professional practice to provide a sense of containment and safety for all concerned.

RESISTANT OR DIFFICULT SHARING

'Gosh, that was a good group! Everybody was crying at the end!' Too often, psychodrama groups can be 'judged' by the depth of sharing. Too often, psycho-dramatists' esteem is raised or dashed by the same phenomenon. Although it is important to embrace the importance of catharsis, and the sharing of distressing and sad feelings, thoughtful, silent reflection can be as therapeutic. Sometimes the sharing can be tense or uncomfortable. Group members are unable to speak, say what they think or feel, leaving a sense of awkwardness and lack of resolution. The reasons for this may be manifold. Perhaps the theme of the drama was awkwardness; perhaps the issues raised are too painful to voice or indeed buried too deep to be understood. Dalmiro Bustos, the Brazilian psychoanalyst and psychodramatist, has often said: 'the greater the resistance, the greater the pain' (personal communication). So, the task of the director is to reflect with the group and struggle to understand the nature of the difficulty or resistance. A comment may be helpful:

Director   I am wondering if we all feel a bit bewildered by John's description
of home.

   or

Director   Perhaps there was something uncomfortable about what Fred was
saying.

Certainly, it is important that the director's esteem does not rely on the group making it alright. The director needs to remember that part of the task of the group is to act as a container or hold discomfort, uncertainty, ambivalence until such time as those feelings can be worked on. Many people may never have had such an opportunity.

I remember a client who was always silent, even awkward at the end of each session, unable to communicate verbally. My assumption could well have been that he was getting very little from the group and that I was in some way failing him.

In those moments, that notion can be translated into a projected response – i.e. *he* is failing me and therefore a waste of time – and a negative, therapeutic response can set in. In fact, this same man, on the last day of the group, was noted to be wearing an uncharacteristically flamboyant tie and was heard to say to a friend that the group had been a very significant experience in his life. Working with difficult feelings is a vital part of the therapeutic work and facilitating the sharing through difficult times is essential.

Dr Donald Winnicott (1971: 43), in his renowned book *Playing and Reality*, describes this point very well. He says:

> It did not seem to me at the end of this session that one could claim that the work of the previous session had had a profound effect. On the other hand, I was only too aware of the great danger of becoming confident or even pleased. The analyst's neutrality was needed here if anywhere in the whole treatment. In this kind of work we know that we are always starting again, and the less we expect the better.

CONCLUSION

So, the task of the sharing phase in a psychodrama group is to provide a safe space for the group members to voice their feelings, thoughts and identifications with the protagonist and other group members and to share the experience of the group process. With the help of the director, what is unconscious can be made conscious and what is projected, claimed, acknowledged and worked with in order to continue the journey towards change.

To quote Winnicott again:

> Psychotherapy takes place in the overlap of two areas of playing, that of the playing and that of the therapist. Psychotherapy has to do with two people playing together. The corollary of this is that where playing is not possible, then the work done by the therapist is directed towards bringing the patient from a state of not being able to play into a state of being able to play.
>
> (Winnicott 1971: 44)

The importance of the sharing is to be able to bring the whole group together into 'a state of being able to play'.

REFERENCES

Foulkes, S.H. and Anthony, E.J. (1973) *Group Psychotherapy: The Psychoanalytic Approach*, London: Penguin.

Goldman, E.G. and Morrison, D.S. (1984) *Psychodrama: Experience and Practice*, Dubuque, IA: Kendall Hunt.

Moreno, J.L. (1953) *Who Shall Survive? Foundations of Sociometry, Group Psychotherapy and Sociodrama*, New York: Beacon House.

Ruscombe-King, G. (1991) 'Hide and Seek', in P. Holmes and M. Karp (eds) *Psychodrama: Inspiration and Technique*, London: Routledge.

Stride, M. (n.d.) 'Reflections of the Experience of Group Analytic Psychotherapy', in T.E. Lear (ed.) *Spheres of Group Analysis*, Naas, Co. Kildare: Leinster Leads Ltd.

Winnicott, D.W. (1971) *Playing and Reality*, London: Pelican.

Yalom, I. (1975) *The Theory and Practice of Group Psychotherapy*, New York: Basic Books.

Zuretti, M. (1994) 'The Global Task: Sharing Time and Space', in P. Holmes, M. Karp and M. Watson (eds) *Psychodrama since Moreno*, London: Routledge.

THE PROCESSING

Chapter 11

The processing

Jinnie Jefferies

INTRODUCTION TO PROCESSING

The term 'processing' is generally used in psychodrama to refer to the phase when the group, led by the director, discuss in some detail the steps that occurred during the psychodrama. Traditionally it takes place some time after the psychodrama has ended. Like many terms used in psychodrama it has come to have its own definition, depending on who is using it and the context in which it is used. Goldman and Morrison use the term to refer to:

(a) processing the dynamics that take place between a protagonist and an other as they interrelate during the enactment session of a psychodrama.
(b) observing the protagonist's journey from selection to resolution.
(c) critiquing the psychodrama session as a learning experience for the trainee director.

(Goldman and Morrison 1984)

Kellerman on the other hand uses the term to refer specifically to the critiquing of a psychodrama for training purposes, in order 'that the student director can learn, understand, analyse and evaluate his or her directing skills' (Kellerman 1992: 164).

'Processing', for Williams refers to an examination of the auxiliaries' experiences of being in role within a psychodrama. It is a time when the major auxiliaries speak of their experiences of being in role and reflect on their feelings and activities in the intervening time; how the roles they took have influenced or affected their interactions outside the session. It is also a time to examine what changes have taken place for the protagonist, how the problem has been resolved in reality (Williams 1989).

In this chapter I shall use the term to refer to the evaluation of the course of action taken by the group, the protagonist and the director, within a psychodrama session. I shall also be looking at what is involved in 'processing', when the director, protagonist and trainer are involved in training and how the concept enables all concerned to integrate what has happened during a session.

Why process and with whom?

Moreno described psychodrama as the chance to dream again. Some would argue that the act of processing detracts from the richness and the magic of the experience. They fear that in processing a session something is lost or taken away. Contrary to this fear I feel that the act of processing can be likened to a hall of mirrors, reflecting back the observed phenomena to all concerned, thus adding another dimension rather than detracting from the experience. I have known it to be viewed as supportive, enlightening and helpful.

The 'processing phase' needs to be clearly differentiated from the 'sharing phase' which has different objectives. The 'sharing phase' in psychodrama sets out to encourage identification with the protagonist in a personal and emotional manner whilst the 'processing phase' focuses on learning and understanding, by evaluating and analysing what has taken place in a less subjective manner. Processing is not focused on the protagonist. It can be seen as a time for the therapist and other group members to give feedback and/or interpretations of the group process that has taken place.

Kellerman restricts 'processing' to the evaluation and the teaching of psycho-drama. He believes it should focus on the trainee director's skills and include the director's analysis of protagonist and group but should exclude working through what is verbalised during the processing. He acknowledges that the protagonist may benefit from additional re-examination and re-integration of the issues raised within a session but believes that this should not be done during the processing but at a later session. By the same token he believes that the conflicts which tend to inhibit the group's development may be worked through at another time. Furthermore he believes that processing becomes a more constructive learning experience when feedback is generally restricted to professional skills and methodological issues, which tend to be easier to assimilate non-defensively and may be shared by the whole group (Kellerman 1992: 164).

While I support the exclusion of 'working through' I have some difficulty in restricting processing to feeding back of professional skills and methodological issues. If we were to accept that the only reason for processing is to teach psychodrama then it follows that we need to ask the question, 'What does it mean to teach psychodrama?' If psychodrama is to be a powerful therapeutic method, used to explore, clarify and resolve group and individual difficulties then the trainee director must understand the dynamics by which the protagonist and/or the group arrive at their present state of difficulty. I cannot see how the skills of the director can be evaluated yet separated from the analysis of the therapeutic process.

Other psychodramatists would agree that processing should include an in-depth analysis of what happened, why and how it happened, but feel the protagonist should not be present, fearful that something of the experience will be lost by being in attendance during the 'process phase' (Williams 1989). It is my view that not to include the protagonist is to rob the individual of a chance to reflect, to internalise the experience, to digest all that has happened through action, to integrate and consolidate the cognitive as well as the affective elements of the work. The protagonist's experience can be likened to having been subjected to a blast of 'psychic surgery', hardly having had time to take breath amongst the flurry of role reversal, doubling, mirroring, catharsis, concretisation and role training. Protagonists have often expressed the need of more than the psychodrama experience in order to complete the healing process. Obviously one needs to be sensitive in assessing the capacity of the protagonist to integrate and participate in the work that has been undertaken.

PROCESSING THE GROUP PROCESS

Moreno's development of sociometry was based on the belief that groups have an internal life of their own and that this life can best be understood by examining the choices made at any moment with regard to each other. He insisted that every group has underneath its visible structure an internal invisible structure that is real, alive and dynamic.

Moreno provided a theoretical foundation for working with the group. He stated that, 'the protagonist must serve as the vehicle of the group and that the theme chosen must be a truly experienced problem of the participants' (Fox 1987: 13).

The 'central concern model', developed by Enneis (1951) at St Elizabeth's Hospital, Washington DC provides a framework for structuring a psychodramatic production from interactions which emerge spontaneously from the group.

Attending to the group process entails a review of the group's contractual relationships, the goals and specific purposes for which the group was formed and the specific areas of content. During the life of a group themes will emerge. These themes will include issues around dependence, independence, potence, impotence and abandonment. The 'central concern model', identifies the 'topical concern' of the group, that is, the concrete concern in which the group manifests interest for a particular therapy session. The 'topical concern', will be broad based and emerge spontaneously from group members' interactions with one another. In the process of identifying the topical concern there is a need to differentiate between the 'manifest content' (the actual words spoken by the group), and 'the matrix of identity' (the development of individual identification with the 'here and now' concerns of the group).

> The group process is an alive and changing process and there will be changes in the 'topical concern' during and after the session, as well as changes in the group's sociometry and the change in the affective theme. It is the role of the director to facilitate and observe this process.
>
> (Buchanan 1980: 45)

PROCESSING THE PROTAGONIST'S PROCESS

Williams makes a plea that 'if psychodrama is to be used as a therapy rather than as a revelation, theology or epic representation it may need to take into fuller account the systemic nature of the problem's maintenance, of which the protagonist should be made aware' (Williams 1989: 80). Goldman and Morrison, likewise argue that whether working with the group or the individual, like other traditional methods of psychotherapy, psychodrama needs to help the client understand his or her process in life (Goldman and Morrison 1984).

Psychodrama is a truly existential method of psychotherapy exploring how 'the here and now' of the moment is shot through with memory traces of past relationships and experiences as as well as anxieties about the future. It concerns itself with the interactions of individuals and groups, philosophical issues of universality and existential validation. Classical psychodrama has its own structure and process to enable the client to explore all of these aspects. Within this structure the client places his or her problem upon the stage. As therapists we are interested in observing and helping our client to understand the difficulties experienced. We want to know what is happening or not happening; how our client perceives the situation he or she finds him or herself in and how s/he responds to the interactions of others; what are the belief systems that motivate the behavioural response and the consequences of responding in the chosen way? Of course we will be also interested in finding out whether our client has experienced similar difficulties in past situations, perhaps with other persons, with other story lines but with similar contextual problems.

Having made our observations we will want to share these observations with our client, revealing their process to enhance their awareness. An example of this would be:

Case study 1: Eric's psychodrama

Eric, the protagonist, a prisoner serving a life sentence for an offence against a woman, shows the group a scene in which he receives a visit from his girlfriend. She spends the visit telling him of the men she has met while he is in prison, the parties she has gone to, the overtures made to her by other men. Eric shows us how angry he gets and states in an aside, 'If it wasn't for the presence of the prison officers I would lean over the table and hit her.' What he doesn't do is tell her how hurt and upset he feels about what he perceives as her rejection and humiliation of him.

Eric is asked to find another scene framed by the context, a scene in which he perceives himself as being rejected and humiliated by a woman. He takes us to the scene of his offence in which he attacks a prostitute who laughs at his inability to have an erection and compares him to her other clients. The result is that he brutally murders her.

Director 'It seems to me that in a situation in which you experience yourself as being rejected or humiliated by a woman (context), you believe that no woman can be trusted, you feel very hurt and upset but instead of sharing this you get very angry and revengeful.

Sharing with the protagonist the observed phenomena was experienced as helpful. It enabled Eric to connect his present behaviour and feelings towards his girlfriend's visit with his offence. Hitherto he had little understanding of why he had committed his crime, and had chosen to see it as 'out of character'. The psychodrama in reflecting back his present 'functioning form', showed that when in a situation defined by context, not much had changed for him in the fifteen years he had spent inside.

Eric's continuing process was to explore the transference issues around these relationships, the origins and contributing factors around the role of the 'revengeful attacker'. It was important for Eric to understand how past experiences and belief systems influenced his present-day interactions; why and how those interactions had become problematic, and why and how he chose to respond destructively to situations, which held memory traces of unfinished or unresolved issues in such a destructive way. We explored scenes from childhood in which he was humiliated and rejected by his mother. Part of his process as the protagonist was to understand the need to acknowledge and express his repressed anger and rage towards his mother and the pain at not being accepted and loved.

In the process of this journey Eric was helped to integrate his thoughts and feelings, and return to the presenting scene in order to practise a different way of dealing with the problem. Eric resolved to speak to his girlfriend on the next visit about his feeling of rejection and humiliation.

Case study 2: Stuart's psychodrama

Stuart came to psychodrama concerned about his relationship with his girlfriend. He has been in prison for eleven years serving a sentence for rape. At the time of his offence he had just left his girlfriend believing that she did not really want to make a commitment to him. He had tried hard in the relationship, taking on a child from her previous marriage and finding extra work even after a hard working day. Whatever he seemed to do never appeared to be enough, however the woman has stayed in contact throughout his sentence but now that he is close to release, he is worried as to whether she is going to commit herself to him.

In exploring the problem we encouraged Stuart to reverse roles with Judy. In role he displays her perceived ambivalence towards him, not being straight as to whether she plans to have a life with him or not. She does this by making suggestions on the one hand that he should find someone else when he is released and then implying that they may have a future. His response is twofold, on the one hand he promises to be a 'good boy', do what she wants, get a trade, work harder in the relationship, take all the blame on himself for the relationship not working, and on the other becomes angry, tells her to 'fuck off'. The director wonders what has changed in their relationship in the past eleven years but decides at this moment that the process Stuart needs to be aware of is his twofold response to her behaviour. He is helped by the concretisation of these responses and is amazed when his process is mirrored back to him by another group member playing his role.

To find a recent past scene in which there are contextual similarities, one in which he is rejected for what he has to offer and experiences himself as not being good enough, we have to go back before his offence to a previous relationship in which we observe Stuart being reprimanded for not doing enough. Once again he is in a situation where he has taken on the woman's children, has decorated the whole house as well as holding down a job. He is hurt and angry for not being appreciated but instead of saying how he feels or expressing his anger, he packs his bag and goes. At the end of this scene he looks at the group and director in amazement. He has shocked himself with the frightening similarity between the two scenes. But now with energy and enthusiasm he is eager, having become aware of his own process, to take us to an even earlier relationship. Here we witness Stuart as a fresh-faced young man having got a job at the local supermarket as a trainee manager. He is chuffed at wearing a suit instead of his labourer's clothes. His girl-friend, and hoped-for fiancée, is waiting for him. She greets him telling him how good he looks in his suit. He is over the moon, until she tells him that he will have to aspire to something more if they are to get a nice house and not live on a council estate. He turns to the group and says, 'Then I knew however hard I tried I would never be good enough, I couldn't give her what she wanted, she wanted more than what I had to offer.'

There is yet another scene in Stuart's psychodrama which helps him to understand the process why he believes that whatever he does is never going to be enough.

Stuart as a small child was the only child of five to be put into care when his mother remarried. It is no wonder that later in life he looks after other people's children from former marriages. He would occasionally go home and try hard to be a 'good boy', with the hope that he would be allowed to stay and would not have to return to the children's home. His mother, however, was ambivalent about his presence, wanting him there but aware that his presence angered her new husband. So despite however 'good' he was, however much he tried to be 'mother's little helper', he had to go back into care. Staying at home had nothing to do with his being a good boy. Unaware of the real factors and that his efforts were not going to make any difference, he became disruptive, angry and unmanageable, confirming for his mother that she had made the right decision and confirming his belief that the reason he was not accepted was because he was not good enough. Stuart believed that if only he could be better behaved and for longer he might just get to stay home.

Stuart found it helpful to understand the process and the contri-buting factors by which he found himself, some thirty-five years later, in a not too dissimilar situation. He is at present resolved to have a meeting with his present girlfriend before his release. He has asked for the group's support to explore his responses, her ambivalence and to decide whether things can be different between them. He knows that to repeat old patterns may result in the displacement of his anger once again.

The processing of Stuart's psychodrama occurred mostly within the session, as we moved from scene to scene. It was also important for him to come back the next week to reflect on what had happened and to ask questions of the director and the group. He was helped, by the group sharing their observations of his process and bringing in other material he had presented in previous groups which related to what he had discovered for himself within the psychodrama session.

PROCESSING THE DIRECTOR'S PROCESS

If psychodrama is to be more than a bag of techniques to be pulled out indiscriminately or a collection of scenes to be randomly explored, or a forum for emotions to be expressed then the director must attend to the psychodynamic process of the group, the psychodrama and his/her own facilitation of the session.

Processing the director's process has come to be associated with training. I would put forward an argument that each of us as practitioners have the responsibility to process our own work before, during and after the session. This is in addition to processing the session for the group and the protagonist.

Of the group

With regard to the group Buchanan alerts the director to his own process in attending to the group process. Before the group assembles the director should explore his own warm-up and the contractual relations of the group. S/he must be aware of his or own personal concerns as they relate to his/her personal and professional life, be prepared to bracket them and begin warming up to the role of group therapist in order that the 'central concern' focused upon clarifies and reflects the concerns and feelings of the group and not the projections of the director (Buchanan 1980).

Of the enactment

All of us who are now practitioners remember those early days of directing when one stood watching a scene mesmerised by the content. The action would stop, a sense of panic would set in, as one was faced with the dilemma, of what next, where to go from here. Each psychodrama has a process, a journey that is individually unique but similar to all psychodramas. It begins with a contract, an agreement between director, protagonist and the group, as to what aspect of life's experience is to be explored. The process for director and protagonist has begun, a process of discovery through action. The psychodrama may follow the path outlined in Elaine Goldman and Delcy Morrison's excellent book, *Psychodrama Experience and Process* (1984).

There are some who would argue that the director's process is one of intuition, of 'following one's nose'. I have heard the directing of psychodrama being likened to 'the following of the smoke signals as given by Indian tribes' (Karp in conversation). Of course the director's process entails spontaneity and creativity but as Blatner and Blatner remind us: 'Spontaneity is not merely impulsivity or random behaviour. There must be some intentionality toward a constructive result whether aesthetic, social or practical' (1988: 64). Similarly a psychodrama, though involving spontaneity and creativity must have as its intention the alleviation of the problem presented, aiming towards a constructive result.

In order to achieve this, the director must have an understanding of the theoretical concepts underlying the therapeutic elements of psychodrama as well as a knowledge of the psychodramatic techniques, and know when and how to use them. In addition the director needs a general understanding of personality development and therapeutic principles. S/he is assisted by an awareness of such concepts as transference and countertransference, defence mechanisms and, of course, a knowledge of group dynamics. As already stated the psychodramatist's concern is for the group as well as for the individual protagonist who holds the group concern. A daunting task, so many balls to juggle in front of so many expectant eyes.

In the enactment session the director's process concerns itself with a clear, specific determination about what is wrong and what has to be put right. The application of psychodrama role theory requires two sets of skills, identification and intervention. The first requires the director to make a role analysis which involves defining the context and within that context looking at the person's:

- behaviour in relationship to other
- the belief system that motivates the behaviour
- the feelings about what is happening and not happening
- and the consequences of the inappropriate response

In order to make an intervention the director needs to have knowledge of the stages of human development. Dalmiro Bustos has developed Moreno's concept of 'role clusters' when describing these stages of development (Holmes *et al.* 1991: 69). The director's process in making an intervention is to identify the dysfunctional role and with which particular role cluster the protagonist experiences difficulty.

Having identified the dysfunctional role and 'role cluster' the director's process moves on to an investigation of the group of conditioning factors where the role or way of responding was created (the locus of role); to an investigation of the specific determining responses that the person made to the stimuli present (the matrix of the role) and an investigation of the specific moment when the response emerged (the *status nascendi* of the role).

The director of course needs to be aware of this process during the enactment but needs also to reflect afterwards as to how well s/he facilitated the process. Did s/he make a correct analysis of what was the determining problem? In processing his or her interventions the director needs to ask whether they made a correct role analysis, whether they were able to distinguish content from context and frame the context clearly for the protagonist. How able was s/he in identifying the dysfunctional role for the protagonist, discovering its locus and making the necessary interventions? How well did s/he handle defence mechanisms, deal with the transference issues, and work with his or her own countertransference?

As for the skills aspect of the method, how and why we use various techniques, the level of our spontaneity and creativity, the relationship we built up with the protagonist, how we conducted the group and dealt with closure and sharing, I refer the reader to Kellerman's director's checklist which alerts the director as to what they need to be aware of within a session, from the warm-up stage to the sharing (Kellerman 1992: 169).

PROCESSING THE PROCESS OF THE TRAINEE DIRECTOR

All of us have to begin somewhere. We need an opportunity to practise our skills, make our mistakes and learn from others. In order to do this it is essential that we feel contained, supported and unjudged. As we take our first steps in psychodrama we totter and fall, forget and panic. It all looks so easy sitting in the audience. In making our first steps we are dependent on the knowledge of a senior trainer whose function it is to process our attempts to become a director.

How this is done will depend on the approach of different trainers. Elaine Goldman requires her students to take notes during the session and think of themselves as directors, picking up clues and making directional choices as preparation for the time when they themselves will step upon the psychodrama stage.

> They are asked to make explicit their 'processing' comments, critiquing and questioning the trainers as well as their fellow students. This process not only challenges the director to validate their choices and decisions but amplifies the learning process. The situation itself begins a mental process for the trainee encouraging him or her to organize their thinking.
>
> (Goldman and Morrison 1984: 95)

Long before the neophyte director takes on the responsibility for a whole psychodrama they must develop the skill of observing the phenomena they are presented with, differentiating between content and context, making a role analysis, linking the past with the present, identifying and intervening, encouraging role training as well as being constantly aware of the group process of which they are part. At the London Centre of Psychodrama and Group Psychotherapy, to assist the trainee in this varied and daunting process we encourage students to break down the learning process.

In the early days of training the psychodrama is divided into manageable parts with the trainee being supported by a 'buddy', another trainee who is also part of the learning process. Each trainee is given the responsibility for certain sections of the psychodrama. The learning is supported by didactic sessions but there is an emphasis on 'processing on one's feet'.

At the beginning of each section the trainee is required to consult with his or her 'buddy', in order to review what is required of the trainee director; what needs to be achieved for the protagonist; what pitfalls need to be avoided; what tools might be used. During and at the end of each section of the psychodrama the trainee returns to the 'buddy', to process the observed phenomena. Meanwhile the training group has been asked to make their own observations, be it an understanding of the problem, identifying the context, making a role analysis or identifying the contributing factors that lead to the dysfunctional role and finally deciding on what interventions need to be made. The aim is not only to encourage all concerned to begin thinking about the 'therapeutic process' and practise observing the phenomena they themselves will be presented with as a director but to add extra support to the trainee director and the 'buddy'. Using this process the trainee director begins to build up a plethora of knowledge and skills to enable him or her to finally embark on a whole psychodrama, confident that they can hold in the head, that which has hitherto been concretised, shared and supported. The processing in a training session takes place alongside the action.

The trainee's 'processing' is similar to that of the director but because he/she is in a position of learning there will be a requirement to evaluate their strengths and weaknesses and overall progress and areas that still need to be focused on in training. An example of this is when one of our trainees when differentiating between content and context would pause, turn to the group and acknowledge, with them, his/her 'Achilles heel'.

PROCESSING THE TRAINER'S PROCESS

Examining the literature, little seems to have been written about the trainer's process, what is involved and what needs to be processed. The function of the trainer is to impart knowledge, to support the developing director to learn and experience directing skills and to process that experience in such a way that it is seen as constructive and empowering. The trainer needs to allow the new director to make mistakes and to explore what is involved in the making of those mistakes. His/her role is to help the trainee begin to develop a confidence in their ability to direct, and help the trainee differentiate between the natural anxiety

attached to the role of director and the anxiety, resistance and countertransference issues that arise from the trainee's own psychological development.
Often the trainee experiences the greatest difficulty when their own personal
material is mirrored by the protagonist. The trainee has to learn that they are
unable to take any protagonist further than their own personal psychological
development and be aware of these 'blind spots'. I speak here not simply of
bracketing one's own issues but of those areas of personal work that remain
unresolved for the trainee and need to be worked through in personal therapy, in
order to free the director to assist the protagonist.

In addition to processing the trainee's understanding of the psychodramatic
process, the trainer needs to assist the trainee in applying their wider theoretical
knowledge to the therapeutic process. This entails the recognition of defence
mechanisms, transference issues and psychological resistances.

The trainer needs to encourage the trainee to critique their own work. Learning
from one another is very exciting but also very threatening, it can evoke negative
transference issues around authority and what may be experienced as a wounding
of the 'self'. The trainer needs to be aware of these issues when they occur, and
flag them up for the trainee. The trainer needs to strive to give helpful criticism in
such a way that it does not engage unhelpful defensive behaviour.

The trainer's process involves keeping a close examination on how these
teaching tasks are performed, where his or her own weakness and countrans-
ference issues lie. It is as important for the trainer to get feedback from the
training group as it is for the trainees to receive it.

IN CONCLUSION

All too often psychodramatists concern themselves with the action, the drama
and the emotional contents. We have a tendency to concentrate on sharing our
experiences, giving little time to reflect on the process, maybe because of some
of the inherent difficulties outlined in this chapter. While acknowledging the
difficulty in its management, processing of all the relevant information and
aspects of a psychodrama session remains a profound and essential learning
experience for all concerned.

BIBLIOGRAPHY

Buchanan (1980) 'The Central Concern Model', *Journal of Psychotherapy, Psychodrama
    and Sociometry*
Blatner and Blatner (1988) *Foundations in Psychodrama*, New York: Springer.
Fox, J. (1987) *The Essential Moreno*, New York: Springer.
Enneis, J. (1951) 'Dynamics of Groups and Action Process in Therapy', *Group
    Psychotherapy*, vol. 1: 17–22.

Goldman, E. and Morrison, D. (1984) *Psychodrama: Experience and Process*, Dubuque, IA: Kendall Hunt.

Holmes, P., Karp, M. and Watson, M. (eds) (1991) *Psychodrama: Inspiration and Technique*, London: Tavistock/Routledge.

Kellerman, P. (1992) *Focus on Psychodrama*, London: Jessica Kingsley.

Williams, A. (1989) *The Passionate Technique*, London: Tavistock/Routledge.

Williams, A. (1991) *Forbidden Agendas*, London: Tavistock/Routledge.

Part III

The application – how is psychodrama used?

PSYCHODRAMA IN ACTION

Chapter 12

The three-layered cake, butter with everything

Olivia Lousada

This chapter presents a description of the function and meaning of three psychodramatic techniques: doubling, role reversal and the mirror technique in the context of psychodrama philosophy and psychoanalytic theory. Psychodrama theory understands these techniques to hold the following meanings: doubling represents the fusional stage with mother; role reversal represents the infant's recognition that s/he is separate from mother; and the mirror technique represents the infant seeing their own reflection (Moreno 1977: 92; Kellerman 1992: 148). I will describe the successful application of these psychodrama techniques and the apparent difficulties they can present in a clinical setting. In this discussion I will link these successes and difficulties to the philosophy of psychodrama and to infant developmental theory associated with psychoanalysis. This has been articulated for me through the remarkable research into infant development by Moreno, Winnicott (1977), Stern (1985), Mahler (1975) and Fraiberg(1989), and has provided me with a further understanding of the more serious psychopathologies. This chapter will be insufficient in describing either Moreno's or psychoanalytic theory of infant development, but will hopefully whet the appetite for further study.

PSYCHODRAMA IN A CLINICAL SETTING

The value of psychodrama in a clinical setting is in its capacity to encourage a client to describe the experience of his internal world verbally and non-verbally. The client, with the help of the group, shows important aspects of his internal life; through representation, action and metaphor. This process is invaluable as a route to the expression of pre-verbal and non-verbal experience. Psychodrama is especially helpful for people who intellectualise feelings or who have little understanding of what is happening to them. It illustrates the context and roles of beliefs and anxieties in the client and the psychosomatic component of psychopathology or physical illness. Psychodrama is the drama of the internal world, full of relationships between figures, 'both [of] people, or parts of people, in the external world, [as well as] to the internal psychic "objects" or representations in the mind that [may] result from these relationships' (Holmes 1992: 8).

Relationships are central to psychodrama and are described by role theory which focuses on the concept that humankind from infancy is spontaneously 'act hungry' (Fox 1987: 206) and reaches out into life in an attempt to form a relationship with it. Spontaneity 'propels the individual towards an adequate response to a new situation or a new response to an old situation' (Greenberg 1974: 76) so giving flexibility to perform a variety of roles in relationships both inside themselves and in their environment. Moreno's emphasis on the importance of spontaneity was borne out by his observation of children's imaginative play and their exploration of roles and relationships.

Unfortunately life often leaves people with many unresolved and turbulent feelings and anxieties which inhibit spontaneity. Repetition of roles created by these anxieties is also an 'act hunger' or 'reaching out' into life. Even if sometimes dysfunctional, the repetition of these roles can also be seen as a natural attempt to resolve conflicting feelings so as to gain or regain internal balance and spontaneity. With psychodrama the client can face this 'act hunger', consider the limited range of roles they use and the roles they perceive to be played by others around them. In rediscovering spontaneity and a wider choice of roles clients often discover new ways of understanding the behaviour of other people as well as themselves.

THE CONTEXT OF PSYCHODRAMA PHILOSOPHY

I now turn to the philosophical context in which infant development, the focus of this chapter is set. Moreno invented psychodrama in 1921 (Moreno 1977: 1). He saw spontaneity as the greatest gift with which man was born. Like all good psychotherapists he wanted nothing less than the dignity of the whole of humankind to be in the focus of his work. His many inventions demonstrated his quest to reach all parts of society, both intimately, locally and world-wide. They included sociometry, the concept of encounter, group psychotherapy, spontaneity theatre and sociodrama: but he saw his greatest invention as psychodrama. This is especially relevant in the 1990s as we struggle with the role of psychotherapy. Andrew Samuels at the 1997 UKCP professional conference proposed that this role needs to be considered in the light of clinical, professional, social, spiritual and political responsibility and leadership.

Moreno's philosophy of psychodrama

Time represents the passage of the psyche which is forever living in the present, manifesting the past, and by so doing, describing the future. *Reality* is the context in which the group finds itself, the who, when, where, what, how and why of immediate experience. These are coloured by the cultural, political, social and personal beliefs of the past influencing the present and so anticipating the future.

Moreno conceptualised Reality through five instruments:

- *Time* represents the cosmos.
- *The stage* represents where and when the event of concern occurs in the past, present and future. The stage represents geography in psychodrama.
- *The group/audience* represents society externally and internally by representing figures in the protagonist's internal world. The group represents history in psychodrama.
- *The director* represents leadership or the parents of the 'family'. S/he holds the role of containment, spontaneity and creativity in the service of the life of the group. The director represents adulthood in psychodrama.
- *The protagonist* is the one most in need and thus represents childhood and creativity in psychodrama. S/he represents the unconscious needs and struggle for spontaneity in the group. It is through the protagonist that the group expresses their pain, and finally their hopes in a scene of reparation, known as surplus reality.

Within this context doubling, role reversal and the mirror technique represent the three early developmental stages necessary to give a child the tools with which to grow into a whole person, as an artist and scientist, who can engage spontaneously and creatively with society, history, geography and the cosmic dimensions of the universe.

THE THREE-LAYERED CAKE

The three-layered cake refers to the three techniques of doubling, role reversal and the mirror technique (Kipper 1986: 168). As already mentioned, psychodrama theory organises these techniques as follows: doubling represents the fusional stage with mother; role reversal represents the infant's recognition that s/he is separate from mother; and the mirror technique represents the infant seeing their own reflection (Moreno 1977: 92; Kellerman 1992: 148). In the tradition of classical psychodrama Moreno saw dyadic relationships at the heart of encounter so role reversal is recognised as the cornerstone of the method.

In my practice I was puzzled as to how to make sense of what happened when clients appeared unable to use the techniques of doubling, role reversal or mirroring. I have always understood psychodrama to be an expression of the group process and have been much informed by the theories of group psychotherapy. However I was left wondering why clients were unable to use these psychodrama techniques. As a psychotherapist I needed to be inclusive rather than exclusive about what I was ready to accept as being creative. It was not until I studied infant observation that I found a possible way of understanding behaviour that had seemed confusing and destructive. Through this study I took the liberty of reformulating my understanding of the use of doubling, role reversal and the mirror technique to represent the three major transitional developmental stages of early infancy as described in psychoanalytic theory. The first, the double, is the fusional relationship with mother and includes the narcissistic stage of baby seeing himself in the mirror of mother's eyes; the second, role reversal, the experience of baby separate from mother; and the third, the mirror technique, the period of triangulation, often called the Oedipal phase or the family phase.

In the infant's process of physical and psychological development these stages emerge in interwoven sequences. When we are working with adults these interwoven sequences can come at us all at once, and as directors, we can be hard pushed to keep up with it all. This is why I have used the metaphor of a cake. In each 'mouthful' of a psychodrama session we taste these ingredients. experience of the present, past and future. It is often hard to distinguish one taste. The only comfort to be had is that psychotherapy provides a context in which the tastes of life can be re-mixed and re-sampled. Some reparation can be found at a point where life appeared to have failed to offer such an opportunity: the cake mix of the internal world can be cooked and recooked at different temperatures so spontaneity is gradually restored.

BUTTER WITH EVERYTHING

'Butter with everything' refers to the director's countertransference. In the quest to describe the unconscious processes of the human experience, countertransference can be called the interpreter of transference and the servant of tele. It therefore needs to be understood in the context of the work and with an understanding of the differences between tele, transference and counter-transference.

Tele

Tele in Greek means '*far, or, at a distance*' (*Chambers Dictionary* 1964). Moreno used it to describe the natural attraction/repulsion/indifference that is *between* people. Tele is at the heart of the concept of encounter. This *between* can be described as 'individuals [having] a certain sensitivity for each other, as if they were chained together by a common soul' (Moreno 1993: 157). Tele is a social concept whilst transference, and countertransference, are the 'psychopathological branch of tele' (Moreno 1993: 161).

Transference

Transference describes the phenomena of the feelings and roles unconsciously projected by one person into another. The roles represent significant others, objects or part objects of the client's or group's 'internal' world. Transference is an expression of anxieties which beset all intimate relationships at times of stress, and can endanger, even overwhelm the telic relationship. This is why all psychotherapists need therapy and supervision, so they can remain empathetic, in a state of spontaneity and creativity, and able to think about the feelings stirred in them by the client/s transference not as an expression of their own transference (which might well be the case), but as an expression of countertransference. They learn to hold their responses as transference and countertransference.

Countertransference

Transference in the group gives rise to countertransference, the feelings that suddenly fill the director when s/he enters a room. They seem to come out of nowhere and are unconnected to anything s/he was feeling before s/he entered the room. It can be felt as strongly as a slap in the face or stomach. The telic experience is cut across by the transference of the group and the response of the director's countertransference and is thus a very important tool in informing the director of the unconscious processes of the group or individual in the group. Understanding the countertransference 'is the therapist's proper emotional attitude – a conscious reaction to the [client's] behaviour' (Kellerman 1992: 99). This is why countertransference has been called 'butter with everything'. Like butter, countertransference holds the loose particles of tele and transference. It binds the fragmented ingredients of the psyche so tele and spontaneity can be restored. Some psychotherapists call the director's transference countertransference. As Kellerman suggests, I find it clearer to call transference the director's feelings connected to experiences from their own life outside the group, as separate from countertransference, the director's responses in the group (Holmes 1992: 100–101).

We are all natural experts of tele and countertransference and use it intuitively from infancy though most of us don't either know or use it consciously, or develop it as a professional tool. Those people who do are usually called healers or witches.

APPLICATION OF DOUBLING, ROLE REVERSAL AND MIRRORING IN PSYCHODRAMA PSYCHOTHERAPY

I will now describe the three techniques and how they are used successfully.

Doubling

Doubling is the 'heart of psychodrama' (Blatner 1973: 24). It is unquestionably the technique which requires most sensitivity, empathy and understanding of countertransference. The double assists the protagonist in finding words to express feelings and thoughts that s/he previously could not adequately express. There are two stages to doubling.

How to double

The first stage: holding

To learn the technique of doubling you take up the body position of the person you wish to double, to become them. You give yourself up to the experience of being that person by learning to notice the feelings brought up in you as your countertransference. You learn to articulate those feelings, you *mirror* the protagonist physically and emotionally to support the protagonist's psycho-physiological experience, so they can enter their experience more fully and become stimulated towards interaction, 'the precursor of the mirror is the mother's face . . . *what she looks like is related to what she sees there*' (Winnicott 1971: 111–112). This sensitivity or contingency (Brazelton and Cramer 1991: 123) is like an imaginary elastic band of tele between baby and mother. Mother responds to the 'tug' from baby and reflects it back watching for a tug back. She relaxes the elastic when the energy is not returned and there is a turning away from the encounter. Mother waits for the baby's recovery and possible re-engagement. This is the start of ego development. So we too, as doubles and directors, track the protagonist.

The second stage: stretching

The second task of the mother, to stretch the infant's experience, has to be done with great sensitivity to what excitement can be withstood by the baby's psychophysical capacity. Similarly, if the empathy between the double and protagonist is very strong, the double may also go so far as to make suggestions or interpretations. This may include 'questions, contradicting feelings and defending against the feelings' (Blatner 1973: 29). It is the rudimentary begin-nings of play.

In the early stages of a group the concern is to find similarities between group members. If action methods are used, doubling exercises surprise the group in how much, as strangers, they can understand each other. The most frequent outcome of this technique is that the protagonist feels supported and the double feels they have been supportive. There is an atmosphere of union, comfort and expectancy.

> Margaret is an anorexic adolescent. She clearly experiences life and the group as cut off from the walled-in emptiness inside her. In her first session, after a doubling exercise, she says she likes having someone listen to her and be with her. This is a small but significant beginning. She has allowed someone to be near to her, in body contact, near her elbow, and in the same position in the seat next to

her. She has allowed someone to join with her feelings, reflecting her internal world, so she has a better sense of her own presence, her ego, in the room.

Some directors double a great deal, and some encourage their group to double. Others will only let the person in action, or the protagonist, double themselves. Some directors don't use doubling at all. It is unquestionably an extremely powerful technique and so most capable of manipulation.

A word of caution

This method can weaken defence mechanisms or coping strategies most effectively. Sometimes this can be too quick, and maintain or increase internal psychic fragmentation instead of enhancing integration. It is therefore important to use doubling with great respect as the protagonist is in the most vulnerable position in their experience of the group.

Role reversal

Role reversal is known as 'the engine of psychodrama' (according to Merlin Pitzele, Zerka Moreno's late partner). Doubling is the first step towards role reversal. It represents the establishment of the ego. Without enough ego development it is difficult to engage in role reversal. There has to be a sufficient sense of the self in order to experience a sense of the separate other. The value of role reversal is to experience what it is like to take on the role of the other, and to experience the self through the other's eyes. 'They see themselves from the other person's perspective' (Kellerman 1992: 90). Role reversal partly comes about through imitation, and partly by exploration. It is an expansion of all the games and play that have made up the fabric of early interaction between the mother and baby. As Moreno wrote, 'it is the intense level of communication between two or more persons' (Moreno 1969: 26) in which the baby sorts out social relationships. Much of childhood play and adult activity is, in one way or another, an exploration of unexplored or unresolved relationships. Moreno observed this as he watched children playing and then re-enacting stories he told them in Vienna. Role reversal is the technique which brings most insight, resolution and hope, and is therefore heralded as the most important invention of psychodrama. Moreno writes with passion about the interaction of the encounter between any two people or dyad which he later called the psychodramatic scene.

> Then I will look at you with your eyes
> And you will look at me with mine.

(Moreno 1977: Preface)

How to role reverse

To learn the skill of role reversal, the protagonist must now become the other role. They are assisted by the director who will interview them as the other person to guide them into role. S/he will ask, 'What is your name, your age at the time of the scene; what is a word to describe the sort of person you think you are? How would you describe your relationship with the protagonist? How are you feeling about this? What is the message you give the protagonist?' This is usually sufficient preparation. The protagonist then chooses a group member to hold this 'auxiliary role' and the drama unfolds.

> Andrew wants to speak to his girlfriend. He is asked to role reverse, to imagine he is she. He thought he spoke from his perception of her point of view, but also discovered, to his surprise, other feelings from being in the role. He was worried about talking to her about the relationship. In role reversal he finds she is very clear headed. He had projected his own fear of falling apart on to her.

Two kinds of role reversal

There are two kinds of role reversal. 'Reciprocal role reversal' is between the self and another person. 'Representational role reversal' (Holmes *et al.* 1994: 274) is between the self and roles or objects within the self. This is often facilitated by the use of symbols and metaphors.

> Tessa is torn between two feelings and is asked to represent them. One is slipping into a black hole, and the other, the lost childhood before father died. The dialogue begins. The black hole is quite unable to hear the childhood until eye contact is made. Through this beginning the pain of unacknowledged grief at the loss of attachment to father and mother begins to emerge into focus.

Role reversal has a number of functions

To gain information

Role reversal gives the group information about the significant other. The director may also interview the protagonist in this role to learn more about the protagonist. 'Many protagonists . . . reveal more about themselves . . . [from] the role of the auxiliary. Getting out of their roles often reduces their original defensive position (Kipper 1986: 163). After the initial interviews role reversal then takes place when the protagonist asks a question of the auxiliary and role reverses to find and give the answer. The reason for this is that only the protagonist knows the answer. This knowledge might be known as fact, believed or imagined. As the work of psychodrama is to reveal the internal world, if fact is not satisfactory, beliefs and fantasy or imagination can bring the internal world alive. Without this accuracy resolution or reparation is impossible. This process of accuracy is in itself a vital element to role reversal.

To understand the role of the other

The protagonist might be interviewed in role reversal by the director to discover if the protagonist's perceptions are as s/he described them. The initial perceptions are often shifted as the protagonist reveals a much deeper understanding of the other person than initially appeared. As I have suggested above, the interviewing can be very precise to capture the dynamics and spirit of the situation. However it is also very important at a deeper level. People often grow up uncertain about how they see the world, and this can come from an experience of being told or understanding that their perceptions are inaccurate if not totally wrong. Hence they cease to trust their natural knowledge, tele and countertransference.

To heighten spontaneity

Role reversal may take place when the emotion has become arrested and the scene is static. 'When the interaction needs to be further intensified, or when it gets close to a dead-end while the main issue(s) remains largely unexplored' (Kipper 1986: 163).

Sophie is talking to father who is unprotective in Sophie's eyes. The auxiliary ego, or person chosen for the role, presents a protecting father. Sophie cannot proceed with her psychodrama as the opportunity of expressing her feelings and consequent possible reparation are denied by the failure of the auxiliary to reflect Sophie's internal experience of an unprotecting father. Sophie role reverses to demonstrate her experience of him so the auxiliary can be more accurate and Sophie can communicate her feelings.

This process can be very important to someone who is not familiar with valuing their own perceptions.

To develop a new role

Role reversal can provoke the protagonist who projects feelings into the group already encountering their own feelings. The outcome can be an eruption of energy throughout the group. The longed-for but forbidden scene takes place in spite of and because of the protagonist's reticence.

Jane wants to confront her father but quickly becomes the terrified child. She role reverses to become the advocate for her own abused inner child but seems to portray an unconvincing figure. Two-thirds of the group got up to double as advocate. This is called multiple doubles. Jane wanted to stand up for herself but unconsciously got the group to be the advocate she too still needed as a model. It reflects the need of this relatively new group. The entire group shares their own experience of childhood abuse and their search for justice. The internalised and active adult who was able to protect the child was a new role for the entire group.

To clarify the projection of feelings into significant others

In role reversal the protagonist may discover feelings in the role of the 'other'. When he returns to his own role a new attitude is approached.

John is furious with his wife and believes her to be angry. In role reversal, as his wife, he bursts into tears and is touched himself by her tender feelings and fear of abandonment. Back in his own role John was faced with his reluctance to own his own tenderness and fear of abandonment. He understands how he had projected his anger into his wife.

To face splitting

Role reversal sharpens the difference between the protagonist's perception and the experience of being in the role of the other person. In the role of the other, John showed insight but in returning to his own role his attitude was not significantly altered. The failure to acknowledge these feelings is often associated with childhood. With the splitting of the internal world made concrete, the first step towards amelioration is taken and the early beliefs and splitting can be reconsidered.

In order to gain from this technique the person needs to have 'a balanced personality, a certain degree of ego strength and ordinary sensory perceptions' (Kellermann 1992: 267). This corresponds with the theory that role reversal reflects the second stage of the infant's developmental process – the recognition of separateness, that mummy is not me.

Role reversal is an essential part of learning about relationships. Adults use it as part of their attempt to understand the world around them. Children spontaneously adopt role reversal in play from a very early age. At its best role reversal can bring insight and hope. It is centred in the here and now and affords variety, playfulness, creativity and spontaneity.

A word of caution

Role reversal should not be employed:

1 when the action is running smoothly;
2 when the protagonist is too threatened or intimidated when they are facing an external or internal figure that stirs up their fear of violence or insanity (e.g. a liar, a sadist, a rapist, a saint, an adversary) (Kipper 1986: 164);
3 with psychotic patients who may respond with terror or take the role for real (Starr 1977: 44);
4 and it should be borne in mind that too many role reversals can be physically and psychologically exhausting.

The mirror technique

The mirror technique has two functions. The first, and most familiar, is essentially dyadic and existential; the second, is essentially triadic and systemic.

The existential function

The existential function of the mirror technique enables the protagonist to watch their own behaviour as others show them in action their own drama. 'It encourages the protagonist to think objectively about what he is showing subjectively' (Kipper 1986: 172). He is physically present but not psychologically. 'The real purpose is to let the patient see himself "as if in a mirror" to provoke and shock him into action' (Moreno 1993: 280). Kipper (1986: 173–175) held that there are 'four elements that may elicit resistance: the content of the issue under treatment, the therapist, the treatment format, and the therapeutic process'. Starr (1977) describes the mirror technique as representing:

> the moment when he sees his image in the mirror and discovers that the image is of *himself* . . . he may touch it, kiss it, or hit it. This action, immortalised in the myth of Narcissus, is translated into an action technique in which the looking-glass image reflects the self as seen by another.
>
> (Starr 1977: 178)

This is the existential position in psychodrama.

How to use the mirror technique

The technique is developed in the following way. The protagonist has become stuck and is invited to step out of the situation and choose someone to show their own behaviour. This method is usually understood to explicitly tackle resistance in the protagonist because it portrays 'non-verbal communication' (Kellerman 1992: 748). At its best the protagonist observes his behaviour and returns to the scene to try another response.

The difficulty is that clients often persecute themselves. In the face of their guilt and shame they can become so anxious they are unable to see or think about their own behaviour. An amelioration of the superego is central to the process of psychotherapy. It is a long and hard task. Any exacerbation of shame and guilt can be counter-productive unless encountered with kindness and empathy; otherwise there can be further internal splitting and increased anxiety.

> Sheila wants to tell her family how vulnerable she feels and how much she needs their support. She proceeds to look after them. She is put in the mirror position to view her own behaviour. After reflecting on the situation she re-enters the scene to try another response. Once back in the scene she becomes wrapped up again in the care of the other figures and is again quite unable to make her own stand. Her isolation, shame and guilt are heightened. She hears nothing of the support of the group. Such is her anxiety.

With the mirror technique the protagonist can look at their own behaviour and how much it falls short of their idea of spontaneity. The protagonist can advise the auxiliary. This can warm them up, or raise their adrenalin so they then want to try the new role.

> Steven is at a meeting with his boss for whom he feels both contempt and hatred. He has gone full of determination to speak his mind. As the meeting commences his energy diminishes, he becomes childlike, and he seeks approval. He is asked to take the mirror position and watch. He notices how much his behaviour changes. He is asked what moment in his life this reminds him of. He goes to a scene in which he confronts his mother who hit him. Again he is asked to take the observer mirror position and he sees himself as intimidated, hostile and passive. After reflection he returns to confront mother more

appropriately. He then finds more spontaneity in his response to his boss. Steven has worked through the transference toward an improved tele.

The mirror technique can enable the protagonist to see their behaviour as childlike. It can occur to them that their internal child had no support and they too as adults have failed to develop the appropriate adult role towards themselves. As an adult the protagonist can then become the advocate.

Susan wants to talk to her dead father about his cruelty to her as a child. She quickly became speechless. In the mirror position she notices there is no one to defend the child in her and returns to the scene as the child's advocate.

A word of caution

The mirror technique is 'a human version of videotape playback. It can be a powerful confrontational technique and must be used with discretion. The protagonist must not be made the object of ridicule' (Blatner and Blatner 1988: 169).

The systemic function

The use of the mirror technique developed as a systemic function in my work because it was an attempt to find a less humiliating approach by which the protagonist could face their own resistance. The importance of this triadic concept is that it sets dyadic confrontations in a context of triangulation. It is not unusual to find members of a group obsessed about their feelings with one parent to the total exclusion of the other. The emotional temperature of the work alters considerably. Dyadic work can often express emotional states: outrage, despair, fury and tenderness. It is often emotionally cathartic, in an atmosphere of life and death. Triadic work can be emotionally wider and so frees up the protagonist to deeper feelings that embrace both the dyadic and triadic relationships. It usually brings a mental catharsis and is in this sense less dramatic and more reflective. There is less emotional elation or despair and more a re-evaluation of the dynamics of the situation. It can lead to a very different understanding of the emotional content of the situation. The use of the mirror technique as a systemic process requires the most ego strength. The protagonist moves from powerful and sometimes regressed feelings, to role reverse into the other roles, and to the role of the watcher and thinker, and back again.

How to use the mirror technique

With this technique the protagonist can watch their own behaviour *and* the behaviour of the other roles. They can consider not only what is going on *between* themselves and each of the parents but also what is the preoccupation *between* the parents. It looks at who or what is being fought over, be they alive, absent or dead, by the protagonist and the other roles in the dyadic relationship. By understanding the meaning of the third figure the dyadic relationship is reconsidered and addressed. Often the protagonist is confronted with facing their role in the family as being far more powerful than hitherto imagined. Tough as it may be, it can clarify the external family experience and challenge the client to think about the repetition in their internal world. By this route we reach the client's resistance from a position of strength and humility rather than through humiliation. This systemic approach looks at the *telic* relationships. We can call this the *sociometry of the family*. Moreno called this the *social atom*. It can include other family members but here we are restricting it to the triangle.

> Hannah never gets what she wants from her mother. Her brother is the favourite just as she is the favourite with father. The war of hatred with mother seems fixed and desperate inside her. In the mirror technique for the first time she wonders why her mother is like this. She role reverses with mother and is interviewed. Father is brought in. The rivalry in the marriage emerges. Hannah sees that, as a child, she has been caught between her parents' needs and lost touch with herself. She watches the interaction between the two parents from an adult role, as a third pair of eyes. Hannah then starts to separate herself, to think about her own needs and destructive behaviour.

In a more systemic approach, we wonder what or who the protagonist and his or her significant others are fighting over. This missing component may be expressed as an idea or belief such as religion, but behind it there will usually be the absent parent or a lost significant other person. Often we come across an apparent impasse between two figures in which reparation feels impossible. In the awkward silence an absence is felt and the collusion of omission of the role is revealed in the dyad and in the group. Hence, when I set space for dyadic work I always hold the third space in mind, as follows:

auxiliary as protagonist   auxiliary as other person
absent person

This third figure will almost certainly have been already introduced to the session in the attitude of the protagonist as s/he watches the auxiliaries. In understanding the triangular relationships the dyadic or fusional stages can be approached with less confusion. We are, at one and the same time, dealing with the external realities and the relationships of the internal figures. 'A parent can watch a scene from his own childhood as a way of gaining insight regarding his own parenting behaviour' (Blatner and Blatner 1988: 169). The purpose of this work is to reduce anxiety and gain insight into the external and internal world, so expanding role choice and spontaneity.

A word of caution

The purpose is not to apportion blame but to take responsibility for the internal drama.

A BRIEF ACCOUNT OF DOUBLING, ROLE REVERSAL AND THE MIRROR TECHNIQUE IN RELATION TO RESEARCH INTO EARLY INFANCY DEVELOPMENT

I now turn to discuss doubling, role reversal and mirror technique, from a psychoanalytic perspective of infant development. Every stage of infant development theory is both healthy and necessary. In an adult the failure to have made an internal integration of these three developmental transitions results in an impoverishment of the psyche and can lead to destructive behaviour and beliefs. Most of us have failed to make these transitions completely. In our work we bear witness to these incomplete transitions and the way in which they are unconsciously communicated. We see that behaviour from these unconscious communications can be understood as a defence mechanism, a survival strategy and a communication of these unresolved internal anxieties. It is through understanding these communications that we get to know the inner world of the protagonist.

The double

The first stage

The double represents the union between mother and baby from the moment of conception to the baby's instinctive letting go of mother after the first few weeks of life. It is the stage of one. This stage of infancy requires intense sensitivity from mother. The effort required is so embracing and obsessive that if it were not connected to pregnancy and the early months of the infancy the mother would be seen as being psychologically disturbed. This effort is devotion or reverie, which most mothers experience instinctively. Devotion is holding both the physical and psychic world of the infant, like an envelope. Devotion in the mother gradually develops during pregnancy and lasts for a few weeks after birth. This organised state of heightened sensitivity recedes in mother as the infant releases her when ego establishment means the baby has developed a sufficiency of 'going on being' (Winnicott 1958: 302–304) through mother's devotion. Mother and baby cannot exist without each other. Such devotion also belongs to the role of director, and is the key note to understanding the role of the double as reflection to the protagonist. Moreno called this stage of development the first 'matrix of identity . . . one total existence' (Moreno 1977: 111). This matrix of identity is made up of 'co-action and co-being' (Moreno 1977: 59–61), or a two-way relation involving co-operative behaviour. The living relationship is a necessary 'basic ration of the experience of omnipotence' (Winnicott 1986: 23) for the infant. Through this encounter is laid the foundation of the first emotional learning process for the infant.

Edward is chosen as protagonist. He messes about, trying to please and rubbishing any help offered. The director feels unable to move and notices Edward has stopped breathing and is frightened. He is asked, if he were to be in action, what parts of himself he would bring. He uses the group to represent different parts of himself which were placed as far away from each other as possible. He feels there is no way in which they can be brought together. He stands in this desolate landscape. He is asked if he is frightened. 'Terrified' is his reply. He has clearly had enough. He stops. He is relieved the group recognises his fear and that he is not overstimulated. Nor has he to pretend. At this stage reparation is premature. He needs to experience the group being able to tolerate and 'hold' his terror. . . . The director's countertransference is to feel riveted to the spot and it doubled the protagonist's early and very present fear of dis-integration. It helps to give meaning to his behaviour and to what looks to him like another apparent failure to function, which he dreads. He is amazed that he revealed the anxiety he tries to hide and he is not punished for it.

After the experience of birth the infant has little physical internal organisation with which to respond to the outside world (Brazelton and Cramer 1991: 113). He must survive his lack of co-ordination and the threat of annihilation.

The first ego organisation comes from the experience of threats of annihilation which do not lead to annihilation but from which, repeatedly, there is *recovery*. Out of such experiences confidence in recovery begins to be something which leads to an ego.

(Winnicott 1958: 304)

Paradoxically it is at this point of separation that the ego begins to form and thus the baby can *also* become bonded to mother instead of enmeshed with her. As 'this environmental condition of holding' (Winnicott 1960: 45) failed him in his childhood, Edward, as a baby, had adopted a 'false self' (Winnicott 1965: 47) to take care of his mother, and in this way failed to discover his own psychic reality through his own omnipotence. If the development of the 'false ego' (Winnicott 1965: 47) is not arrested it makes the second part of this stage of development very difficult to overcome as the ego is not sufficiently formed.

The second stage

To stretch or expand the capacity of the baby's responses mother instinctively starts to initiate action and watches the baby's response, modifying it when the s/he is overstimulated. Her initiations strengthen the infant's ego, just as the double stretches the protagonist. The baby's range of interaction expands as the ego forms. Separation and bonding become more established. During this time most babies experience split feelings of love, hatred and envy and respond to the confusion of feelings with the psychic defence mechanisms of splitting, projection and introjection. Melanie Klein called this 'the paranoid schizoid position' (Klein 1955: 268) which can be overwhelming. A holding environment is needed in order for the feelings to be contained otherwise the psychic defence mechanisms of splitting, projection and introjection can remain unreconciled. Loving and hating, rather than being reconciled as two parts of the whole person, are split further asunder.

Jane, a young woman, is willing to be chosen as protagonist but then stands smiling and vacant. The director feels wiped out and angry. The psychodrama reveals the underlying anxiety that mother nearly died at her birth. Jane is anxious that her spontaneity for life will cause her mother's death. She is equally anxious that the group will not be able to hold her anxiety or rage. She is caught between her wish to get back inside mother and her fear of being overwhelmed by her. She fears that if she attacks her mother she will die and they will both be destroyed. She becomes grossly dependent on the double or she does not use it at all. Jane's ego strength is not grown sufficiently for her to embrace her loving, hating and envious feelings. She cannot experience herself as both separate and close to her mother. The director's countertransference is to feel it is life and death. This helps reveal the communication as very early pre-verbal development in infancy.

Doubling can unearth the earliest aspects of pre-verbal infancy which have not been weathered successfully: the early need to be held, to survive the fear of disintegration, gain ego strength, separation and bonding (Winnicott 1965: 37–55). It is not always the case that doubling is comforting. Far from it. It can raise many anxieties in both roles. The protagonist may find the double intrusive, irrelevant or irritating in some way. They may feel overwhelmed; or they may even lean on the double to articulate their experience and then deny it. On the other hand the auxiliary as double meantime, may be intrusive, invasive, unengaged or grossly out of step with their protagonist and quite unable to join the protagonist in their internal experience of the world.

Mary has been a child-parent so long that she cannot bear to be doubled whilst she herself is a willing and effective double for others. There is no comfort or feeling of union of mother and infant in her. Mary's underlying anxiety and defence mechanism which disguise her need to be 'held' are revealed.

Role reversal

Role reversal reflects the second stage of two objects, mother and baby as separate in the infant's mind (Holmes 1992: 60). It gradually emerges from the stage of one. The feelings engendered in the infant can be overwhelming and need a holding environment to contain their natural ego defence mechanisms of splitting, projection and introjection.

Wendy's mother suffers post-natal depression at her birth. Mother's fear of hurting the baby was projected into the world around so she could play the protector. As an anorexic adolescent, Wendy is faced with the painful journey of discovering bad objects inside and being terrified. Through role reversal she can discover mother means well. This enables her to start to face her own persecution also unresolved in mother. Wendy role reverses with the dependent and independent parts of herself and eventually creates a new role between these extremes from which she can think. The games between these two polarisations both reflect the interaction between herself and her mother, and her own internal struggle for separation and bonding.

Role reversal represents the emergence of games, which have already started in tiny interactions between mother and infant. These games gradually develop. At best they express the main lines of harmony and of conflict in the parent–infant relationship (Fraiberg 1974). They provide an outlet for aggression without losing sight of what can be tolerated. The infant discovers s/he can initiate interactions and can control psychic boundaries. These games can be 'stretching', not abusive; but the line of what is tolerable is an important and fine one. It is in this arena that the mental, emotional and physical boundaries of the infant's psyche can be punctured.

With role reversal the ego capacity for coping with frustration (Winnicott 1958: 304) can evolve from the paranoid/schizoid position to 'the depressive position' (Klein 1955: 268) or separation when the small baby can tolerate mother as a separate object. Role reversal is not possible without sufficient ego strength; there has to be enough sense of 'me' in order to create a 'me and you encounter'. This may seem absurd but it is not infrequent that we come across a client who is unable to role reverse. Normal practice in psychodrama is to ask the protagonist to represent the significant 'other' first. The protagonist may become very anxious. At such a time we can ask them to find a space to represent themselves, and to then choose an auxiliary to represent themselves. Having established their presence in the room they can usually proceed to role reverse with the 'other'. Here is both a demonstration of how enmeshed the client is with mother and a conceptualisation of separation.

Esther's psychodrama is about her relationship with her mother, but she refuses to role reverse with her. She hunches up, sulks and is furious. She communicates to the director she feels far too much is expected of her. She is asked what it is about mother that is so unbearable. She says that mother finds her too demanding but also has too high expectations of her. Esther can then let herself role reverse with mother who appears preoccupied with her own experience of the world. Experiencing this, Esther is able to be in touch with how abandoned and persecuted she feels. Role reversal helps her gain insight into the difference of how she feels and how her mother feels. This enables her to face the pain of her own internal world; how enmeshed she is with mother; her sense of self is poor, swinging between anxiety, terror and rage. One set of feelings overwhelms another in a chaotic way. This mess is so intolerable to Esther that she takes control by trying to make mother have therapy in an attempt to make her create a world in which she can develop a sense of herself as a daughter. It always fails. Role reversal helps her face the depression she feels about her imperfect mother. In mourning the longing for a perfect mother she can then start to recognise some good as well as bad objects inside herself.

Mirror technique

I now return to the mirror technique as a systemic function. This final socialisation function represents the third developmental process necessary to the small infant in acquiring the psychic fabric to facilitate his well-being in the world. I call this function triangulation, but it is also known as the Oedipal stage of psychosexual development (Winnicott 1986: 137–141). The father or the third figure enters the internal world of the infant and heralds another enormous transition in terms of ego development. Triangulation is the psychic plane in which jealousy emerges.

> the child develops an in-love type of relationship to the father . . . [involving] . . . hate . . . fear of the mother . . . however . . . the child returns to the mother . . . sees the father objectively and the feelings of the child can [also] contain hate and fear for the father [so experimenting] with disloyalties . . . perceived tensions and jealousies.
>
> (Winnicott 1986: 138)

Through this process the child learns that his feelings contain love and hate. If all goes well enough, the baby learns that s/he can love both parents, feel loved by them and see that they also love each other. Such a completion is brought about by the parents protecting each other from the excesses of the baby as well as protecting the baby from the excesses of each other.

In our work as psychotherapists we see little of the sufficiently completed process of infant development. More often we see an internal world of distorted relationships between three internal figures or objects which are at best strained and at worst vicious.

To return to Steven. What is omitted from the previous description is the role of his father. Before proceeding with the scene with his mother he is asked about father. Here we meet a man whose strategy for living is to let mother be the controlling figure. This triangulation alters our understanding of Steven's experience. He is struggling with the part of him, father, that wants to give in, as well as the part of him he fears is like his violent and frustrated mother. He feels contempt for his father and hatred for his mother. These two feelings, as well as his need for approval, he feels also towards his boss.

Triangulation clarifies and makes concrete the internal triangular conflicts with which the difference between perception and reality also have to be struggled. Steven projected his violent hatred into his mother, and took in, or introjected the passivity of his father as a defence against his murderous feelings. This left him in a passive despair, as he increasingly saw himself like father. There was no internal balance or harmony. The outcome was that Steven failed to internalise a triangular relationship which might have protected him from a bleak internal landscape in which some form of psychic murder was always imminent.

When looking at a relationship between two people, especially if they are family figures, we must always ask where is the third. Clients often believe they are entirely responsible. This may be to defend against helplessness or rage. Clients are often baffled as to why the communication they so long for is absent in a dyadic relationship. With the mirror technique it often emerges that jealousy or envy in the parents distances them from their children. The outcome is that a healthy experience of triangulation is not experienced and integrated in the protagonist's internal world, and their psyche can be left in a precarious state.

To return to Esther. When father is brought into the scene, it is quite clear that Esther is his favourite. Esther has never seen this favouritism as something that might come between her and her mother. Consequently Esther is always trying to put things to rights and is mystified as to why she is failing. As the daughter she is caught in the unresolved issues between the parents. The result is that Esther splits her caring feelings into father and her jealous feelings into mother and hates both of them. Once she can see that she can do nothing about the marriage she can start to pay attention to the marriage of the loving and hating feelings inside of her.

Abuse is always a distorted triangular experience. It is therefore imperative to check the nature of a dyad in terms of the triangle, otherwise we may find we have colluded with the abusive situation. Through triangulation we see the lack of parental protection experienced by the protagonist, who can find this more difficult to face than the abuse itself. The abuse always speaks of too much from one parent and not enough from another, or too little from either parent. With the latter the protagonist's desperation may draw them to seek attention elsewhere and they are then at risk.

Andrew finally discloses to the group the abuse he experienced from a family friend. He goes off to tell his parents. He returns feeling neglected and unsupported. We turn to the nature of the lack of support, and his experience of his own internal objects. His apparent affability masks his deep hatred of himself and belief that he is unsupportable and unwanted. The work around his experience of his parents and upbringing has hardly begun.

Triangulation is important in helping develop the female and male objects inside us. However much we like to believe that either sex can perform all functions we cannot offer the unique balance of the triangle, where, at one and the same time there is a balance between the male and female energy which stimulates, holds and contains.

Joan has a bullying father and a passive mother who fails to protect Joan from the excesses of father. Joan tends to be self-effacing like mother and feels she must not hurt father. It is very difficult for her to experience herself as getting anything good or feeling protected for fear of the rage she projected into father but felt towards her mother. To be passive is to believe that Jane's feelings are as dangerous as she experiences father's behaviour. Mother's passivity confirms this. Jane lives in a frightening internal world in which there is violence or passive manipulation. Through this understanding Jane feels she can now start to consider her capacity to be assertive.

Finally, triangulation is important as it completes the psychic development of relationships from one to two to three internal objects which form the internal balance between action and stillness, creative and destructive forces, and the capacity to tolerate uncertainty, contradictions, ambivalence and mess without fear of being overwhelmed. Without triangulation this balance cannot be achieved.

CONCLUSION

I have given a brief outline of the three techniques of doubling, role reversal and the mirror technique. I have described their function and meaning in relation to 'holding, separation and triangulation'. As I said at the start, all three parts of the cake confront us at once. Through bringing psychoanalytic research of early infant development alongside psychodramatic philosophy and practice I have briefly articulated one way of explaining the confusion and complexity that can arise from the experience of some clients' response to doubling, role reversal, and the mirror technique. In every bite is the possible taste of the need for holding, separation and triangulation. Every bite of the cake is both bitter and sweet. It is bitter because of the un-contained vicious feelings which have frightened their owners for so long. It is sweet because of the longing for reparation of the tele and spontaneity. We taste these hopes and fears through the butter of countertransference which informs us at these moments of apparent failure in psychodramatic practice.

BIBLIOGRAPHY

Blatner, A. (1973) *Acting In*, New York: Springer.

Blatner. A. and Blatner, A. (1988) *Foundations of Psychodrama*, New York: Springer.

Brazelton, T. and Cramer, B.G. (1991) *The Earliest Relationship*, London: Karnac.

Fox, J. (ed.) (1987) *The Essential Moreno*, New York: Springer.

Fraiberg, S. (1974) 'The Clinical Dimensions of Baby Games', *Journal of American Academy of Child Psychology* 13.

Greenberg, I.A. (ed.) (1974) *Psychodrama, Theory and Therapy*, Norwich: Condor.

Holmes, P. (1992) *The Inner World Outside*, London: Tavistock/Routledge.

Kellermann, P.F. (1992) *Focus on Psychodrama*, London: Jessica Kingsley.

Kellermann, P.F. (1994) *Role reversal in Psychodrama* in P. Holmes, M. Karp and M. Watson (eds) *Psychodrama since Moreno*, London: Routledge.

Kipper, D.A. (1986) *Psychotherapy through Clinical Role Playing*, New York: Brunner/Mazel.

Klein, M. (1955) *Developments in Psycho-analysis*, London: Tavistock.

Mahler, M.S. (1975) *The Psychological Birth of the Human Infant*, New York: Basic Books.

Moreno. J.L. (1969) *Psychodrama, Third Volume*, New York: Beacon House.

Moreno, J.L (1977) *Psychodrama, First Volume*, New York: Beacon House.

Moreno J.L. (1993) *Who Shall Survive?*, Student edition, Roanoke, VA: American Society of Group Psychotherapy and Psychodrama, Royal Publishing Co.

Starr, A. (1977) *Rehearsal for Living*, New York: Nelson Hall.

Stern, D. (1985) *The Interpersonal World of the Infant*, New York: Basic Books.

Winnicott, D.W. (1958) *Collected Papers: Through Paediatrics to Psycho-analysis*, London: Tavistock.

Winnicott, D.W. (1971) *Playing and Reality*, London: Tavistock.

Winnicott, D.W. (1977) *Playing and Reality*, London: Tavistock.
Winnicott, D.W. (1986) *Home is Where We Start From*, London: Penguin.
Winnicott, D.W. (1965) *The Maturational Process and the Facilitating Environment*, London: Hogarth.

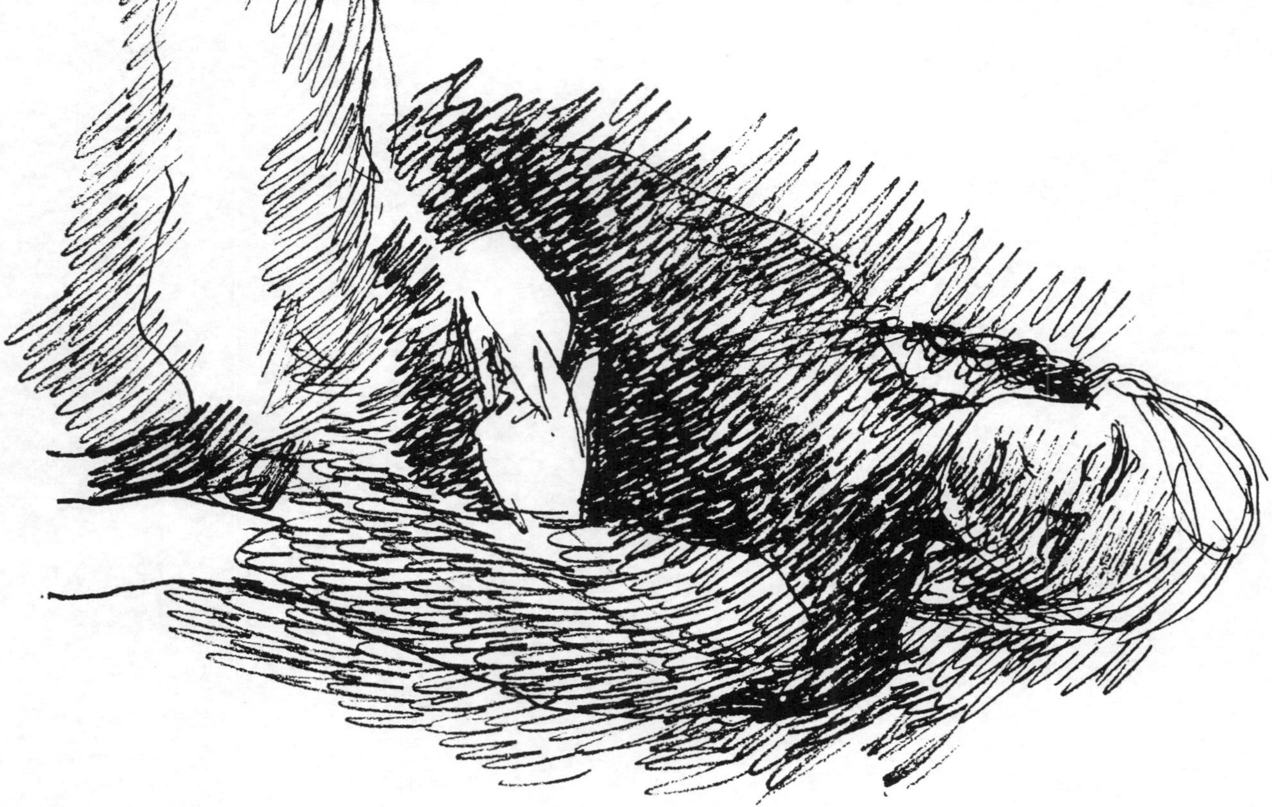

Chapter 13

The psychodramatic treatment of depression

Chris Farmer

This chapter illustrates psychodramatic interventions in four people with common manifestations of major depression which was unresponsive to medication alone. The cases are judged to be typical of routine psychiatric practice; all four people participated as protagonists in a sample of sessions directed by the writer over a period of one month.

Depression is defined medically as a condition of intractable low mood and dispirited attitude that is associated with sluggish function of brain (as in retardation of thought) and body (in particular, poor appetite, constipation, loss of weight, lack of libido, and a reversal of the diurnal rhythm of sleep and energy patterns). The quality of depressive ideation is particularly distinctive, consisting when severe of profound pessimism and a self-devaluation of the patient's achievements accompanied by a remorse for perceived past failings. The joy of living is replaced by hopelessness, abject despair and suicidal intimations.

Most cases today present to a less extreme degree, perhaps on account of earlier detection and the prescription of the newer anti-depressant drugs, but the increasing numbers of patients who are taking them in their ever-advancing refinements suggest that there are many for whom other approaches to treatment are as necessary as ever. The writer finds it helpful to consider part of the brain as like an organ such as the stomach, skin or bowel that may be constitutionally vulnerable to certain kinds of stress: once targeted, the emotions, thinking and bodily activity governed by this area of brain become affected and out of the direct control of the mind. Like asthma, dyspepsia or colitis which respond to physical treatment, the brain function may recover with anti-depressant drugs, but it would make sense to address the original psychological stress upon the brain – particularly insofar as it is a matter of functional activity rather than structural damage.

Major depression (American Psychiatric Association 1994) is chosen to illustrate this section because it has the highest lifetime prevalence of the serious formal psychiatric illnesses occurring in the general adult population. Aside from any biological predisposition, personality, lifestyle, personal relationships and precipitating events are all contributing factors. It is generally the final common path of many different life experiences, usually involving loss, especially of relationships or roles. A classical account of the aetiological aspects of psychological medicine, and an authoritative description of depressive conditions in particular, is provided by Lewis (1966: 1153). Starr (1977: 303) illustrates a variety of methods of working with depression using psychodrama.

Psychodrama addresses the present-day experience of depression, its context (particularly past and present relationships), and its origin. Typically, attention flows back and forth in scenes examining these three areas of enquiry, until the protagonist acquires the spontaneity to find new roles to replace redundant ones, re-edit previous life narratives and create a fourth area of new possibilities for the future.

The first example is a record of one psychodrama session. In the remaining three, material is presented from a series of sessions. For the sake of authenticity the overall framework of each story has a broadly factual basis but identifiable features have been altered to protect privacy.

CASE ILLUSTRATIONS

Jill

This is a report of the action phase of one session. Since the information was gleaned while Jill was working as a protagonist, it is recorded, as it emerged, in the present tense.

Jill, aged 26, lives with two children, estranged from her husband and all close relatives. The main presenting features are hopelessness and loneliness. She is slow to warm up, but an initial present-day scene in her home shows her attempting to alleviate the sense of futility of her monotonous life with bulimic behaviour. It is the only way to relieve, albeit temporarily, her experience of emptiness that she feels, literally, in her body.

Through a simple time regression (walking anti-clockwise, hand-in-hand with the director) she finds herself starting her bulimia at the age of 13. She has been recurrently depressed ever since.

In the following scene of her family life at this time, the *locus nascendi* of her life problems is explored. Jill's parents have no happiness in their marital relationship, which is sustained, first by the mother's fear of material insecurity and need for comfort from her children and, second, by the father's sense of loyalty and self-esteem in being a consistent financial provider. There is pressure upon Jill, as last of five children, to be fat and socially underdeveloped, so that her leaving home would be delayed.

These issues become apparent to the group, and also to Jill herself, as she speaks in the roles of the various family members. Auxiliaries from the group then fill these roles, so that Jill is enabled to experience a typical home scene: father complains incessantly to mother about how hard-working he is and how little mother appreciates him. Mother is, ironically, relieved that he drinks heavily as it makes him soporific and less inclined to be physically violent. Jill sits between them, pretending to follow a soap opera on TV. She eats crisps.

When she watches a mirror of herself, the realisation comes to her that her older siblings are out of the scene. Jill remains in the room as a silent referee – a child in front of whom neither parent would wish to fight – and a tangible justification for the continuation of the marriage. She can also see that she has colluded in maintaining the situation, for she does not want to have her parents fighting in her absence. Now Jill can see how she has provided some measure of meaningfulness for her parents' marriage, but to the exclusion of any purpose in her own right.

The psychodrama proceeds with Jill becoming involved in the normal, everyday, arguments with her parents that she had never had as she grew up – the *status nascendi* of the therapy. It is then that she realises that she has been attempting to replicate within her own failed marriage the family life of her mother. The action concludes with a rectifying scene with the mother in the present day.

While it is not possible to extract one detail or scene of a psychodrama in isolation from the rest as the single decisive intervention, it is helpful to look at what might be regarded as the turning point. With Jill, it was a 'catharsis of integration' (Moreno 1993: 57), as she watched the auxiliary mirroring herself as the 13-year-old in the presence of her parents. At that moment she appreciated how her own sense of meaninglessness reflected that of the futility of her parents' relationship. She could then look with sympathy at her parents' own plight. Finally, she could connect this with her emptiness and her bulimia.

When 'depression' is experienced as a lack of meaningfulness, the discovery, experientially and intellectually, of its origin can come as an enormous relief; Jill found a 'reason' for her sense of pointlessness, derived from a new historical perspective, one that could now be revised with a fresh narrative.

Sue

This more complicated case addresses serious personality traits and long-standing emotional issues. Fragments are presented from different psychodramas undertaken over a period of some months.

An early psychodrama shows Sue, a woman in her late 40s, as a bitter recluse since her divorce some years previously. In her small flat she avoids all social contact, except when telephoning the doctor with hypochondriacal complaints. Her friends and relatives have lost patience with her. Her social atom is almost depleted.

It was hard to work with Sue as she devalued any therapy and avoided conversation with other group members. At home she ate little, lost weight, slept poorly and became apathetic towards her housework. She claimed that her family and friends had given up on her. While sometimes maintaining that she deserved to be abandoned – as is typical in depression – she could also be aggressive and then blame others for not standing by her. Her isolation was becoming self-perpetuating.

Eventually she gives a hint to the nature of her anxieties when as a group member she attempts to leave a psychodrama session at a point where the protagonist is displaying a great amount of anger. Sue is confronted by the director; people do not walk out in the middle of psychodramas. That is a basic rule and Sue realises this very well. In fact the director is himself angry with Sue and she knows it.

Sue's flight from a scene of anger, however, suggested that in her everyday way of life she was also attempting to escape from an intense rage of her own. Furthermore, she was so frightened of it that she denied it and projected it into others. Through the process of projective identification, the staff felt this anger in such a way that they too were frightened to express it to Sue, as though it would demolish her. (Sandler 1988 provides a review of such unconscious fantasies and mental mechanisms, while Holmes 1992 furnishes a full application of object relations theory to psychodrama.)

In a later session, Sue as the protagonist provided two clues to the understanding of her depression. First, she showed scenes of her teenage life in a fishing community where her mother and father had both died very young, leaving Sue with a physically ailing grandmother. This prevented Sue (who is bright) from going to college.

The second clue to the nature of Sue's depression was her subsequent style of coping with these deprivations. Scenes revealed how she avoided the full impact of her grief by overfunctioning: as the senior sibling, as a career woman and finally as a mother. A further scene portrayed her marriage failing and her resorting to alcohol. When her children left home she felt it to be a repetition of the abandonment experienced when her parents died. She reacted by trying even harder with her dysfunctional coping styles and became ever more proudly independent and aloof, until she alienated her family and friends.

Having understood unmanageable childhood grief as the likely original source of Sue's uncontrollable anger, the director then sought to help Sue to feel secure enough in the group to handle this. She needed the group to assure her that her anger was rightful and that the group was safe. The director's insistence on her not leaving during the earlier psychodrama session had given her the message that anger and fear were to be (and therefore, implicitly, *could* be) contained within the psychodrama group.

> She is encouraged to play with the bataka. The group enthusiastically cheers her on. 'I feel stupid', she says, waving the bataka in the air. However, when she does give one tentative whack on the back of her chair, a fleeting smile crosses her face.

Perhaps, to avoid sadistically venting her anger upon others, she had instead inflicted it upon herself by stigmatising herself as a figure of shame.

> This possibility becomes more evident when she is encouraged to whack more energetically with the bataka, for she then addresses the chair as herself. 'You stupid bitch', she mockingly shouts, as she strikes the chair. 'You have been f——g up Sue's life. . . . I don't believe in bad language. . . . You silly wretched b——.'

This appeared to be a fundamental feature of her depression: she had directed her anger inwardly, by way of humiliating herself, because she had been too afraid, and concerned for the consequences, to express her anger consciously and directly towards others. Instead, she had metaphorically thrashed herself. In psychodrama, we dissuade people from 'beating themselves up'; that is the very trait that many protagonists are attempting to overcome. However, by using the chair to represent the part of Sue that tormented herself, she was enabled to externalise her self-destructiveness – to concretise her tyrannical self-persecutor – and to allow herself to get in touch with her innate spontaneous aggression, humorously and physically confronting the internal oppressor. Segal (1975) in her discussion of Klein's concept of manic defence organisation against depression points out that such issues of control, guilt and denial of independence require working through to achieve reparation.

When Sue had worked through the conflict that had been raging within herself, she could face the dependency needs that were hidden behind it and begin to accept the care offered by the staff. It was this that made the final work with Sue – the repair of her social atom – possible. In a vignette some weeks later:

> Sue revisits her flat. She sets the chairs out to represent her current family. Sitting in the chair representing her eldest daughter, she explains from her own perspective how their relationship has broken down. It becomes clear that these grown-up children will not take the first step in talking with or visiting their mother. From the experience of previous fights, they have no reason to believe that their mother wishes for any contact. They are so hurt and angry that they will not take the risk.

Sue, however, by this time had accepted the advice and support of the staff. She had finally accepted her share of the responsibility for the fights. She wished for a reconciliation.

The staff then took steps, through the social worker, to enable this message to get through to the relatives. They tentatively began to respond. So frightened were the parties of meeting each other that a staff member was needed as an auxiliary ego for the reunion to feel safe.

Violet

This lady in her late 70s had a series of three sessions alone with her therapist: psychodrama *à deux*. She had what used to be described as 'involutional melancholia' (a major depression with a pattern of features that relate to later life), having become depressed after her son's death two years previously. She had persevered with maintaining the outward pattern of her life, but she could not grieve. She had lost weight, she could not eat, she woke early (hardly able to face the day), and she could not look to the future. She complained of panics, palpitations and nausea.

Fortunately, three important aspects of her mental functioning were retained: her intellectual faculties, her motivation to get better and, in particular, her insight, for she was aware that she had unresolved grief and she stated that if she could only cry, she would grieve her son's death and recover!

Two significant features that struck the psychodramatist as possibly interrelated were her presenting physical symptoms (nausea, headaches and tremor) and her inability to cry.

In the role of her deceased son she describes his terminal illness. He has cancer of the throat. He cannot swallow and the radiotherapy gives him constant nausea.

These features coincided with some of her own somatic symptoms so well that the therapist surmised that she had identified with the deceased son; she had taken upon herself some of the features of his illness as a way of holding on to him, to avoid emotionally letting him go. (See Freud 1917 and Abraham 1924 for the significance of identification in grief.)

Accordingly her son is 'resurrected' in the form of a cushion in a chair where he usually sat (this psychodramatic enactment takes place in her home). She is able to speak to her son, reverse roles with him and experience him (with the therapist in the role of her son) speaking as he was unable to do while he was dying, owing to the exigencies of his illness and the unnatural 'rationed' time that she was allowed to be with him. For the first time since his death she begins to cry.

Two weeks later she was somewhat better, but the discomfort in her abdomen persisted and she still could not weep to the degree that she knew was needed.

Violet is asked to reverse roles with the sensation in her abdomen. She sits on a stool, hunched up, and becomes 'Violet's painful memories'. She then recalls the death of her husband some thirty years earlier. The therapist suggests that they go back to that event.

As the scene proceeds, Violet exchanges roles with her husband and with her son (both represented by cushions) just before her husband dies. She relives the experience of her husband slumping in the chair in the kitchen and her son feeling his pulse before calling the doctor. The fear becomes focused and experienced for what it really is: terror for the husband and alarm on behalf of her son.

By seizing upon the plight of her husband and her son, she had avoided the full experience of her own devastation. Indeed, it was very possible that she had sought to protect herself from the full intensity of the separation from her loved ones by allowing a part of herself to become, in fantasy, merged with them, first with her dead husband, and later with her son, holding them inside herself as a way of avoiding the full agony of the grief that she had needed to suffer, in her own right, before she could accept their deaths at a deeper emotional level. She had not cried for her husband until exactly one year after his death.

In a further session, two weeks later, her depressive mood had lifted but her conversation was still an effort in the middle of the morning. It was now time to address the existential here-and-now; what did it mean for her to be in her home on a routine, everyday, morning? 'I just stand and stare', she reported.

> The therapist has her stand and stare. As she gazes out of the window the therapist doubles with her. Eventually, after a long lapse of time, he feels as though he is waiting for something, and puts this into words.
>
> Together, they now attend to what 'waiting' means for Violet. She is patient because she would otherwise be impatient.

She has achieved this reversal through the defence mechanisms of denial and reaction formation.

Once they had, together, acknowledged her underlying impatience – a tenacious withholding of a deep exasperation – she could concretise this feeling and wrestle with it.

> She wrings a bath towel with all her strength. She gasps. She is encouraged to breathe in as she straightens her back and to exhale as she bends her body and squeezes the towel. She is urged to voice a sound. What does that noise convey? 'A growl.' Gradually, as she straightens and bends, inhales and exhales, squeezes and relaxes, she assumes a rhythmical motion which amplifies the energy. At length the pitch of her voice rises, so that, when eventually the action ceases, she speaks with animation and conveys her sense of sheer relief at having come through her ordeal.

Through persevering with a struggle between her patience and her impatience she reached a catharsis which released the spontaneity that had been locked up in her unresolved grief.

On a further visit she was entirely clear of her depression and eagerly planning a holiday. Follow-ups over the following year confirmed that she remained well.

Angela

Examples from a series of three sessions show how the development of her relationship with the other group members complements her work as a protagonist and as an auxiliary.

Aged 50, Angela had been miserable and underfunctioning for twenty years. No medication had helped; for the first ten years benzodiazepines had curbed an excessive irritability, but at the cost of inducing a profound apathy. She was stubborn and aggressive – to a point of being 'bloody minded' – using vitriolic sarcasm to silence her soft-spoken husband.

The underlying crisis was the imminent departure of Angela's granddaughter, Tracy (the only other member of the household), to university, leaving her ill-fated husband as her only companion at home. To her credit, Angela was at pains not to dissuade Tracy from pursuing her career.

Her progress over the course of some weeks is shown in three discrete psychodramas:

First psychodrama

Angela, using quick sequences of monodrama, compared her present family relationships with her experiences as a child. Scenes oscillated between present and past to provide a narrative report of the development of deep conflicts over envy and her fear of it – in herself and in other people.

1   In the present day Angela ensures that Tracey has all the care that was denied to herself by her own mother.

2   In her own childhood Angela was favoured – above her mother – by her father and his own extended family, and consequently suffered from her mother's intense jealousy.

3   Rapport between Angela and her mother had always suffered from poor bonding after Angela's difficult birth. When Angela developed into a bright and clever child, her mother became so envious and resentful that in fits of fury she would attack Angela with a knife.

4   In a scene depicting her husband enjoying the company of her daughter, Angela was painfully reminded of the relationship she had lost with her own father. She tried to maintain her self-control, but envy got the better of her and with her vicious tongue she skilfully berated her husband and denigrated her daughter.

The granddaughter was not her husband's child and so the position did not resemble that in Angela's own childhood too closely. This averted the intense rivalry that had existed between Angela and her daughter. Indeed, Tracey was seen as a gift from the daughter to appease Angela.

Second psychodrama

Angela took the role of a nurse in various scenes from her early truncated career. She showed her effectiveness, sensitivity and resourcefulness to an increasing degree as the action developed.

Feeling from her home experience that these skills were resented and devalued, she had underfunctioned for many years.

Angela declares that she has not dared to allow herself to show her care for people for fear that this would be regarded as 'weakness' or make her vulnerable to those, like her mother, who could become envious towards her.

The closing scene is a theatre recovery room. As a theatre nurse she tends to the patients (represented by members of the group) and discovers that she can, after all, be recognised and appreciated for her qualities of caring and empathy.

Third psychodrama

Angela's final psychodramatic insight came not as a protagonist but as an auxiliary ego.

She is chosen to be an authoritative and very businesslike husband to Sue. In this role as a husband, Angela proves how articulate, practical, determined and capable of handling people she can be. Sue has clearly recognised, through tele, these features in Angela, who by bringing panache to the role shows again what she might achieve in the future.

In the sharing phase, Angela confesses that she inflicts upon her husband the violent rage that her mother had delivered upon her as a child. Her misuse of benzodiazepines had been to suppress feelings and impulses which otherwise would have brought torment to her husband and family. Angela reflects ruefully upon the time when she had successfully run her own business; unfortunately, when thwarted, she had directed her energies to running her family like a business, and 'wearing the trousers'.

Angela, thus, through a series of psychodramas, gained insight into the development of life-long personality traits that had arisen in large part from her attempts to cope with the envy and physical abuse from her mother that were incurred by being close to her father. The significance of envy, its denial and projection in obstructing the course of the paranoid-schizoid position is explained by Segal (1975).

In psychodrama Angela felt safe enough from envy between herself and the group members to re-live scenes previously too painful to contemplate, and thereby to experience herself in vulnerable or dangerous roles. She was finally able to get in touch with her sensitivity and to accept her energy, wit and fluency as fortunate endowments that could be used to enhance the well-being of other group members, rather than be stored as ammunition for threats or punishments. Having accepted and confronted the enviously abusive mother inside her, she could begin to separate herself off from this internalized figure and be Angela in her own right.

THE FLEXIBILITY OF PSYCHODRAMA IN CLINICAL USE

These four cases feature people with very different personalities, life experiences, levels of insight and requirements for containment. They illustrate the wide variety of presentations of depression and some of the many possible ways by which psychodrama may be employed in its management. Their therapy entailed different relationships with the group and a very varied therapeutic timespan.

They show (apart from Violet's 'psychodrama *à deux*') how the role and function of the group itself in its infinite flexibility can be crucial. With Jill the group formed the context for the warm-up to the drama of the action, provided the auxiliary egos, gave support and shared, as in a 'one-off' session. For Sue and Angela, however, the continuity of the group over periods of weeks and months was indispensable. The building of trust in working together, through interactions with the protagonist that included an interlocking of group and auxiliary roles with very real relationships, led it to become a holding environment that enabled sufficient time for the therapeutic process to attain its resolution. Sue required the firm boundaries of an on-going group to contain primitive anxieties and impulses related to fear, aggression, hate and envy. For Angela, the real relationship with the whole group over a long series of sessions, including her engagements as an auxiliary ego for other protagonists, was crucial in rectifying issues of envy and for gaining respect and acceptance from the value that was placed on her by the other group members.

Aside from the group issues, each protagonist had a distinct presentation, a particular history and required different assignments from their psychodramas. Jill's single classically framed session provided the necessary insight to bring understanding and meaning to the pattern of her life in the light of a review of her childhood family relationships. This then enabled her to relinquish a redundant role and to begin to rehearse more functional family roles. Sue's depression had come after the breaking down of life-long attempts to defend against anxieties from childhood abandonment. With the group as a container – for her fears of further painful rejection and for her struggles to fight against her need for acceptance – she was finally able to contemplate the reality of the depletion of her social atom and consider how it might be repaired.

Violet, by contrast, was at the start only too aware of the need to resolve her grief. She was able to work through her losses in a non-group setting with a focus, in particular, upon the techniques of concretisation (including physical struggle), doubling and, especially, role-reversal with her deceased son.

Finally, Angela, who had experienced life-long recurrent depression, had required a very interactive engagement with the group to re-work and revise narratives emanating from her childhood in order to understand the deeper significance of the threat of the imminent departure of her granddaughter.

DIRECTING PSYCHODRAMA WITH DEPRESSED PATIENTS

The writer believes that an understanding of clinical depression is helpful in interpreting the significance of a patient's condition for the group. However, the protagonist's life and experience are explored, and the sessions conducted, in much the same manner as in non-clinical settings. The 'depression' does not have to be reified and seen as something autonomous and separate from the subject's psychic life and its implications for the patient. Depression is most significant in terms of relationships with self and others – present and past – particularly where, as is common in depression, the future is hard to contemplate.

The director should be aware of the effectiveness of psychodrama in attending to depressed people and should convey trust in the method to work with their anxieties and needs. A therapist's optimism is remembered with appreciation when at the time it would appear to have been disregarded. Nevertheless, depressed people may show great difficulty in shifting their mood or raising their sights. They may therefore be slow to warm up and, with their spontaneity hard to access, not inclined to volunteer to work as the protagonist. Depression is often associated with a sense of a burden of inappropiate guilt, and since spontaneity cannot be forced, the protagonist can well do without having to feel that something is owed to the director or the group.

Very depressed people cannot easily focus their mind upon anything but 'the depression'; spontaneity of thought and feeling may be at a standstill. It is then useful to learn how this stasis may mask other issues or stand in the way of resolving them. Indeed, it is often by defining, with the help of the protagonist and the group, what in life is so restrictive as to be reflected in the patient's locked up thoughts and feelings, that it becomes possible to examine the precursors and the future implications of working through the depression. In this way alternative descriptions and definitions can be arrived at, paying particular regard to role theory and sociometric status.

Just as suicide can be considered as a two-person event at the very least (whatever side of the grave), so may depression itself be viewed from a sociometric perspective. It is helpful to begin by finding out who else is involved, or – which has much the same significance – who is specifically *not* aware of the patient's condition at this time. Once a protagonist begins to relate, especially through role reversal, to significant people in their lives, then the opportunity to recover more functional roles (for these are often very constrained in depression) begins a process of warming up to the spontaneity for further action.

There is, finally, for those involved in the psychodrama of depression a level of significance that goes beyond the personal and the clinical domain to the more fundamental process and meaning of human life. Freud considered that life might be thought of as a process of mourning from the moment of birth over the loss of physical and psychic union between mother and infant. If this is so, then our hopes and disappointments – and the letting go of our expectations in the maturity of age – can be viewed as marks of the vicissitudes in the endless struggle with our own grief. The transcending of despair and desperation through an acceptance, in the experience of true sadness, of the reality of death and loss, can be considered as integrative for the soul and conducive to human psychic growth. When the truth of life and death hits us dramatically, be it on the stage or in life itself – as in the death and funeral of Diana, Princess of Wales – the collective catharsis leaves us with new meaning for one another and a reaching out together in the sharing and acceptance of life. The psychodrama of depression reflects the drama of life and is healing for the whole of the group.

THE PSYCHODRAMA METHOD'S WIDE APPLICABILITY

This fairly random selection of cases is taken to show the diversity and flexibility of psychodrama in addressing one diagnostic group by taking account of each individual person's unique life experience. As the process unfolds underlying aspects of the condition are revealed which in turn suggest further options for the director. This indication of its adaptability hopefully conveys a sense of how this powerful method through its versatility can be applied effectively to other clinical conditions.

SUMMARY

These examples show just some of the ways in which psychodrama can address clinical depression and, by implication, other clinical conditions. They are presented in detail to show how the complexity needs to be addressed, and, where life-long issues are involved, work needs to be carried out over time and from multiple perspectives. Psychodrama needs to engage with the person who is depressed before it can attend to his or her 'depression'.

Depression is prone to occur after key relationships are threatened or broken – through discord, distance or death. If family roles have not been fulfilling or mutually compatible, the depressed person is left with conflicting emotions and confused thoughts that result from unfinished dialogues with absent parties. Many patients harbour deep inside a smouldering anger that they fear releasing. Psychodrama provides an arena for completing these unresolved interactions.

BIBLIOGRAPHY

Abraham, K. (1924) 'A Short Study of the Development of the Libido, Viewed in the Light of Mental Disorders', in *Selected Papers on Psychoanalysis*, London: Hogarth Press (1927): 418–501.

American Psychiatric Association (1994) *Diagnostic and Statistical Manual of Mental Disorders (DSM IV)*, Washington, DC: APA.

Freud, S. (1917) *Mourning and Melancholia*, Standard Edition 14, London: Hogarth Press: 237–258.

Holmes, P. (1992) *The Inner World Outside*, London: Routledge.

Lewis, A. (1996) 'Psychological Medicine', in R. B. Scott (ed.) *Price's Textbook of Medicine*, London: Oxford University Press.

Moreno, J. L. (1993) *Who Shall Survive?*, Student edition of Moreno 1934, 1953 and 1978, Roanoke, VA: American Society of Group Psychotherapy and Psychodrama, Royal Publishing Co.

Sandler, J. (ed.) (1988) *Projection, Identification, and Projective Identification*, London: Karnac.

Segal, H. (1975) *Introduction to the Work of Melanie Klein*, London: Hogarth Press.

Starr, A. (1977) *Psychodrama: Rehearsal for Living*, Chicago: Nelson Hall.

Chapter 14

Permission to interact

A who, how and why of sociodrama

Ken Sprague

Asking why one should concern oneself with social problems or try to change the status quo is like asking a mountaineer, 'Why climb Mount Everest?' The answer will probably be, 'Because it is there'. It seems to me that the same can be said of social difficulties; they are there. They surround us and turn the world into a vale of tears rather than the garden of Eden it could be.

Across the entire world human achievement in technology and science is extraordinary. In art and music, humankind often reaches the sublime. Yet our cruelty in torture and warfare world-wide still descends to hellish behaviour. The link road to that behaviour is all too evident in everyday personal relationships.

Nobody is without the rotten seed and no country is without it. When Great Britain was the richest and most powerful nation on earth, its government allowed 1 million of its own people to die of hunger in the Irish potato famine. We all still suffer the consequences of that murderous period.

Yet change is in the air. In 1997 the nation came together in mourning for Diana, Princess of Wales. It was a phenomenal response, the like of which I have never seen and we are unlikely to see again. There are very few ways in which people feel able to concretely do something about how difficult the world is. Diana provided an opportunity. People responded by showing that they are not forever cabbages waiting to be cut and cooked.

People want something better, more just and more caring. They are, like the stars or the stones, part of mother nature and they are evolving with her. Their uniqueness lies in being able to dream and act upon their dreams. They dream and work to make life better for their children than it was for them. It is a rather endearing human habit but it drives dictators and bureaucrats stark raving mad because dictators aim to take decisions for people rather than empowering them to make their own choices. This century has produced many examples of such madness. Hitler, Mussolini and Stalin are the obvious names that spring to mind, but most nations can provide candidates. The crazed African dictator who had himself crowned as a Napoleonic Emperor may have seemed a joke to the rest of us but his own people did not find him very funny. (His crown, by the way, was made in London. Imperial connections and illusions of grandeur are a long time lingering!)

If I make it to the millennium I will have lived three quarters of the century or roughly about the same time that Dr Jacob Levy Moreno's ideas and action methods have been available to us.

As a boy I began to learn about history and was advised to study my historians first; I would then know what kind of history to expect. This is because all historians of necessity write subjectively. So before going any further let me declare my own history, so that you will know what to expect from me. I have worked as a baker boy, a coal miner, political activist, trade union newspaper editor and graphic artist. I gained my psychodrama certification in 1980 and my sociodrama recognition in 1990. I have always drawn pictures and now work as an artist, psychodrama educator/practitioner and a sociodramatist.

As a teenager I used to visit, most Saturdays, a second-hand bookshop in London's Red Lion Street. It was run by a kindly old anarchist with silver hair and a pointed beard. We used to do a sort of sociodrama on my visits. His 'warm-up' was collecting old Jack London books and repairing them for me with sellotape and brown paper. I 'warmed up' by saving pence, mainly on my lunch and buying the books for a shilling or two depending on their rarity and his recycling. The 'action' came when we swapped Jack London anecdotes and he turned his shop into the adventurous landscapes or dismal opium dens that Jack had written about. His customers were press-ganged into participation.

'Catharsis' came when I made the actual purchase and read great stories like *The Iron Heel* and *The Jacket* or was disappointed by *Little Lady of the Big House*, a pot-boiler written when Jack was desperate for money. 'Sharing' came when I left the shop and my friend called after me in a loud voice, to the consternation of the rest of the street, 'Remember the status quo anywhere in the world must be bloody well changed.'

I loved the sound of his voice, loved his dramatic, defiant presentation and shared it in turn with my friends and now with you. I also came to realise just how profound his words were and are. For me, they are the bedrock of Moreno's action methods.

WHO WAS MORENO?

Moreno was not a doctor in pursuit of respectability or comfortable medical status. This man was a revolutionary, but not the revolutionary of barricades and blood-letting. He had seen the results of violence in the aftermath of the First World War. He rejected the methods being debated in arguments rumbling through Vienna for political and social change. Hitler was there formulating his Nazi ideas. Trotsky, calling for permanent revolution, lived in a room above Moreno's theatre.

Moreno chose to follow his own road. He had been a student at the University of Vienna when Einstein was a professor there. Although he may never have attended any of Einstein's lectures, I suspect that Moreno shared with Einstein the idea that 'the only justifiable purpose of political institutions is to assure the unhindered development of the individual' (Einstein 1943). I believe that this led Moreno to develop a philosophy and then a method to give his ideas life; a method that is based upon the individual's active participation, not upon systems of controlling the individual.

From the start, Moreno set out quite deliberately to change the status quo. He saw that his calling as a doctor was limited if he only treated personal health and suffering.

He understood that each of us is born with gifts of spontaneity and creativity. For him these represented potential well-springs of health: personal and social. He recognised that our industrial, profit-hungry society does not value or encourage people's innate creative potential. Therefore that potential needs support and training if it is to develop.

'The scene' was Vienna after the First World War. Moreno had the job of organising camps of displaced persons. These were people who had lost everything. They had seen their dreams smashed into tiny pieces. He set about helping them to dream again. Later he worked during the day in a big children's hospital and in the evenings helping the city's prostitutes to organise their own protection. He also started his Theatre of Spontaneity in which life's daily problems could be re-enacted, followed by testing of possible solutions.

Every healer or therapist learns, sooner or later, the contradiction of helping people toward recovery and then sending them back into the conditions that made them ill in the first place. Moreno took on the task of treating society as well as the individual within society.

WHY *SOCIO*-DRAMA?

Sociodrama is a group method of education. It gives us the opportunity to use our imagination to practise living in the sociodrama group without being punished for making mistakes as we might be if we did the same thing in everyday situations. The sociodramatic method provides a training ground for collective action and education. It has three aims: 'an improved understanding of a social situation, an increase in participants' knowledge about their own and other people's roles in relation to that situation, and an emotional release or catharsis as people express their feelings about the subject' (Wiener 1995).

A group of people come together to look at a particular subject of local difficulty. It may be a problem with school bus arrangements or safety questions. The group may number five or fifty. During the Malvinas War my great friend Dalmiro Bustos used sociodramatic methods in a football stadium with over 700 Argentinian parents desperate for news of their sons. The numbers vary but the method is basically the same. Instead of simply discussing, stating personal opinions or riding individual hobby horses the group used action methods to search beyond the personal to wider, more universal truths.

Sociodrama is closely related to psychodrama and has the same basic structure of three distinct stages. These are the warm-up, the enactment and the sharing.

There is of course usually an earlier stage of planning the sociodrama, attracting the participants and arranging the venue. It also makes good sense to have a later stage for assessing and analysing the session.

1   *The warm-up*   In this stage the participants are warmed up to one another and their new surroundings. There are two aims: first, to create a cohesive group of people ready to work and learn from each other and, second, to build a safe place where each person can express their ideas, thoughts and feelings openly and without fear of attack or ridicule.

2   *The enactment*   Some people call this stage 'the Action'. In all three stages people are 'active' in mind and body, therefore I prefer to use the title 'Enactment'.

The stage is set and the scene begins. Participants take on roles and develop the enactment. The director (sometimes called 'conductor') acts as guide, helping to deepen the levels of role-playing from stereotype to typical and, with skill and luck, to archetypal. The aim here is to bring the enactment to a more advanced and effective state. In other words, to help those taking part to grow and expand. It is a considerable task for director and group that requires serious preparation and training. As in psychodrama the action of 'role reversal' where a player moves out of one role and into another role often provides the high learning experience. Role reversal is regarded as the engine of the method.

3   *The sharing*   In the third stage of the sociodrama people share what they have learned and how they learned it. This sharing allows ventilation of feelings and thoughts that did not get expressed during the enactment or those things that have been learned from other people during the session. We might also call this stage the cool-down period allowing participants to divest themselves of roles they have assumed during the action and, in so doing, help them return to normality.

Action methods by their very nature raise deep emotional feelings, disturbing thoughts and passionate experience.

In *News From Nowhere* William Morris has his hero travel home on the underground railway, stewing discontentedly over the meeting he had just taken part in. He thinks of the wonderful arguments he could have put forward, regrets the clever interventions and opportunities for expression missed. Most of us have experienced this kind of inner struggle and self-reflection. We set ourselves up for it each time we attend gatherings that will arouse our intellect and emotion. However, we don't usually have time to stew in William Morris's comfortable railway carriage. More likely, we climb into a motor car and join hundreds of others in the race homeward. This is dangerous. It does make sense to 'cool down'.

Action-method directors are using a method that resonates from the body and mind of the protagonist, the group and the director. Directors should be non-judgemental, empathic and objective, but I believe they must be involved. Their own experience and feelings are important to the session, but in the right place at the right time. That place and time is the sharing stage. Any other expression of the director's own material can be self-indulgent.

In developing the technique of 'sharing' Moreno introduced a unique democratisation. It allowed the group to see their director first and foremost as a human being like the rest of us. In doing so Moreno also protected the director by giving him or her the opportunity to share their own life experience in sharing time.

The difference between psychodrama and sociodrama is that psychodrama looks at the roots of personal problems while sociodrama looks at the soil in which our collective roots have been formed – or deformed. A good example of such deformation occurred recently when an English company director defended on television his company's sales of weapons to the dictator of Indonesia with these words: 'There are more people killed in Northern Ireland than in East Timor. The difference is that in East Timor they do it in blocks of two hundred and in Northern Ireland it is one or two a day.' This deforms by prompting an indifference to human suffering. No wonder some sociologists think society's sickness is not just critical but possibly terminal.

As a cancer survivor I know something about that. There is nothing like a life-threatening disease to concentrate the mind and make us greedy for life and love. Maybe the very gravity of our world's troubles will help propel us into the twenty-first century with new hope and determination. Maybe it also heralds a massive opportunity for sociodrama: an idea whose time has come.

The phrase 'pre-millennial-tension' was used in a *Times* newspaper article to describe the current stressful world situation. That night I 'nightmared' the following story: I saw my own birth in the 1920s and my life stretched out before me like a pathway through a landscape of suffering. Warriors were dying amid their broken swords and rules of warfare. They were replaced by aeroplanes dropping high explosive on women and children, now regarded since the bombing of Guernica as legitimate targets. Scientists worked frantically developing weapons solely to make large holes in people.

Then I saw atomic weapons making possible tens of millions of casualties. A big American general gave the chilling command 'Overkill anything that moves' (Sprague 1969). Around him lay piles of Vietnamese children. I saw young English friends sent to their deaths to protect 'our oil' under Arab soil. I saw tanker disasters polluting the sea bed and our shore line before the oil reached the refineries, let alone our motor cars. The cars stood in shining colours across the landscape; I could not see the grass any more. Thousands of working people went in and out of factories using their talents to build death-dealing machines. Indeed, our country's economy depended upon it. Men in pin-striped suits sold guns to the world's most repressive regimes. I was blinded by media people scrambling words and turning the English language on its head. All around me people's brains were being washed with jingoistic soap powders. Two of our pilots were shot down over Baghdad and were beaten up. We were outraged, we hid from ourselves the truth that those young men, well-fed, well-dressed and well-educated in their faster-than-sound machines, were not dropping teddy bears to poor children.

I awoke sweating and remembering that after one raid during the Gulf War, Western journalists reported wading ankle deep through human fat. It was the residue of more than 200 people, men, women, children and babes, crowded together in a shelter hit by a British laser-guided 'clean' bomb.

All this carnage has actually taken place during my life as technology has exploded. It has left most of us reeling with its complexities. We are technology addicts and slaves to machines. Encyclopaedic knowledge is now available to us all in our own living rooms at the touch of a button or the movement of a 'mouse'. And yet . . . and perhaps this was the message of my nightmare: our general failure to communicate authentically with one another, whether person to person or nation to nation, remains a major problem. Solving this problem could be described as a sociodramatic task.

Let me first deal with the failure to communicate adequately on a personal level. My nightmare was concerned with national and international problems but it is a mistake to see the big issues as more important than the personal issues. Personal is where it all begins. I learned a relevant message about this on return from Argentina after the Falklands/Malvinas War. In Buenos Aires I had been involved in sociodramas dealing with the conflict and saw it through our 'enemies'' eyes. I had learned of their suffering, their losses, their 'disappeared ones' and I had shared their anguish.

On my return to London I ran a session in which an old lady worked on the loss of her cat. I questioned my involvement: I had come from the horror of General Galtieri's regime and Margaret Thatcher's warmongering to the apparent triviality of a cat's death. What on earth was I doing? By the end of the session I had understood fully that the cat was the only thing of importance the old lady had in all the world. Suffering is not measured by size, but by its effect on the individual. In her session we encountered one another at a deep level of human understanding and were the better for it. Encounter of that kind is, in my opinion, sociodrama's mission and a bridge to changing the world.

This mission travels a parallel course to what I call 'green thinking' and to what I think Moreno meant by being cosmic men and women. There is a continuum from early societies that lived in harmony with nature, people like St Francis of Assisi, the 'green' activists of our own time and the visionaries of sanity who will take us into the new century.

Our primary task is not to save the rainforests or stop fox hunting, although we may support such campaigns. Nor is it to preserve the birds and their breeding grounds, although these might be ideal themes for sociodramas. Our aim is to save our humanity, which is essential at this stage of evolution if all our other efforts are to succeed.

All this constitutes the raw material of sociodrama. Similar conditions of suffering and abuse, I believe, led our national poet Percy Bysshe Shelley to remark, 'This, ladies and gentlemen, is a bad way to live.'

Perhaps the British people were expressing something similar when they gave such a landslide victory to Tony Blair and his New Labour Party in 1997. I don't think it was Tony's blue-suited spin doctors who won the day, but the utter revulsion of the great majority of our people from the sleaze, the arrogance and the sheer crookedness of those holding power for so long. Power corrupts, whoever holds it. The situation now needs to be broadened into mass democratic participation far beyond the walls of Parliament. Politics, social caring and support for those in need are much too important to be left to the politicians. They are 'people's business, and are the socio- part of sociodrama.

BUT WHY SOCIO-*DRAMA*?

Life itself is essentially dramatic. Actors, playwrights, sociodramatists, drama-therapists are the product of this drama. They hitched their wagon to a natural process; the drama came first. Let me give an example of how it works, not from a sociodrama session, but from a life situation.

I had been commissioned to paint a huge mural around a theatre auditorium in Torrington, North Devon. The theme was local creativity, the customs, festivals, fairs and regattas of the region. In North Devon every village has annual festivities and you cannot experience them in any depth without seeing the bones of English history poking through. The pagan and early Christian cultures, church politics, royalist and parliamentary battles are all there. The on-going struggle of life and death binds them all together and is perhaps most clearly seen in the Mummers Plays. In order to create the mural I felt the need to refresh my experience of the Mummers.

I had many drawings of Mummers but they were all at least 10 years old and I needed updating. My friend, Norman Saunders White, found that a Mummer presentation was to be performed in Dorset.

We arrived on a wet night at an isolated village hall. The place was not inviting, uncared for and damp. There was an atmosphere of middle-class stuffiness. I felt like going home. Small groups of woolly-jumpered people sat at plastic covered trestle tables in silence. An older man, looking like the local bank manager, stepped on to the stage and apologised for being no good at what he was about to do. Our hearts sank. We were given hymn sheets and asked to sing. There was no accompaniment and nobody wanted to sing. The problem was magnified considerably because the hymns were printed in small type on brightly patterned paper. My glasses were in the car. The singing was pathetic and I saw a handful of younger spirits easing themselves toward the door.

Suddenly there was a ripple of movement and the whisper went round, 'The Mummers are here!' A wind of change came to blow the stuffiness away. It was magical. A be-ribboned man led a hobby horse between the tables. It nibbled at men in check jackets and nudged twinsetted ladies. Tension had been introduced. Something was going to happen. We were being challenged!

The man in coloured ribbons announced: 'The horse is looking for the maiden who kicks all her bedclothes off when she dreams of her lover.' There were some meaningful glances and we all knew who it was going to be. A large-bosomed, glamorous young woman in the front row also knew. The horse advanced, retreated and finally lunged, teeth bared, toward the beauty. She screamed, we hooted and the hobby horse darted past her to embrace an old lady in the back row.

The beauty was delighted. She had been honoured without embarrassment. The old lady was charmed by the now most respectful horse.

Before the audience could become smug and self-satisfied, the horse himself announced gruffly that he was looking for the boy who stole sugar from his mother's table. People moved to the edge of their chairs, children tried to pretend that they were not really there at all. The exception was one small boy in the front row. His face was pinched and he wore wire-rimmed spectacles. The horse sniffed several children but we all knew it was going to be the lad with specs. We empathised with him, wanted to protect him and thought the horse was overdoing it. Unfair indeed! When the horse nabbed him, the little lad stood his ground. We saw the horse's astuteness. The lad was hero of the moment.

The entertainment and education continued. It was simple Punch and Judy stuff, but the atmosphere had totally changed. People had been given permission to interact. The drama had contacted individuals, connected them to others emotionally and produced the conditions for real encounter. People previously separated by propriety, by class and by personal shyness had become an involved and supportive group. That is what drama does.

WHY DOES SOCIODRAMA WORK?

It works through taking the dramatic course I have just described of *contact* leading to *connection* which builds a safe environment for the group to work. The 'safe place feeling', and it is worth repeating, is necessary if people are to trust the process. This applies to psychodrama also.

The tasks of the sociodrama director and group are to guide the educational process according to the theme of the session, to promote group enactment, and to encourage further social action beyond the walls of the session.

HOW DOES IT WORK?

I want to take examples from my own experience of sociodramas dealing with the AIDS problem. Each is from the early period when the subject provoked fear and panicky reaction based upon ignorance and prejudice.

The first example took place in Helsinki. I co-directed a session with my friend and student Martti Lindqvist. The day was advertised as an exploratory meeting using action methods. The audience attracted were therefore concerned people, mainly social workers, doctors and those working in health care. Martti had been the best selling writer in Finland for three years running and was a respected journalist. He had written an article in a leading Finnish newspaper which was arousing interest and comment on the question of AIDS.

As each participant came through the door they were handed a copy of Martti's article photocopied on to a large sheet of white paper. This provided plenty of room for note taking. Each person was welcomed and asked not to spend too much time greeting friends but to read the article and write down their reactions in the space provided. In this way an atmosphere of seriousness and urgency was established.

A circle of chairs was arranged with an open space in the middle. It was a sort of theatre in the round arrangement. There was no rush, but people were encouraged to complete their writing, put the papers into the centre and take a seat. As they sat the pile of papers grew and people began to talk to one another about their reactions. They were now asked to take a paper from the pile – not their own paper – and read out pertinent comments. A volunteer scribe was found and she recorded comments upon a large blackboard and began to categorise them. The audience joined in to arrange the comments in clusters – knowledge, personal experience, conjecture and prejudice. In this way the proceedings were focused. The circle was broken and a small dais was introduced and surmounted with a rather grand throne-like chair. With some humour, in sharp contrast to the proceedings so far, Martti was made King and introduced, to most people's surprise, as the author of the article. We had removed his name from the photocopies. He certainly knew more than most of us and held his own under question, attack and supportive back-up. At this point, as director, I introduced doubles, for Martti and doubles for questioners. This broadened the whole proceedings and almost everyone was involved. There were not enough chairs as latecomers arrived. Some people were standing and had been joined by others who wanted a better view. Right at the back stood a man slightly apart. We were creating an isolate.

Martti had left the small stage and the throne was removed. I spoke directly about what I saw happening, that we seemed to be pushing one group member away and remarked that he had not spoken and asked if he would he like to do so? There was a pause, a moment of tension throughout the room. He then burst forth in a torrent of abuse at AIDS sufferers and particularly at homosexuals. He concluded that they should all be transported to an isolated island off the coast of Finland and an atomic bomb dropped upon them. There was a stunned silence and then outraged response, but he did not leave the room. I asked what proportion of the people of Finland he thought his views represented and he became calmer and his voice less prejudiced. He said the majority of people he knew were terrified and his less outrageous views probably represented a large proportion of people – maybe even a majority. A discussion followed and this I believe was a mistake. As directors we should have developed the dramatic action. We should have given him supportive doubles which would have relieved his isolation. More importantly, it would have given a safe opportunity for us all to express the fears we were *afraid* to express and the prejudices we were *ashamed* to express.

In this way we could have evaluated the reality we were up against more fully and confronted our own inner weaknesses. We would also have kept contact with the man who expressed himself so outrageously but with some courage given the do-gooder liberal climate he must have been experiencing.

The blackboard was cleaned and the group began to formulate a future action list. It was written up by the scribe and small groups formed to carry the work forward in areas of their own interest or work involvement. The most successful of these continuing social actions was the creation of a similar sociodrama, live on Finnish national television conducted wonderfully by Martti Lindqvist.

Both the first session and the TV programme were advertised sociodramas attracting, in the first case, a specialist audience and in the second, a broader, national audience. Both were arranged sessions on a stated subject. The first session was successful and produced a high degree of encounter and further action. The participants were pleased with their collective achievement and remained talking together long after the session closed. Interestingly, it was the man who expressed such offensive views who asked me whether I had transport and a place to eat. It turned out that we were staying with his wife at his home, but he did not know that at the time. Their flat was next to a synagogue which neither of us had ever visited. That evening we and our partners attended the service and he and I sat together with the men while our wives were half-hidden in a corridor. So here we were, two men taking part in a cultural tradition new to us both, neither of us Jews, both of us with very different politics and social views on the AIDS problem but, hesitatingly, liking each other. The episode taught me that personal contact is an important factor in change-making. It is also a basic factor in the process of authentic encounter.

The second session took place in Australia. I was a group member on a summer sociodrama practicum. Warren Parry was the director. Spontaneity training was the subject. We were asked to choose a scene and people it. We built a public bar with a jovial landlord, a worried barmaid wife, a 20-year-old daughter (very attractive) and drinkers. Warren encouraged us to overplay the roles and we thoroughly enjoyed being stereotypical characters.

The director now encouraged us to deepen the roles, leave the scene if we desired and come back as the characters we felt emerging within us. The stereotypes disappeared and were replaced with everyday characters and as the action developed, a couple of *archetypes* were produced. This was particularly obvious in the case of the mother; her role changed from blowsy anxious (stereo-type) to concerned friend (typical). The final remarkable change in her was from *a* mother to *the* world mother (archetypal).

The session was going well, the daughter's boyfriend had arrived and invited her away for the weekend. Mother agreed, father was unsure. Warren now made an intervention. The father received information that the young man had AIDS. Our spontaneity was fully tested by this revelation and our education considerably enlarged by the enactment that then took place. The session was for training and education in a closed group.

The third session I would call real 'life drama'. It took place at Holwell during a week-long workshop with Zerka Moreno, Merlyn Pitzele, Marcia Karp and myself.

Halfway through the week a group member demanded that another member be asked to leave the workshop and the premises. It was a shock announcement taking most of us by complete surprise. The speaker said she was spokesperson for three others; it was a big group, and they had learned that the person they wanted removed had been nursing AIDS victims. Remember, this was in the early days of 'catching it from the lavatory seat' hysteria.

The group split down the middle, half asking a highly embarrassed member to leave, the other half supportive but unsure how to proceed.

Merlyn asked for a break to allow the group to consider its position and to come together in two hours for a sociodramatic investigation. Marcia, my partner, and I phoned our local GP's group practice for some information leaflets. One doctor agreed to come and give a brief lecture on medical knowledge and protective action. There followed a question and answer period. Merlyn then spoke on the question of prejudice and witch-hunting. He was a determined enemy of both. Wide discussion and enactment followed. The accused member spoke movingly of his experience nursing dying friends and of his commitment to their need. Doubles were introduced and hypothetical scenes of role play followed. If I remember rightly, Marcia, Merlyn, Zerka and I acted as 'rolling directors', co-directing as seemed appropriate.

The session was successful, calmed fears and tempers, educated us all and dealt directly with group dynamics. We also made a future action list for personal work after the group dispersed at the week's end. The session was a spontaneous reaction to a real-life drama. The man stayed, having taken an active part.

The fourth session was advertised as a workshop on AIDS and took place during a training week at Holwell Centre. The group built a scene representing 'society'. It was peopled with doctors, nurses and members of society with differing views. A doctor played an AIDS victim. He was attended, sympathised with, shunned, vilified and protected. He developed a low-profile role, saying little and being very ill. He was outstanding. The enactment was remarkably rich and expressive. I made, having learned from Warren, an intervention. I quietly passed a note to the doctor which said 'Die'! He lapsed into unconsciousness, turned in his bed and quietly died. The action and interaction continued and it was fully 11 minutes before his nurse (a nurse in real life also) noticed that he was dead. No one else had seen his passing. There was a shocked group catharsis. We had created a mirror of society at that time. There was endless talking, newspaper articles and television discussions and meanwhile, few people were aware that hundreds were actually dying of AIDS.

Some weeks later I conducted a similar session in Norway with social workers and heroin addicts with almost identical results. All six examples I have given were educationally successful and had high degrees of sociodramatic encounter.

By *encounter* I mean people met at an emotional level, responded spontaneously to the situation and opened themselves to an immediate creative exchange in the here-and-now. They confronted each other directly, face to face and on equal terms during an educational enactment.

MISSION-ENCOUNTER

This definition of encounter is I suggest an essential part, a first step in sociodrama's mission to bring about creative change. I want to give an example from real life of what happens when 'encounter' is missing.

Some years ago a student and fine colleague got himself into trouble. He was unclear about professional boundaries, was reported for misconduct and had to face disciplinary investigation. The circumstances were not straightforward and the investigators had an onerous task. The matter ended by the man dying before the case was concluded. The old adage 'let sleeping dogs lie' may be appropriate. However, I want to talk of a more recent event connected to this investigation. I found myself, by a series of coincidences, working in the area that my colleague had lived and where his widow still lived. I made enquiries, took the day off and called on her.

It was a grand summer day. We lunched together at a riverside pub and walked in the forest. She began to unburden her sadness at losing her man and expressed great anger at the organisation that had 'hounded' (her word) him. I saw her anguish but thought she was being somewhat unfair to his professional organisation, of which I was also a member. As kindly as possible, I said: 'Your anger is understandable, but you are being one-sided. Your man was at times his own worst enemy. He was uncooperative and didn't even answer the committee's letters.' There was a pause. She clamped her hands to her mouth, stared at me over her fingers and said 'Oh God! That was my fault. I was so worried about his health and the effect of all the stress, that I never showed him the letters. I put them on the fire before he came home in the evenings!'

What a tragedy! There was no encounter. It needed someone to knock upon his door or make a phone call and say 'Why don't you answer our letters?' He would have replied 'What letters?' and the outcome might have been different.

I am not suggesting that my friend's death would have been avoided, that no one can ever know. I am suggesting that his widow would not now be so embittered and I would not now be so disappointed at the lack of encounter, his and theirs.

As it is, the human factor of a woman attempting to protect her loved one is understandable. In turn the seemingly dismissive and uncooperative behaviour of the man promoted irritation and formality from the committee, most of which could have been avoided by applying the principles and the philosophy of Moreno's method. To put it in a nutshell, organisation yes, but never at the expense of encounter.

ENCOUNTER PLEASE

All over the world sociodrama is growing. As it does so disputes inevitably arise, personalities fall out with one another and splits occur. It is the unavoidable result of growth. I have experienced it in many countries, have urged my colleagues to use the problem-solving method of sociodrama with their own difficulties. I have to say that rarely have I heard of it being so used. Why? How come this remarkable action method so effective in our training, in our work with patients and clients, is so rarely used upon ourselves? This, ladies and gentlemen, to paraphrase Shelley, is a bad way to live, and it is time for a change.

Hardly a week goes by without evidence of sociodrama's international contribution to sanity and creative development. The written material on socio-drama is considerable. My colleague and former student Dr Ron Wiener has written *Using Sociodrama* (1995), a fine publication from which I have already quoted. It is printed by Leeds University at an affordable price. James M. Sacks and colleagues, in their superb *Bibliography of Psychodrama* (1995) includes over sixty books and articles on sociodrama. Today there has arrived on my desk 'Sociodrama as a Social Diagnostic Tool: Our Experience in Paraguay' (Carvalho and Otero 1994). So there is no shortage of written help. Dr Ron Wiener runs on-going postgraduate training in sociodrama with the backing of Leeds University and recognition from the British Psychodrama Association. I believe we are moving toward the time of international meetings of sociodramatists. The Stockholm Group Conference on Social Disintegration 97 and the presence of many sociodrama/psychodramatists on its advisory board, organising committee and among its workshop leaders was an indication of this progress.

As the creative work of sociodramatists spreads, the need for organisation, for high standards and ethical models will, as ever, arise. I have suggested that our method's mission is 'Encounter' as a bridge to change for the betterment of humanity.

The 103rd Archbishop of Canterbury, Dr George Carey, recently wrote of his role model, the first archbishop, St Augustine: 'Augustine knew that organisation matters. Indeed, one of the features of his work was to provide the basis from which our parish system has grown. He did not, however, let organisation get on top of mission' (Carey 1997).

JOYFUL ENCOUNTER

Lastly, I want to put in a word for what I will call a fourth aim in sociodramatic endeavour. It applies also to psychodrama. I have spoken of 'aims' in terms of education, therapy and further action beyond a particular session.

There is a fourth possibility that should not be underestimated. It is the practice of enjoyment. The action of doing something for the sheer fun of doing it is an important factor in both personal and social health.

Let me give a final example.

I was in Australia for my sixtieth birthday, New Year's Day 1987. I really wanted to be at my home in Holwell, England, with my family. I also wanted my new Australian friends to be there to meet my family. Tom Wilson, director at the Wasley Centre, arranged the answer. He organised a session in which we built my home kitchen and filled it with my daughters and sons, my partner Marcia and my Mum and Dad. My sister's family were there, my first wife, who died, and our brain-damaged children who also died. Friends, long since gone, met new Australian Wasley Centre people and we had a 'ball'. Psychodrama for Ken became sociodrama for us all as Australians introduced their own families. The aim was *fun*. The resulting birthday party was wonderful laughter-filled enjoyment.

Of course, next day, as we processed the 'encounters' within ourselves, we saw that education, therapy and future action were also present but they were never our aim. They are in such circumstances a bonus. I can heartily recommend such delight.

REFERENCES

Carey, Dr G. (1997) 'The Saint I Seek to Follow' *Weekend Telegraph* 29–30 March.

Carvalho, E. and Otero, H. (1994) 'Sociodrama as a Social Diagnostic Tool: Our Experience in Paraguay', *Journal of Group Psychotherapy*, Winter.

Einstein, A. (1970) A collection of photographs and quotations issued by the San Francisco Museum of Science.

Morris, W. (1970) *News from Nowhere*, London: Routledge and Kegan Paul.

Sacks, J. (1995) *Bibliography of Psychodrama*, Psychodrama Centre of New York.

Sprague, K. (1969) *Arrogance of Power*, folio of prints and quotations issued by the Molehill Press.

Wiener, R. (1995) *Using Sociodrama*, Department of Adult Education, University of Leeds.

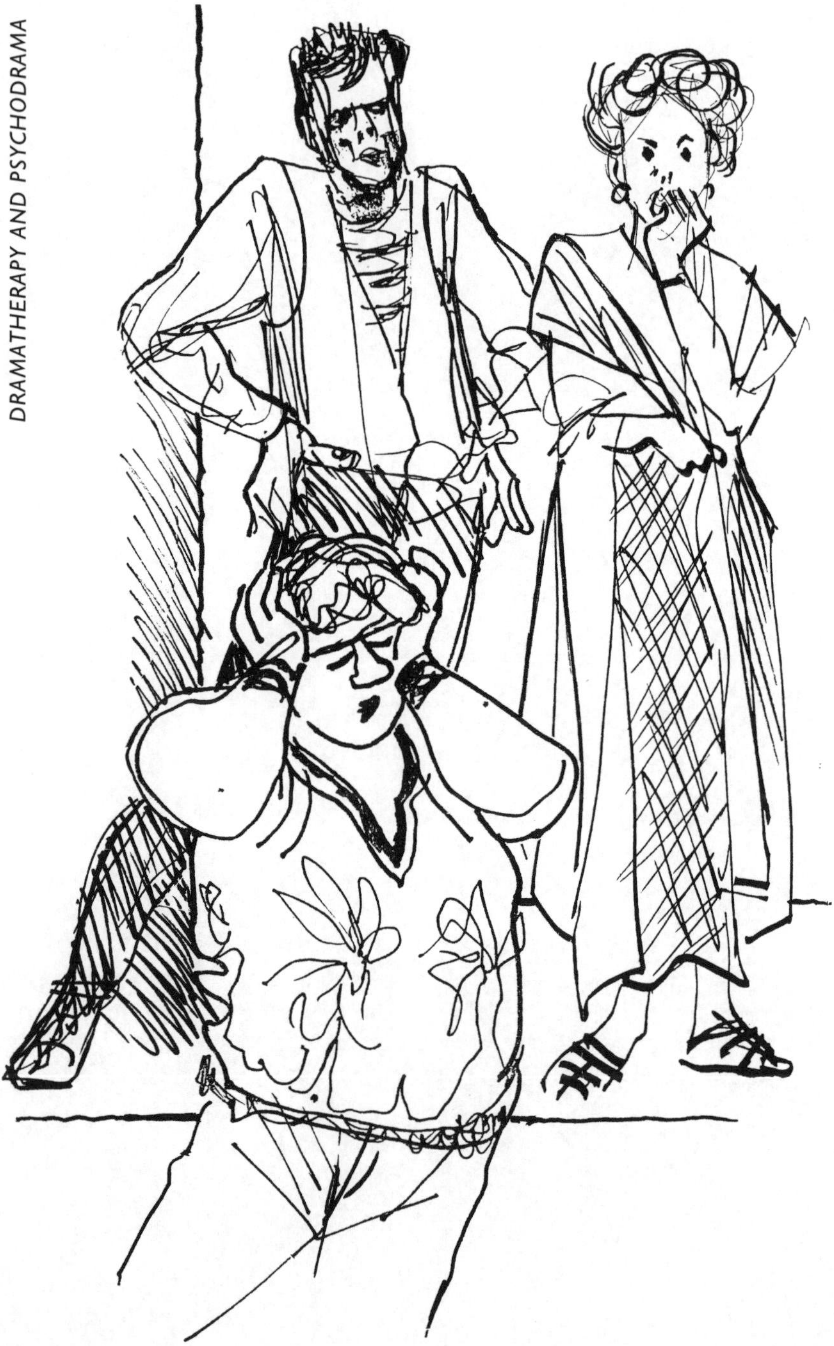

Chapter 15

The relationship between psychodrama and dramatherapy

Dorothy Langley

Which came first, the chicken or the egg? The foundations of and relationship between psychodrama and dramatherapy are as complex as the answer to the inscrutable question. The two forms of therapy are intertwined and their individual origins are obscure. That Moreno invented psychodrama is undeniable. We have his writings for reference, confirming that he based his work on dramatic expression. Dramatherapy is also based on the dramatic process, and the healing powers of that process were present long before Moreno saw their potential. He harnessed those elements to create a powerful method of therapy, but the healing in drama had been recognised for centuries (Jones 1996: 46). Both therapies use drama as the medium for change. In this chapter, some of those healing aspects – catharsis, metaphor, ritual, role and theatre – will be examined. Their use in both psychodrama and dramatherapy will be explored.

CATHARSIS

The term *catharsis* originally applied to physical purging, and was first used in the context of drama by Aristotle (1992: 11) who related it to the emotional reaction of the audience in Greek theatre. Watching the tragic plays, the audience became vicariously involved in the feelings and events portrayed by the actors, resulting in an emotional display of anger, tears and/or laughter. After the performance, they would experience a feeling of well-being – the catharsis, or flood of emotion having created a sense of cleansing of all the pain, grief and distress in their own lives.

Moreno used the notion of catharsis as part of his psychodramatic process. He says that, whereas Aristotle focused on the final stage of catharsis, he was himself interested in the initial phase (Moreno 1946/1980: 14). Unlike the audience in Greek theatre, in psychodrama it is the actor or protagonist's catharsis that is the centre of attention. The audience in psychodrama may well have their own emotional experience, and this becomes evident in the sharing. Kipper tells us that Moreno described two kinds of catharsis, *action catharsis* of the protagonist, and *catharsis of integration* which is experienced by identification (Kipper 1986: 15).

Popular belief at one time appeared to be that a great display of anger or grief was essential for an effective catharsis. This fallacy caused considerable prejudice in the 1950s and 1960s. The general feeling amongst the staff at the hospital where I then worked was that 'all this emotional stuff is dangerous'. Since then emotional discharge has become more acceptable, but is still sometimes associated with 'acting out' in a negative sense of uncontrolled behaviour.

Experience has taught me that an altered facial or bodily expression can indicate a cathartic reaction that is just as valuable to the protagonist as any noisy outburst may be. However it is expressed, catharsis is not an end in itself, but a means to an end. It cleanses the emotional channel, getting rid of debris in order to clarify the 'here-and-now' feelings and allow the protagonist to move forward. An example of this is when a protagonist is allowed to vent anger felt towards an overprotective mother. When the anger has been expressed, she can then confront the mother, lucidly state the wrong she feels she has incurred and gain a new perspective on the situation, an option which was previously inaccessible for her because of the welter of repressed feelings.

Catharsis is not always necessary in psychodrama, and the therapeutic effect is no less because of its lack. It was Zerka Moreno during a workshop at Holwell who finally settled the matter for me. 'The protagonist does not owe the director a catharsis' was how she expressed it. However, Kellerman in his study of therapeutic factors as perceived by participants, ranks emotional abreaction as more helpful than behavioural learning (Kellerman 1987: 408–419).

Whilst acknowledging that catharsis can happen, dramatherapy does not emphasise it. The total emotional experience is what is important. It is interesting to see that Jones (1996: 99) does not list catharsis in his chapter on core processes.

METAPHOR

We are all familiar with the symbolic use of an artefact to represent an emotion or object, for example the orb and sceptre that represents royal power. Metaphor takes a step further from reality, and uses one word to describe another 'as if it were' that object, e.g. he is a raging bull. To say 'he is like a raging bull' is a comparison that emphasises the person. To use the metaphorical statement 'he is' when everyone knows you are talking about a human and not an animal, removes the emphasis from the personality to the quality expressed. Jones states that it is the common quality of each that links the two (Jones 1996: 222). Jaynes suggests that metaphor is a means of understanding the unfamiliar by substituting something that is familiar (Jaynes 1990: 52). He says that we create images that do not really exist in order to explain the inexplicable, and gain a sense of understanding.

Grainger (1990: 101) says that dramatherapy uses *acted* metaphor to 'express the intangible quality of human experience'. The action has to be seen to be understood. Bolton (1979: 128) states that drama is metaphor – the two being synonymous. He describes the experience of 'it is happening to me now' as a function of dramatic play (1979: 54). Certainly the 'as if' factor is paramount in both dramatherapy and psychodrama. It is the interpretation of metaphor that differs with each.

In psychodrama the metaphor is explicit. The use of a stage area indicates the presence of an audience, and with it the application of what Aristotle termed a 'suspension of disbelief' (Jones 1996: 44), which surely must be necessary for metaphor. The audience knows that the events in the story being presented on stage are not really happening in the here and now, yet are able to believe in them as if they were. The performance is real and happening at the moment, so there is a reality to be experienced.

Psychodrama is focused on an individual in the group and his/her specific problems. The whole process is seen through the eyes of this protagonist. The group assists by becoming auxiliaries and taking on roles within his/her action. The issues may be shared by other group members, but this is not stated until the final stage of 'sharing'. Throughout, the internal thoughts, feelings and insights of the protagonist are being expressed, and are therefore apparent to the other group members.

Dramatherapy does not necessarily use a theatrical structure. When it does, the model is usually one of *using a script or known story* as the metaphor. Lahad (1994: 180) states that the use of remote story as a metaphor is the difference between psychodrama and dramatherapy. He maintains that the dramatherapist has a choice of identifying the figures and roles that are used, or working entirely through the metaphor. The psychodramatist, however does not have that choice because the identification is apparent.

If theatre is not being used in dramatherapy, the action may take an issue raised by an individual, but worked on at a personal level by *all group members*. Role play and improvisation may be the means employed to create the metaphor, but on an individual basis. Each group member selects or is allocated a role, and plays it as he/she wishes, usually without intervention from the therapist. In this model, it is not necessary to interpret the metaphor. Sometimes it is more therapeutic to allow the group to reflect for themselves without being aware of the metaphorical content of the action.

Shuttleworth (1985: 5) states that the dramatherapist should not interpret the metaphor or allow comment from other group members. In psychodrama that is inevitable. As auxiliaries share their experience of the role they played, they are commenting on the metaphor.

In my experience, I find it important to bring the group to an awareness of the metaphor and consideration of what it means to individuals unless either one or both of the following factors are present:

1   the group members do not have the intellectual ability to comprehend the significance of metaphor, or
2   the group members are unable to conceptualise the process of metaphor

through confusion about their inner and outer worlds (e.g. through psychosis, confusional states or dementia).

It is my opinion that the main therapeutic value lies in the reflective process. If reflection can be achieved on a conscious level, then the insight gained can be assimilated fairly quickly. If this is not possible, then it may happen at an unconscious level, possibly over a longer period of time. Unlike psychodrama, the interpretation is not obvious to other group members unless the individual chooses to verbalise it.

As psychodrama requires a certain level of cognitive understanding and participation, dramatherapy is a more appropriate process for people whose cognitive abilities are severely limited or impaired.

I believe the essential difference is that the metaphor of theatre can be seen and heard. The metaphor of dramatherapy is experienced emotionally and is not immediately obvious to the outside world.

ROLE

The term 'role' originated in the theatre, as the scroll that contained the words an actor was to say. Later, sociologists took the word into their vocabulary as a description of a person's place in society. Moreno, with his interest in both disciplines, developed a role theory to encompass both. He identified three main categories of role. The somatic roles such as that of breather, eater, sleeper, etc. are physical and the first to be experienced. Psychodramatric roles, such as that of hero, explorer, film star, etc. develop within the imagination and fantasy life. Social roles, such as occupational, family, friend, etc. are the last to be acknowledged. There can be conflict between the categories of role as in those of sleeper (somatic) and mother (social) when a child wakes in the night. Conflict can also occur within the same category, e.g. when the daughter role conflicts with that of wife. Moreno maintained that the roles exist first, the individual taking on the role as he/she perceives it enacted by another. For example, the behaviour of a mother determines her daughter's perception of the role and consequent behaviour in motherhood. Roles are learned and can be revised, relinquished, lost, modified and redefined (Blatner and Blatner 1988: 105). Moreno sees roles as interactive, most roles having counter-roles, existing only in relation to other roles, e.g. the pupil in relation to the counter role of teacher.

Moreno believed that the more roles a person possessed, the greater the quality of life. Psychodrama is based on his role theory and aims to extend current roles, create new ones. and reassess one's perception of both old and current roles. In order to do this, one has to look at how the roles were created, and find the place of origin or *status nascendi* as Moreno (1946/1980: 55) termed it.

Bennett (1977: 119) tells us that performance in a role requires:

- knowledge about the expectation of performance
- skills required to perform it
- motivation to embark upon it

Psychodrama allows the experience of all three. In the psychodramatic action, the protagonist presents a current problem, which he may not necessarily associate with role. The director will help him to identify a dysfunctional or redundant role, and through a series of enactments, return to the scene where the role was created. Past feelings are restimulated, and there may be a cathartic reaction. Exploration can then enable the protagonist either to reassess the present role or, if necessary, create a more effective one. The protagonist may then try out new roles, and learn how to operate within them successfully by a process of role training. Clayton describes a system of role training that incorporates other therapeutic models (Clayton 1994: 143). He distinguishes role training from psychodrama by the fact that role training focuses on, and builds up one single role, or one aspect of a role.

Although, in psychodrama, fantasy may be used as a warm-up to and within the action, ultimately the protagonist will work on the real roles he/she has in life.

Landy has created a dramatherapy role model in which the client works entirely through fantasy roles. He sees the healing potential in the stance a person takes in the 'me' and 'not me' paradox of the theatrical and/or therapeutic actor. He maintains that the client is capable of working therapeutically whilst he/she is between the state of 'being' and 'not being' – reality and imagination (Landy 1993: 46). Although clients work within an identified role, the process allows a flow in and out of role during the reflection which guides them to understanding. He describes a method of working in role, identifying sub-roles, and exploring qualities and alternatives of role.

Jennings says that it is the embodiment of a theatrical role or scene that engages all our senses and thoughts (Jennings 1992a: 5). She describes the use of the play *King Lear* in a series of 'therapeutic journeys'. Selecting appropriate themes, roles and scenarios from *King Lear*, she worked with a variety of groups who were able to identify with the characters and their situations. Her intent was not necessarily a therapeutic one. She describes the use of the play to assist staff to reach some understanding of their clients.

Discussing a role method of dramatherapy, Meldrum describes three types of roles: biological, occupational and social (Meldrum 1994: 77). She says that the dramatherapist working within this model will be aware of the range of his/her own roles as well as that of the clients. She advocates the use of drama games, story telling, role play and script to enable clients to find a more effective way of behaving in their current roles, and to extend their role repertoire.

It is important to consider the role of the therapist in both psychodrama and dramatherapy. The psychodramatist is given the title of director. He/she is the person who has an overview of the action, and guides the protagonist through the psychodrama. The director is on-stage or near the action throughout (Moreno 1946/1980: 256) and is responsible for the aesthetic as well as the therapeutic performance. Yablonski sees the director as the prime co-ordinator and catalyst of the session (Yablonski 1981: 111). There is an unlimited range of other roles available, but the director needs to consider his own ability, the needs of the protagonist and the context. He says that a director may choose to 'double' an auxiliary or protagonist, thus taking on a role within the psychodrama.

Kellerman has revised Moreno's description of the roles required of the psychodramatist (Kellerman 1992: 46). He suggests the director's role constitutes the interrelated roles of analyst, producer, therapist and group leader. These are reality roles and do not include the director taking on a theatrical role.

The role of the dramatherapist in a group is described by Landy (1992: 98) in terms of a basketball coach who aims to help the group to find a strategy that will lead to an individual knowledge of social roles. He stresses the importance of aesthetic distance in which human relationships are considered in terms of the degree of closeness or separation present. Over-distanced people are considered cold and self-protective, and under-distanced people are experienced as too excitable and vulnerable. The ideal is a balanced state. He considers the role of most therapists to be over-distanced, but finds that of the dramatherapist less rigid. Along with others, Landy does enter into theatrical roles within clients' role plays. He describes (1992: 101) the flexibility required by the participating dramatherapist. There is a need to find a balance of distance as well as selecting roles that create a boundary between therapist and client. Involvement in role play is more usual in one-to-one therapy, but may take place in a group setting.

The dramatherapist 'in role' is described in the same book by Read Johnson (1992: 112). He identifies three major roles: a psychological one as a transference figure, a dramatic one as a character in the drama and a social one as therapist. He goes on to list some modes of participation available to the dramatherapist. They are: witness or mirror, director, sidecoach, leader, guide and shaman. Individual dramatherapists will select roles and modes relevant to the needs, abilities, limitations and context of the group.

The dramatherapist has a wide choice of roles, structures and means of participation at his/her disposal. The psychodramatist, working within the theatre structure also has a variety of roles, but his/her means of intervention are limited by that structure. Chesner compares their therapeutic roles (1994: 130). Both, she says require empathy and need to be in tune with the whole group. While the psychodramatist is map-reader, guide and director, the dramatherapist proposes dramatic structures and invites exploration of the group. Her conclusion is that psychodrama requires a more directive approach, and dramatherapy allows a less directive one. She speaks in general terms, and notes that there are individual differences in both professions.

I have become aware of a 'client-centred' approach becoming more popular with psychodramatists. In my own practice, I have developed a method of following the protagonist rather than leading him/her. Nevertheless, as director,

I am on stage and obvious. Moreno (1946/1980: 256) recommends three positions for the director, but maintains that they should not be rigidly held. I am required, among other things, to be responsible for the setting of scenes, suggesting the use of auxiliaries, ensuring an aesthetic presentation, guiding the action and providing a secure environment for the whole group. As a dramatherapist, I am not central to the action, and although responsible for all of these tasks at some time, I operate from the sidelines. Ideally, the group decides its own structure, develops its own improvisation, and follows through ideas, working either individually or as a group. I provide only the security and maintain the boundaries required for it to function. In either role, I feel that the less I intervene, the more the group acts as its own therapist.

THEATRE

Moreno tells us that theatre has been associated with healing since Aristotle described its cathartic effect (Moreno 1946/1980: 14). Wesker describes how theatre can be therapeutic for the actor (Wesker 1993). So both sides of the proscenium arch hold potential for therapy. Jones traces the more recent development of therapeutic theatre and dramatherapy. He looks at the influence of theatrical techniques, and the relationship between dramatherapy, hospital theatre and educational drama (Jones 1996: 53–70).

Artaud provides a therapeutic link. He questions whether theatre was actually intended to define character and resolve conflicts and later suggests that its real aim is to 'express objectively secret truths' (Artaud 1977: 30, 51). If we consider these secret truths are the client's inner world, then herein lies the therapeutic value of theatre for both actor and audience – to view subjective matters objectively.

Moreno's discontent with the way in which theatre and play-writing was heading, prompted his Theatre of Spontaneity (Moreno 1946/1980: 39–40) and eventually psychodrama. One of the fundamental differences I see between dramatherapy and psychodrama is the fact that psychodrama has a theatrical structure. There is no set structure for dramatherapy, although the therapist may choose to use theatre.

Some dramatherapists practise a theatrical model of dramatherapy. Meldrum, in a workshop with dramatherapy students, identifies her theatrical model of dramatherapy with that of a theatre production. She usually uses script, and works in the same manner as with a theatre group. She maintains that it is the intent that distinguishes the two. The theatre group's intent in exploring text is to enhance performance, whilst the dramatherapy group explores text for personal insight leading to therapeutic change (Meldrum 1995: 1).

Anderson-Warren describes a dramatherapist and nurses working in collaboration with a community theatre company in the production of a melodrama and play with a hospital-based dramatherapy group. She argues that this is not theatre in therapy, but that the therapy lies within the application of theatrical structures (Anderson-Warren 1996: 133). Unlike Meldrum's theatre model, the work culminates in a production before an audience. The involvement of a professional theatre company adds another dimension to the range of therapeutic input. The company personnel act as ancillary therapists, contributing their skills in the 'application of theatrical structures'.

Mitchell describes a para-theatrical model of dramatherapy with an out-patient group (1992: 51). Basing his method on a process he learned through his study of Grotowski's work, he created a structure for spontaneous activity. The ritualistic element of drama is emphasised, and group members encouraged to contribute their own ideas to the sequence of events. This is very far from the 'proscenium arch' style of theatre, yet valid in its attempt to move away from a rigid script and stylised representation.

I have written elsewhere (Langley 1982: 24) of a nurse/dramatherapist in a psychiatric hospital who produced a scripted play which was so successful, it was followed by an improvised nativity play. The group revealed musical and performance skills that had been unused for a long time. As a result of this, they were stimulated to produce a concert consisting of sketches, songs and a stand-up comic (quite a feat for someone just emerging from a depression!). The group were long-stay patients in a psychiatric hospital, the productions were intended to entertain fellow patients, and increase their own confidence. It also re-stimulated lost roles, enhanced their self-esteem, and demonstrated an ability to relinquish the 'sick' role if only for a brief period.

There are many structures available to the dramatherapist, which, for dually trained therapists can include psychodrama. The psychodramatist, however has the structure devised by Moreno, and any other form would be considered a 'warm-up' to that method. Psychodrama is, however, flexible, since within that structure there is the possibility of using voice, dance, music, movement, art and even script.

The model a dramatherapist uses will be determined by several things:

- the needs, abilities and limitations of the client group
- his/her own interests and training
- the limitations of the space provided
- the philosophy and understanding of the organisation within which he/she works

The psychodramatist will consider the same criteria, but it is the definition of the pychodramatic training that ultimately determines the way in which he/she works.

RITUAL

Drama evolved from the early rituals of primitive man (Harwood 1984: 18). Life transitions, grief and sorrows, fears and celebrations were all expressed and communicated to and with others through ritual. Grainger sees ritual as a means of communication without words: 'Ritual says things we cannot say any other way.' That communication is mainly through its shape of beginning middle and end, and the emphasis is on experiencing rather than explaining (Grainger 1990: 123). This tripartite sequence is present in both dramatherapy and psychodrama. Chesner describes three stages that are similar in the process of both therapies. They both contain a warm-up, but in dramatherapy the aim is not to produce a protagonist, but to form an expressive and cohesive group. The action stage of psychodrama is paralleled by the development phase in dramatherapy, and the sharing is likened to the closure, which may be a group ritual or simply time for reflection (Chesner 1994: 125).

Scheff says that ritual is a way in which individuals and groups distance themselves from shared emotional distress. He names three central elements of ritual:

* recurring shared emotional distress
* a distancing device
* discharge

All can be identified as elements of psychodrama and exist within dramatherapy (Scheff 1979: 118). The potential for healing can be seen in both Grainger and Scheff's statements, and the relevance of ritual in therapy becomes clearer. Jaynes describes rituals as 'behavioural metaphors', linking communication and culturally accepted belief. When they are enacted without belief and feeling, the heart has gone from them (Jaynes 1990: 439). Belief in the ritual may seem obscure in therapy, but there must be faith in the medium of drama and the method in operation. A therapist and client who work without belief share a meaningless experience.

In time, ritual progressed from its early associations with hunting and communal distress to also be connected with magic, witch doctors and healing, in particular shamanism. The shaman is both priest and therapist, working through magic and ritual to attain healing for individuals and communities.

Landy points out that the shaman makes use of role-playing, chant, stylised movement, make-up, and costume in his healing rituals which often lead to catharsis (Landy 1986: 69). He suggests that psychodrama can be seen as a bridge between shamanism and psychotherapy and that Moreno's 'life and work embodied a confluence of magic, science and religion' (Landy 1986: 70). Jennings describes a shamanic model of dramatherapy in which the movement between two realities – dramatic and everyday – is facilitated by ritual (Jennings 1992b: 239). The roots of both psychodrama and dramatherapy may be seen in shamanic and ritual healing.

Ritual is acknowledged by psychodramatists less frequently than by drama-therapists, but it is nevertheless a component. Kellerman suggests that the entire process of psychodrama can be regarded as a ritual (1992: 135). He says that the most common use of ritual is to facilitate people to deal with unfinished business such as saying 'goodbye' to a dead parent. Most groups create their own rituals of entering and leaving the therapeutic space. These may not be specifically stated, but take place by unspoken mutual agreement. The dramatherapist may make this explicit and encourage other rituals that facilitate security. Kate Hudgins and Mary Frances Toscani use ritual within the 'therapeutic spiral' to create and maintain a safe place for working with people who have been abused, and Antony Williams, in Australia, also intentionally uses ritual. On the whole, the psychodramatist is less likely to emphasise rituals, accepting their silent acknowledgement by the members. The creation of a specific ritual within a psychodrama may enable the protagonist to move from one role to another. In both dramatherapy and psychodrama the intention is to facilitate change. The dramatherapist will select the appropriate mode of action for the group. The psychodramatist will select the dramatic mode most appropriate for the protagonist within the structure prescribed by Moreno. Both will be invoking ritual during the transitional period of psychic change.

IN CONCLUSION

I have considered catharsis, ritual, role and theatre as healing elements of drama, and shown how they are present in Psychodrama and Dramatherapy.

The main *differences* I see are:

Psychodrama	Dramatherapy
Has an essential theatrical structure	Can have a variety of structures
Selects one person to work for the group on his/her own issues	Is more likely to work with group issues either as a whole or individually
The metaphor is explicit	The metaphor is not necessarily explicit
The director is on-stage or in the wings	The dramatherapist may not be central to the action
Catharsis is seen as fundamental to most psychodramas	Catharsis is considered less important
Ritual is not necessarily invoked	Ritual is explicitly invoked and acknowledged

The main *similarities* are that both:

- use drama as the medium for change;

- emphasise the importance of role;
- can embrace the whole range of dramatic elements;
- distance the clients from their issues, enabling a clearer and less painful approach;
- work towards resolution of conflict through metaphor.

Both dramatherapy and psychodrama are powerful methods of treatment. The power lies in their dramatic roots and careful application with selected groups. In all events it is not the model but the motivation and co-operation of the client combined with the philosophy, training, understanding and skill of the therapist that makes for success.

REFERENCES

Anderson-Warren, M. (1996) 'Therapeautic Theatre', in S. Mitchell (ed.) *Dramatherapy Clinical Studies*, London: Jessica Kingsley.

Aristotle (1992) *Poetics*, trans. T. Buckley, New York: Prometheus Books.

Artaud, A. (1974) *The Theatre and its Double*, London: John Calder.

Bennett, D. (1977) 'Psychiatric Rehabilitation', in S. Mattingly (ed.) *Rehabilitation Today*, London: Update Books.

Blatner, A. and Blatner, A. (1988) *Foundations of Psychodrama*, New York: Springer.

Bolton, G. (1979) *Towards a Theory of Drama in Education*, London: Longman.

Chesner, A. (1994) 'Dramatherapy and Psychodrama Similarities and Differences', in S. Jennings, A. Cattanach, S. Mitchell, A. Chesner, and B. Meldrum (eds) *The Handbook of Dramatherapy*, London: Routledge.

Clayton, M. (1994) 'Role Theory and its Application in Clinical Practice', in P. Holmes, M. Karp and M. Watson (eds) *Psychodrama since Moreno*, London: Routledge.

Grainger, R. (1990) *Drama and Healing: The Roots of Drama Therapy*, London: Jessica Kingsley.

Harwood, R. (1984) *All the World's a Stage*, London: BBC/Secker and Warburg.

Jaynes, J. (1990) *The Origins of Consciousness in the Breakdown of the Bicameral Mind*, Boston: Houghton Mifflin.

Jennings, S. (ed.) (1992a) *Dramatherapy Theory and Practice 2*, London: Routledge.

Jennings, S. (1992b) 'The Nature and Scope of Dramatherapy Theatre of Healing', in M. Cox (ed.) *Shakespeare Comes to Broadmoor*, London: Jessica Kingsley.

Jones, P. (1996) *Drama as Therapy, Theatre as Living*. London: Routledge.

Kellerman, P.F. (1987) 'Psychodrama Participants' Perception of Therapeutic Factors', *Small Group Behaviour* Vol. 18, No. 3: 408–419.

Kellerman, P.F. (1992) *Focus on Psychodrama*, London: Jessica Kingsley.

Kipper, D.A. (1986) *Psychotherapy through Clinical Role Playing*, New York: Brunner/Mazel.

Lahad, M. (1994) in S. Jennings, A. Kattanach, S. Mitchell, A. Chesner and B. Meldrum (eds) *The Handbook of Dramatherapy*, London: Routledge.

Landy, R. (1986) *Drama Therapy*, Springfield, IL: Charles C. Thomas.

Landy, R. (1992) 'One-on-One: The Role of the Dramatherapist Working with

Individuals', in S. Jennings (ed.) *Dramatherapy Theory and Practice 2*, London: Routledge.

Landy, R. (1993) *Persona and Performance*, London: Jessica Kingsley.

Langley, D.M. (1982) 'Theatre and Therapy', paper presented at an Art Therapy and Dramatherapy conference, Hertfordshire College of Art and Design, 22–23 April.

Meldrum, B. (1994) 'A Role Model of Dramatherapy and its Application with Individuals and Groups', in S. Jennings, A. Kattanach, S. Mitchell, A. Chesner and B. Meldrum (eds) *The Handbook of Dramatherapy*, London: Routledge.

Meldrum, B. (1995) 'Theatre Model of Dramatherapy', handout for South Devon College students.

Mitchell, S. (1992) in S. Jennings (ed.) *Dramatherapy Theory and Practice 2*, London: Routledge.

Mitchell, S. (1994) 'Therapeutic Theatre', in S. Jennings, A. Kattanach, S. Mitchell, A. Chesner and B. Meldrum (eds) *The Handbook of Dramatherapy*, London: Routledge.

Moreno, J.L. (1980) *Psychodrama, First Volume*, New York: Beacon House.

Read Johnson, D. (1992) 'The Dramatherapist's Role', in S. Jennings (ed.) *Dramatherapy Theory and Practice 2*, London: Routledge.

Shuttleworth, R. (1985) 'Metaphor in Therapy', *Dramatherapy: Journal of the British Association for Dramatherapists*, Vol. 8, No. 2: 8–18.

Wesker, A. (1993) 'Master Class', *The Sunday Times* 11 July.

Yablonski, L. (1981) *Psychodrama – Resolving Emotional Problems through Role-Playing*, Gardner Press.

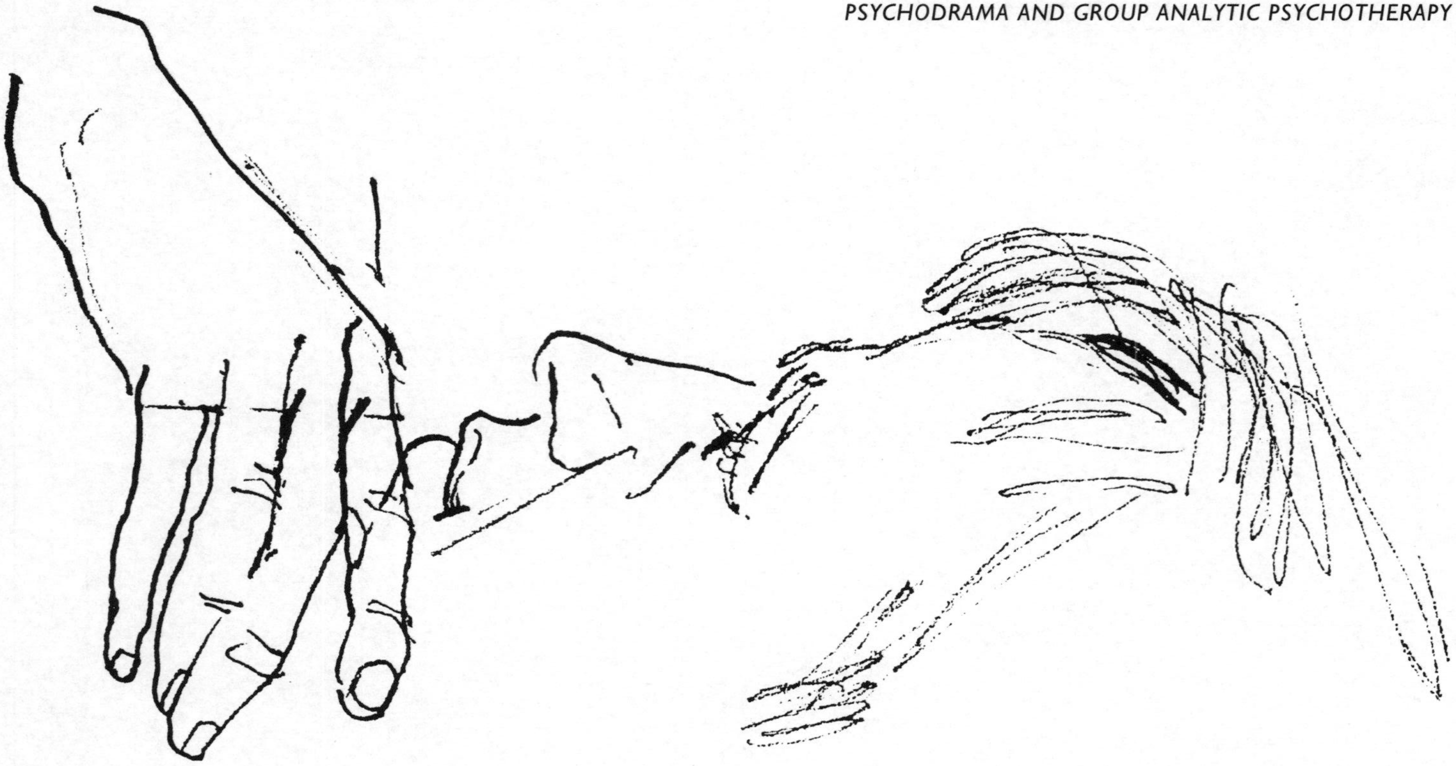

Chapter 16

Psychodrama and group-analytic psychotherapy

Kate Bradshaw Tauvon

INTRODUCTION

In this chapter I aim to give you an introduction to the principles and practice of group-analytic psychotherapy and in that way present a way of thinking which can enrich psychodrama practice. An appreciation of group-analytic principles can provide an instrument which helps a psychodrama director:

- to understand what is going on under the surface communication in a group;
- to lessen the director's anxiety around silences in the group;
- to demystify certain aspects of a group's behaviour;
- to understand transferential and countertransferential issues, related both to the leader and to other group members;
- to anticipate that each group member will project on to the group, experiences of earlier groups in their lives, in particular their family of origin;
- to understand the process in a group over time; that is the steps and crises in the developmental stages of a group's life.

These developmental stages involve the initial anxiety and ambivalence around joining a group; the 'honeymoon period'; a critical period where a person loses their old defences and often feels worse although she may function better in life outside the group; and the period of separation. Agazarian and Peters describe them rather differently: '(1) dependence: flight; (2) counterdependence: fight; (3) power: authority issue; (4) overpersonal enchantment; (5) counterpersonal disenchantment; (6) interdependence: work' (Agazarian and Peters 1981/1989: 132).

I discovered in 1974, as an Occupational Therapist at the Maudsley Hospital, that those who had an ego-structure and life-situation which tolerated group membership progressed more quickly in group therapy than when seen individually. The methods of group therapy which inspired me to learn more about them were psychodrama and group-analytic psychotherapy. I first studied and worked with psychodrama and then twenty years later trained as a group-analytic psychotherapist. I had trouble maintaining both methods' purity but learned whilst both approaches are of great value and the theory of both can enrich the work of the other, that when actually running a group, one *method* only should be used at a time. Integrating the different theories is difficult if the specific advantages and power of each approach are not to be watered down.

A number of group therapists are today trained in both psychodrama and group analysis but members of a psychodrama group can be thrown into confusion if the leader, who is trained in both methods, does not hold to a specific therapeutic culture in the group. Even if the group leader can themselves mutate between the roles of psychodrama director and group-analytic conductor it can be anxiety provoking, confusing and even anti-therapeutic for group members if they do so, since the roles invite different responses.

Having an awareness of how and against what social and political background both theories evolved can help us to take to us the richness of both theories whilst placing them in context.

THE EVOLUTION OF PSYCHODRAMA AND GROUP ANALYTIC PSYCHOTHERAPY

Psychodrama

As Peter Haworth has described in his chapter on the history of psychodrama, Moreno's first contribution to group work was to develop sociometry, the mapping of social networks. By 1931 he had integrated sociometry, group psychotherapy and psychodrama so that they became different aspects of the same three-dimensional method. In 1932, Moreno presented his results from his research in Sing Sing prison to the American Psychiatric Association; an event which is recognised as the historic moment at which the term *group psychotherapy* was first used.

Group analysis

Trigant Burrow, a psychoanalyst, had in the mid 1920s written a couple of papers in which the term 'group analysis' had been used, but it was Wilfred Bion, a hero of the First World War, who grew up in colonial India, who lay the foundation stones for the group-analytic movement. Based on his research started in 1942 at Northfield Hospital, with men who were military casualties of the Second World War, he developed a scientific approach to group therapy. In his experiments he began from a similar principle to that of Moreno, namely to observe the pattern of behaviour of the groups of men. He was to define the qualities which contribute to a 'good group spirit' (Bion 1961/1991: 25–26) which are summarised below:

- A creative common purpose, whether offensive or defensive.
- Common recognition by the group members of the 'boundaries' of the group and their relationship to those of larger units or groups.

- A flexible 'group character' which involves the capacity to absorb new members, and to lose members without fear of losing group individuality.
- Freedom from rigid exclusive sub-grouping; each member is valued for his contribution to the group and has free movement within the group; the group must have the capacity to face discontent within the group and must have the means to cope with it; the minimum size of the group is three.

Siegmund Heinrich (S.H.) Foulkes, known to his colleagues as Michael Foulkes, was a German Jewish psychoanalyst trained in Vienna in the 1920s, who moved to England in 1933. He was to follow Bion at Northfield Hospital and there made use of the method of psychodrama in the early part of his career. 'Moreno [had] established links with the Tavistock Clinic and was to cooperate closely on the international scene with Foulkes who had visited him at the New York Institute in the 1940s' (Marineau 1989: 147). It is unclear in Foulkes's books and essays why he gave up the use of the psychodramatic method but in 1940 he held his first group, in which he invited his patients 'to carry out as far as possible "free-associations" in a free-flowing dialogue' (de Maré 1983: 222) and thereby was to be seen as the founder of the group-analytic method. It seems, from what Foulkes has written on the subject of psychodrama, that his training in this method was simply too limited to be able to use it to best advantage and he was not especially versed in Moreno's metapsychology. This view has been confirmed by Zerka Moreno and Anne Schützenberger. Foulkes considered Moreno's theoretical concepts to be significant in the field of group psychotherapy and in accord with many viewpoints expressed by himself (Foulkes and Anthony 1957/1965/1973: 242). He has described in his book *Introduction to Group Analytic Psychotherapy* (Foulkes 1948/1991: 54 and 115) two successful applications of what he called 'Enactive Therapy' which resembled both psychodrama and sociodrama. Moreno's definition of group psychotherapy, 'one person the therapeutic agent of the other, one group the therapeutic agent of the other' is a dictum which applies to the world view of both men.

Moreno's dream when he started Beacon (New York) in 1936 was of a World Centre for Psychodrama, a world organisation which would promote the development of creativity and spontaneity in addressing conflict resolution and the making of political and life decisions. Foulkes also aimed to bring about social change through maximising the capacity of individual members of society to participate fully.

> The concrete realisation of the part which social conditions play in their troublesome problems, the social front of inner conflicts so to speak, gets people thinking in a critical way and makes them experience the part they themselves are playing, both actively and passively as objects as well as instruments of these conditions – an altogether desirable contribution to their education as responsible citizens in participating in a free and democratic community.
>
> (Foulkes and Lewis 1942 quoted in de Maré 1983: 222)

The development of the concept of group psychotherapy led to the foundation, in 1957, of the International Council of Group Psychotherapy, of which Moreno was the first president, with Michael Foulkes and Serge Lebovici as vice-presidents. This organisation was to grow and continues to thrive today known as the International Association of Group Psychotherapy (IAGP) (see Marineau 1989: 150 and 167).

Malcolm Pines, a leading group analyst in Great Britain and internationally, is well versed in the theory and practice of psychodrama and states:

> The structure of the group, that is the patterns of the relationships that are relatively stable and continuous, can be altered either by bringing about planned and deliberate changes in these patterns, as for instance by Moreno's use of the sociogram to clarify to the participants the nature of their relationships, or by the group-analytic method of the gradual evolution of awareness by the members of the group themselves of the ongoing patterns of relationships.
>
> (Pines 1983: 273)

The following general outline gives the basic frames of the two methods. However there are vast variations in the style of different therapists of both schools.

The basic frame of a group analytic psychotherapy group

The basic frame of an on-going psychodrama group

Time

One, to one and a half hours, usually once a week with holiday breaks announced by the conductor.

The conductor arrives precisely at the agreed time of the start of the group and leaves precisely at the agreed time of ending, regardless of what is occurring in the group. Group members assemble in the group room at the agreed time since, in line with group-analytic thinking, they should not meet other than within the therapeutic frame.

The group does not have a pause. Time boundaries are strictly observed.

Time

Often two and a half, to three hours, once a week during term time with holiday breaks announced beforehand.

The group, sometimes joined by the leaders, may meet up to half an hour or so before the arranged time for the group to start, to drink coffee and talk informally and then go to the group room at the agreed time. This is in line with Morenian philosophy, seen as conducive to supporting the social development of the group, in the spirit of encounter and equality.

The group may have a short pause at a suitable point. An extension of the ending time may be negotiated with the group if extra time is deemed necessary to appropriately complete the action and sharing phases. Occasionally a whole day's workshop or a residential week-end is arranged in conjunction with weekly groups.

Advance warning of leaving a slow-open group is usually at least 4–6 weeks.

Advance warning of leaving a slow-open group at the end of a term may be given at the beginning of a term.

Place and equipment

The room is as neutral as possible offering quiet and simple comfort, available for the group to meet on all occasions. Chairs, preferably of the same sort, are placed in a circle so that all the participants can see each other.

Place and equipment

Psychodrama theatres seldom have a stage as Moreno had but some do. The room, preferably available each week, frequently has a varied range of easily moveable chairs; mattresses; coloured pastels, paints or pens and drawing blocks; batakas (soft firm batons); coloured materials; coloured lighting and/or lighting with dimmer switch; some soft toys and a flip chart and white-board. Residential week-ends may be held in another location.

Membership

Usually 6–8 members. Members, who are selected on the basis that they do not know each other beforehand, are requested not to have contact outside the therapy room. Should they do so, they are requested to feed back to the group the relevant facts. The group is most often led by a single conductor who is trained in the method. The group selection is made by the conductor on the basis of 3 or 4 individual interviews and the composition is arrived at on the basis of the conductor's clinical judgement.

Membership

Usually 8–14 group members, related to the therapist's competence and preference, client group and room-size. A group of this size is a helpful resource, offering choice when it comes to selection of auxiliaries, leaving several group members to witness the drama. A group with two co-therapists has more flexibility. Group members are usually selected in that case by both therapists on the basis of one interview.

Since the psychodrama method has been thoroughly described throughout this book I will describe the group-analytic method in more detail.

THE GROUP ANALYTIC METHOD

According to Foulkes (Foulkes 1948/1991: 70) before the group starts the conductor is aware of group members' hopes and fears concerning 'cure'. Their coping mechanisms are seen as being the best defence they have been able to build up against their psychological conflicts, which they have been unable to resolve. If this is so, why should anyone else be able to understand them? There exists some sort of tacit hope that the conductor will understand that the situation is impossible to change, since change would involve intolerable pain. In these circumstances explanations, pity, advice, medicine or encouragement are all seen to be of very little help in disentangling the group members' problems and will more likely provide the basis for excuses which will prevent conflict resolution.

> If he is, however, brought into a situation, which he himself is continuously helping to create, to shape, he is forced to come out into the open with his own reactions, and their contradictions. He meets himself in the situation, projects his own personality and phantasies into it, and that he cannot escape, nor can he help facing the others and their problems, in whom he sees himself as a mirror.
>
> (Foulkes 1948/1991: 70)

For these reasons, on starting a group, the conductor offers the minimum of instructions to the group members, who are invited to engage in a free-floating discussion, sharing whatever comes into their minds. It is group therapy's counterpart of the free association of psychoanalysis but differs from it. I will say more about what occurs in such a group later in this chapter when describing the leader's role in a group-analytic setting.

Basic tenets of group-analytic psychotherapy

Group-as-a-whole

In the concept of the group-as-a-whole, the group is considered an entity. Foulkes describes this (Foulkes 1964/1984: 70) as an interpersonal, transpersonal and suprapersonal network or matrix. He uses the term 'matrix' here in a different sense than that used by Moreno. The group-as-a-whole can be seen as one 'being', an organism which is different from and greater than the sum of its parts. The group-as-a-whole expresses the communication of its various parts through its different voices, that is the voices of its individual members. This is rather like one person having a range of complementary or contradictory thoughts, and feelings. It allows a therapist to think of the group in its entirety, to wonder 'What is the group doing now?' or 'What is the group telling me?'

Transference

Transference (in contrast to the psychodramatic concept of tele) has been discussed in detail elsewhere in this book (see chapter on principles of psychodrama and for further reading Holmes 1992).

> It is the experience of feelings, drives, attitudes, fantasies and defences toward a person in the present which do not benefit that person but are a repetition of reactions originating in regard to significant persons of early childhood, unconsciously displaced onto figures in the present.
>
> (Greenson 1967: 171)

Group members will project on to the leader and other group members, experiences of earlier groups in their lives, in particular their family group, and much of the work of the group is to make conscious this repetition.

Boundaries and containment

The boundary of the group is defined by time, space and persons. Much of the work of an analytic group focuses on events that occur on the edge of a boundary in relation to the group's process – what is said and not said and why? Why does someone come late? Why was someone obliged to talk about something that happened in the group with someone who isn't a group member?

Abstinence

The needs of the client should not be immediately satisfied. The conductor should contain his wish to be 'helpful' and the group member be given the space to deal with his own conflicts with the support of the group. There should be no physical contact between the conductor and group members or between group members.

Work phases and basic assumption phases

Groups obstruct the fulfilment of their own stated aims sometimes by falling into one of three defence patterns. This is a dynamic which occurs in all groups, which I take up in more detail later in this chapter, as it is important for psychodramatists to consider.

Interventions

These may take the form of questions, observations or interpretations but due to the principle of abstinence, rarely answering questions or entering discussion. Humour is usually seen as defensive and therefore to be questioned.

THE PSYCHODRAMATIC METHOD

On-going psychodrama therapy groups, as all psychodrama groups, begin with some kind of warm-up which may take the form of free discussion. A psychodrama warm-up phase may resemble a group-analytic psychotherapy group but the director's therapeutic style is less distanced and interpretations as interventions are not used. The director shares relevant personal information supporting tele and encounter rather than encouraging transference but may pay attention to transferential issues which are usually later worked with on the stage using the method of psychodrama. Transference themes may be focused on as warm-ups to the forthcoming action.

Social contact between group members outside of group time is not dis-couraged and may be positively advocated. Group members may meet or talk on the phone between groups, some may go out to eat together after the group. They are asked to relay relevant information from such contact back to the group as secrets held outside the group drain the energy from it. The individual integrity of someone not wanting to take part is respected. Before saying more about the leadership of a psychodrama group I will present some thoughts about leadership of psychotherapy groups generally.

LEADERSHIP OF THERAPEUTIC GROUPS

A leader may be neutral, transparent, even charismatic but is always a role model for group members. The role of leader assumes different forms depending on the method being used and the phase of a group's development. It is relatively easy for a leader to get a group to follow them and may on that basis be judged effective (see Agazarian and Peters 1981/1989: 109) but since an aim of group psychotherapy is to re-activate the capacity of group members to self-lead, the successful leader will not only have the capacity to get a group to follow them but will also lead them in a direction towards achieving this goal. 'A group structure in which one member is god, either established or discredited, has a very limited usefulness' (Bion 1961/1991: 56).

Yvonne Agazarian defines the word 'leader' (Agazarian and Peters 1981/1989: 108) as being 'a title publicly designated within a system such as a group, carrying with it the *potential* for power, authority, responsibility, and accountability'. A group therapist is the leader of a group but adequacy in the role is dependent upon whether the group therapist has any power over, authority in, responsibility to and accountability for the group. This definition is just as relevant when describing the role of a psychodrama director. Marcia Karp has in the first chapter of this book listed twenty-three of the key tasks of a psychodrama director. If one translates 'protagonist' in psychodrama language to mean 'voice of the group' or 'person speaking' in group-analytic language and likewise 'stage' to mean 'group space', many of these key tasks can be seen to be just as valid within a group-analytic frame. Where the leadership differs is largely in the psychodrama director's role of theatre producer which brings with it additional responsibilities.

Stock Whitaker (1985/1989: 378) discusses the responsibilities of a group leader and distinguishes between responsibility *to* a group and its members; responsibility *in* a group, whilst actually leading and responsibility *for* a group.

A leader's responsibility to *a group*
- The leader has an obligation or duty to do everything he can, to the best of his ability to work towards his overall purpose of utilising the group for the benefits of the members.

A leader's responsibility in *a group*
- to be clear about instrumental purposes
- to be attentive to events as they unfold
- to be ready to anticipate and note the consequences of his/her own behaviour
- to regulate his/her own behaviour according to how it bears on instrumental purposes

What the leader is responsible for
This is less clear. One can consider for example if the leader is responsible
- for outcome
- for whether or not persons actually gain from a group experience
- for what actually happens in sessions

On reflection one can say that the leader is in part responsible for all of these aspects but that she actually does not have total influence over the situation and therefore cannot be singly responsible for them. The group leader does not have the power to determine the outcome but does have a powerful influence on the outcome. She has the power to render a positive outcome impossible for some members and can spoil a group – cause a group to be unhelpful or even to be damaging for some members – by the way she behaves. The leader's influence is, however, only one of a number of factors which determine outcome and not necessarily the most important one. The leader's behaviour does have consequences for the group.

> The conductor of a group may feel guilty if things do not go well. Some-
> times this is appropriate, if he has made avoidable errors. Sometimes it is
> inappropriate, if unwished-for outcomes have occurred which are outside his

control. What is appropriate to feel responsible for (and guilty about), one can argue, depends a great deal on power, limitations on power, and how one uses power.

(Stock Whitaker 1985/1989: 379)

Leadership within a group-analytic setting

The therapist who has composed a group owes them an explanation but in a group-analytic setting it is deemed to have no meaning to present what was expressed earlier in this chapter concerning the hopes and fears group members are assumed to bear with them to a group. The therapist's aims are together with the group members to bring about a creative, permissive atmosphere, within which such a discussion as Foulkes described can occur between group members.

It is not so important what the therapist says as what he does, which is to support the group in doing its work, only intervening when they lose their way or when unconscious processes are surfacing which can be helped towards consciousness by an appropriate question, observation or interpretation. Bion stated that 'unless a group actively disavows its leader it is, in fact, following him.' (Bion 1961/1991: 58).

Leadership within a psychodrama setting

The chapter on the psychodrama director in this book covers this topic thoroughly. In a psychodrama group the leader's role should clearly be that of psychodrama director. I would add though, that an appreciation of group-analytic theory provides a frame of reference for group behaviour which occurs in all groups, which in turn enables a psychodrama director to predict and relax in the face of what can otherwise be incomprehensible signals. In group-analytic groups I am enormously helped by an appreciation of psychodrama role theory; a capacity to think in images; and a developed capacity both to double and to mentally reverse roles.

WORK GROUPS AND BASIC ASSUMPTION GROUPS

Bion's observation of groups

Consider that a group has a setting, a purpose and forces which cause it to move towards and away from fulfilling its purpose. Bion observed that at times a group behaves in ways which are totally at odds with its stated purpose, 'as if' it is exposed to some invisible threat. *This applies to all groups.* He observed that there are always two active tendencies within any group: what he called the *work group* and the *basic assumption group* (Bion 1961/1991: 59).

Work group

A work group engages in behaviour towards fulfilling the stated aims of its leader and group members. It is engaged in conscious here-and-now communication – what in psychodrama is described as creative, spontaneous encounter in which people work co-operatively together with a task. The interactions are governed by tele rather than transference. The function of a work group is essentially the translation of thoughts and feelings into behaviour which is adapted to agreed reality, and therefore a main task of the leader is to raise a group's awareness when basic assumptions are reigning. 'The group has to struggle towards the work task in the teeth of being dragged back into primitive group behaviour dominated by the basic assumptions' (Hinshelwood 1987/1990: 260). When a group is functioning well in work mode it is working towards what Stock Whitaker and Lieberman have called an 'enabling solution' to its focal problem (Stock Whitaker 1985/1989: 52). This is in contrast to what is termed a 'restrictive solution' where a group deals with its fear at the expense of its wish. Restrictive solutions, often the easiest and evasive, limit the boundaries of a group and impede useful investigation and experiences. When a group finds an 'enabling solution' it contains and confronts its fear, allowing free expression and a greater potential for development.

Basic assumption group

Bion described three kinds of basic assumption activity: 'dependency', 'pairing' and 'fight-flight', which he interpreted as attempts to defend against primitive anxieties aroused by group membership (Bion 1961/1991: 146–153). When the anxiety level in a group rises beyond the capacity of its members to deal with it on a conscious level, it can easily fall into chaos.

> When this happens a basic assumption group results. Contact with reality is lost and the group can be considered to be functioning using psychotic mechanisms. Bion observed that in groups without clear tasks, or in a group under stress, there was a tendency for them to lose contact with external reality. Then the members begin to function *as if* they were but a part of a single organism, 'the group', a psychotic regression occuring both in individuals and in the group as a whole. . . . Individuals within the group become like inner objects within a single psyche in which splitting and projective identification are the main defence mechanisms.
>
> (Holmes 1992: 179)

A group in a basic assumption phase has unrecognised goals, which distract from its main functions and express transferential rather than reality-based communication. Group members' behaviour leads in the direction of one of the three basic assumptions, which hampers the group's work.

The three implicit basic assumption goals are:

1. Dependency. The group behaves as if the members are helpless and know nothing, the leader is omnipotent, and the source of group survival.
2. Pairing. The group behaves as if the group will give 'birth to' a saviour who will solve the group's problem. Two people in the group emerge to play reciprocal roles in this Messianic solution as the focus of the group's attention, support, affection, hope and fantasy.
3. Fight–Flight. The group behaves as if the group survival is dependent upon immediate action, either fight or flight. This pressure towards impulsive action results in the group behaving as if it were a mindless mass.

(Agazarian and Peters 1981/1989: 50)

The leader is by definition inevitably drawn into this process and also loses touch with external reality becoming what Bion called the 'creature of the group' and losing sight of the agreed task. This process does not have to do with the leader or the individual group members *being* psychotic in a clinical sense, it is the group-as-a-whole which behaves in this way. The 'spell' is broken on leaving the group when rationality returns. However, if a group does not or cannot deal with its basic assumption tendencies its work will be impeded and such a group will in time disintegrate. It is one of the group leader's tasks to steer it back on course. Since the root of the problem is that the group is being driven by anxiety, the leader needs to reflect on what it is that is 'too hot to handle' and how the group can be brought back to its task.

Basic assumption and work phases in psychodrama

Psychodrama is an action method which might mean, since things are happening all the time, that these things are automatically constructive. It can be worthwhile, though, to reflect on Bion's basic assumption phases in relation to a psychodrama group. How much of what happens can be seen in the light of dependency, pairing or fight-flight behaviour? When is the group actually working? It is much less obvious in a psychodrama group when such behaviour is occurring as it can be masked by other activity. It can occur at any point in the life of a psychodrama group and can be seen in the warm-up phase, the protagonist selection, the action phase or in the sharing. I will describe some examples to illustrate times when groups seem to have fallen into basic assumption phase.

Dependency

The group behaves as if the members are helpless and know nothing, the leader is omnipotent, and the source of group survival.

At the point of protagonist selection two other potential protagonists have clearly stated what they would like to work on, both feel they could work now or could work in a future session.

Anne   I don't know if I can remain in the group. I have felt lousy all week. Things get warmed up in me each session and then I go home and can't function. I got blind drunk the other day. It can't go on like this. I have to be able to hold my life together but I don't know what to work on.

Anne, who has been a member of this group for two years, is selected by the group to work and the other potential protagonists re-join the group and sit to watch how the drama will unfold.

Director   (to Anne) You said that things get warmed up in you. What are they?
Anne   I can't really say.
Director   What makes you aware that you are warmed up?
Anne   I just feel lousy.
Director   In what way do you feel lousy?
Anne   I just feel lousy.
Director   Do you have an idea of what you would like to work with now?
Anne   No. Can you decide?
Director   No, but maybe I can help you decide. You've raised a number of points that could be useful to look at on the stage for example – what would have to be different to be able to do your work in the group? (The director takes a chair on to the stage to represent this option and each of the subsequent ones.) What is it you get warmed up to that you take home rather than talking about here? What do you think and feel when you feel lousy? What led up to you getting drunk?
Anne   (looking at the four chairs and then the director) Do you think I should look at what happened when I got drunk?
Director   OK. (The director directs Anne to set the scene leading up to when she got drunk. The drama unfolds.)

The content of the session is less interesting to focus on here than the relationship between the protagonist, the group and the leader. At the end of the session Anne gets furious with the director whom she says has steam-rollered her, first into working and then all through the action and that this anyhow wasn't what she wanted to work on.

The director, despite considerable experience in this role, has fallen or been sucked into omnipotence. Why? As co-therapist I too felt that Anne had been steam-rollered. The group chose Anne who signified considerable ambivalence in being protagonist. Since the other protagonists were only too happy to procrastinate, one could say that they were also expressing ambivalence, although I did not think of that at the time. So why wasn't this ambivalence worked on?

The protagonist here, in group-analytic terms, is seen to represent 'the voice of the group' or what the group-as-a-whole wants to communicate. The group seems to be saying 'Help me. I don't know what to do. You are the one that knows what's best for me.' The director responds by becoming more and more active and directive, it is the director who takes the chairs on to the stage and accepts working with the scene without confirming that it is that scene that Anne chooses. She only asked *if the director thought* she should work with that scene. At the end of the drama the single-mindedness expressed through the direction must be countered as Anne is just as ambivalent at the end of the drama as she was at the beginning.

After a session like this everyone feels disappointed. If we return to what was said concerning the therapist's awareness before group members even join a group, it seems we have fallen into the trap of colluding with the idea that the leader will understand that the situation is impossible to change. But when a person joins a group the hope is always that it will be possible to come through the pain to something better. Anne, at least in part, hopes to be able to trust the group enough to be able to share with them the things that trouble her. She hopes to find a more adequate solution to her conflicts than getting drunk. She and the group hope to find an enabling solution rather than choosing to fall into dependency.

Pairing

> The group behaves as if the group will give 'birth to' a saviour who will solve the group's problem. Two people in the group emerge to play reciprocal roles in this Messianic solution as the focus of the group's attention, support, affection, hope and fantasy.

The group, which is led by two co-therapists, comprises eight members who have been in the group for some time and two relatively new members one of whom is Jane, a single parent. The group has recently had a break for a couple of weeks which has been difficult especially for the new members to deal with but nothing has been said about this. Harry has been a member of the group for a year and a half, and has been working on finding a way to have a more real relationship with his wife instead of living in a dream relationship with all other women. We are talking in the warm-up phase.

Jane   I feel very alone. No one helps me at home and I have to work all the time.
Harry   I feel alone too. I feel close to my children but Annette is depressed all the time and doesn't make any effort to meet me. I admire you so much Jane. You know what you want and go for it even if you get tired sometimes.
Jane   I don't want to live my life alone but I am too exhausted at the end of the day to go out.

Ruth   Why do you stay with Annette, Harry? I don't see that she has anything to offer you.

This is the beginning of a phase in the group in which Harry and Jane become a pair. The group actively support this behaviour and focus great interest on them. The work of the group often revolves around them and all attempts from the directors to question their locking on to each other are quashed. The pair raise criticisms about the way we lead the group. The warm-up phase should be shorter; there were too many role reversals in the drama last week and so on. The behaviour can be seen in the light of the group's reaction concerning the recent break at a time when they needed us. I am reminded of Bion's comment that 'All basic assumption groups include the existence of a leader, although in the pairing group, the leader is "non-existent", i.e. unborn (the awaited saviour of the group)' (Bion 1961/1991: 155). They replace us with the unborn leader. Hope is better than acknowledging and experiencing the pain of abandonment.

Only by continuing to take up the hurt and angry feelings around the issue of abandonment can the energy tied up in the pair be returned to flow freely in the group.

Fight–Flight

The group behaves as if the group survival is dependent upon immediate action, either fight or flight. This pressure towards impulsive action results in the group behaving as if it were a mindless mass.

Sue   (arriving 20 minutes late) Sorry. The traffic was awful.

Dan   You always come late.

Sue   What do you mean?

Dan   You have the same excuse every week. Why don't you give yourself more time to get here?

Sue   (sarcastically) Oh Mr Perfect! I left home in good time. It's not my fault the traffic was so bad.

Mary   But you could leave earlier. You mess up the warm-up every week by coming late.

Sue   Oh, so I'm not wanted here, well I'm not staying here to be criticised. (Goes out crashing the door after her.)

Michael   Did you have to say that Mary?

Mary   (angrily) Oh, so it's my turn now is it? (Goes out crashing the door after her.)

This hit-and-run technique of communication is troublesome for both the group and the leaders. Things can usually be dealt with if people stay in the room but energy is split if someone leaves. This splitting mechanism of sending the 'bad' in each of us and in the group-as-a-whole away, in the hope that only the 'good' in us will stay, offers temporary relief but does not solve the problem of living with and integrating both of those aspects in each of us. It doesn't take long otherwise before the process has to be repeated. In the case of Sue and Mary, does someone go after them and if so whom? If no one goes, time is spent on worrying about the consequences.

Sue	(comes in with Mary, both still a bit tearful) I know I come late every week. I don't know why but I get anxious if I come on time anywhere.
Mary	(to Michael) It's really hard for me to say what I think. I couldn't stand it when you made me feel I'd said something wrong.
Michael	I don't care if Sue comes late. It's up to her. It doesn't mess up the warm-up for me.
Director	I think it's time we choose a protagonist. Who is ready to work?

Working

A work group engages in behaviour towards fulfilling the stated aims of its leader and group members. It is engaged in conscious here-and-now communication.

John's son committed suicide a few years ago, an event which has locked John in social and emotional paralysis and isolation. John wants to show the group what happened to him after that event and is working on stage. His son had jumped from a high building and was transported to a place of rest. One scene has already been enacted – hearing from the police by phone that his son is dead and receiving an offer from the policeman to take John to see his son. The second scene is set, an auxiliary takes the role of the dead son lying on a table.

John	(Comes in silently with two policemen (auxiliaries), sits down and wails from the depths of his being.)
1st policeman	(immediately) What a terrible thing!
John	(to director) No, he doesn't say that.
Director	(to John) Reverse roles and show us what he says and does.
John	(as 1st policeman) – That's enough sir! (Takes him by the arm and roughly starts to pull him.)
2nd policeman	(Takes John's other arm and starts to pull him out of the room.)
Director	Reverse roles.
John	(Stands up and says angrily) I have to be alone here a while. Would you mind waiting outside?
Director	(Signals to policemen to do that.)
John	(Approaches his son and takes his hand. He sits and looks at him, rests his head on his son's stomach and cries deeply.)

Many in the group are crying too. It is a moment of existential pain which earlier has been too great to meet. After a while the director asks John if he would have liked to have someone with him in this place. He nods and says he wishes his son's mother could be there. They have been separated for many years. She is brought into the scene so that he can break the isolation he has lived in since his son's death and even grieve the loss of earlier relationships. In the sharing phase, group members are able to express painful losses in their own lives. A necessary step towards engaging in life maximally.

Bion wondered 'whether the group approach to problems is really worthwhile when it affords so much opportunity for apathy and obstruction about which one can do nothing' (Bion 1961/1991: 47). That is seldom the sense in a psychodrama group but the general criticism group analysts have of psychodrama is the lack of time given to silence, to reflection and to allowing group members to come to their own conclusions. The psychodrama director is often imagined to over-control the content and process of sessions rather than allowing these to unfold.

It is my experience that psychodrama groups are most often in working mode, perhaps because the method demands it. The group has a task to fulfil in producing a psychodrama, whereas in a group-analytic group the task has to be grappled for. In the fight-flight illustration of Sue and Mary, they were able to come back and talk about their fears instead of fleeing. We were then able to work with the fear on stage. Earlier intervention by the directors might have stopped them from leaving the room but they were able to come back and deal with the problem themselves. Waiting, the principle of abstinence, can be more productive than being 'helpful'. Many experienced psychodramatists, among them Zerka Moreno, have for example considerably limited the use of the double, having seen that the therapeutic effect for a protagonist is greater if she finds her own expression rather than receiving the immediate help of an auxiliary.

> Moreno talked about psychodrama as an encounter between equals. . . . Meeting one's equals and sharing emotions, pain, history, fun, and laughter can be a most healing experience. The nature of protagonist-centred psychodrama allows for this to happen. The powerful inner-object relationships are not ignored, nor are their influences on everyday life dismissed.
>
> (Holmes 1992: 180)

I would like to make a bid for psychodramatists to have an awareness of the principles of group analysis but whilst working with psychodrama to be loyal to the method. Psychodrama has developed since Moreno devised the method just as group-analytic psychotherapy has developed since Foulkes. Being open to these developments and other theoretical standpoints is enabling and enriching of psychodrama.

BIBLIOGRAPHY

Agazarian, Y. and Peters, R. (1981/1989) *The Visible and Invisible Group*, London: Routledge.

Bion, W.R. (1961/1991) *Experiences in Groups*, London: Routledge.

de Maré, P. (1983) 'Michael Foulkes and the Northfield Experiment', in M. Pines (ed.) *The Evolution of Group Analysis*, London: Routledge and Kegan Paul.

Foulkes, S.H. (1964/1984) *Therapeutic Group Analysis*, London: Karnac.

Foulkes, S.H. (1948/1991) *Introduction to Group Analytic Psychotherapy*, London: Karnac.

Foulkes, S.H. and Anthony, E.J. (1957/1965/1973) *Group Psychotherapy: The Psychoanalytic Approach*, Harmondsworth: Penguin.

Greenson, R.R. (1967) *The Technique and Practice of Psychoanalysis*, London: Hogarth.

Hinshelwood, R.D. (1987/1990) *What Happens in Groups: Psychoanalysis, the Individual and the Community*, London: Free Association Books.

Holmes, P. (1992) *The Inner World Outside: Object Relations Theory and Psychodrama*, London: Routledge.

Marineau, R. (1989) *Jacob Levy Moreno 1889–1974*, London: Routledge.

Moreno, J.L. (1946/1977) *Psychodrama, First Volume*, 5th edn, New York: Beacon House.

Pines, M. (ed.) (1983) *The Evolution of Group Analysis*, London: Routledge and Kegan Paul.

Stock Whitaker, D. (1985/1989) *Using Groups to Help People*, London: Routledge and Kegan Paul.

ANNE ANCELIN SCHÜTZENBERGER

Epilogue

Anne Ancelin Schützenberger

J.L. Moreno once said to me that to become a psychodramatist one needs training, *creativity* and *courage* to start to try it out.

It is, too, a way of life, an art as well as a science. In a way, using psychodrama when working with groups, is to use one's whole potential, science, art and creativity. It helps others to grow and to use all their possibilities, all their potential, what they are, what they could be, what they might be.

For Moreno, psychodrama is a *matrix* of identity, in a *locus* of identity, the group, and the psychodramatic stage is a womb from which the person is born again. It is a place to relive the *past* traumas, to heal them via *catharsis*, group support, *surplus reality* and by working through. It is to understand and explain the *present*, to prepare for the *future*, to try on new roles, possible roles and impossible roles (like being a flying bird, a medieval pilgrim, a twenty-first-century climber, a friend of Socrates, a deep sea diver, a baby . . .).

It is a *safe* place to express all kinds of feelings, joys and sorrows; a person can cry, shout, beat, jump, run, laugh, experiment new roles, feel understanding and support – try out family situations, professional situations and dangerous situations.

Studies and education are supposed to prepare you for your future. They offer background and training for everything . . . except for the essential, how to succeed in a job, how as a doctor or nurse to have *bedside manners*, how to face a class as a teacher, how to be a parent or a spouse, all that could be rehearsed in or via psychodrama and role playing.

We are actors of our own life.

Psychodrama is putting our *inner world outside* (Holmes 1992), acting *one's life on the stage* (J.L. Moreno), understanding and *cleaning up the past* and *training for the future*, a *rehearsal for life* (Schützenberger 1997; Starr 1977).

It has a *clinical use* and a *non-clinical* use, for teaching children, adults, foreigners, disabled people and for *training* doctors, actors, priests, nurses, foremen, managers, salesmen, social workers, theatre and movie directors, customs agents, policemen, administrative staff, staff in industry, the military and hospitals, mothers, children before entering school or surgery, debutantes before a party, diplomats or engineers before working in a different culture; teachers of language, grammar, difficult matters, history and geography, Bible; for rehabilitation after hospital or prison, teaching cancer patients to be *exceptional survivors* (Bernie Siegel: 1986) – the list of applied fields and examples is endless.

We have been taught life roles by our parents *in their time*, but how do we know how to act in *our* time?

As Alvin Toffler puts it in *Future Shock* (1970), the future is facing us more quickly than we expect, with more frightening novelty and more changes than we can handle.

How to be prepared and *prepare others* for the future? How to survive? How to keep the legacy of the past and still invent new ways for the future? What to do and how to react? What role to play? Moreno's *Who Shall Survive?* (1934/1953), written in the midst of the unemployment of the Depression, so actual now, offers the motto, the hope, the tools and training for more open eyes, more flexible views, a more open mind, and to be able to see and grasp new situations, and invent new answers through the development of *spontaneity and creativity*. Spontaneity and creativity are different words for intelligence. They include emotional intelligence, insight and intuitively, the right action.

Freud has made a fine contribution to human enquiry. As Moreno explained once comparing psychodrama with psychoanalysis, 'To drive a car, it is better to look ahead, and on the sides, and not only in the rear view mirror.'

BIBLIOGRAPHY

Holmes, Paul and Karp, Marcia (1991) *Psychodrama: Inspiration and Technique*, London and New York: Routledge.

Holmes, P. (1992) *The Inner World Outside*, London: Routledge.

Moreno, J.L. (1934/1953) *Who Shall Survive?*, Beacon, NY: Beacon House.

Moreno, J.L. with Moreno, Z.T. *Psychodrama, First Volume* (1946), *Second Volume* (1959), *Third Volume* (1969), Beacon, NY: Beacon House.

Moreno, J.L. and Moreno, Zerka (eds) (1960) *The Sociometry Reader*, Glencoe, IL: The Free Press of Glencoe. (25 contributors, including A.A. Schützenberger.)

Moreno, Z.T. *et al.* (1998) *Surplus Reality* (in preparation).

Schützenberger, Anne Ancelin (1965) *Précis de psychodrame*, Paris: Editions Universitaires (Handbook of Psychodrama, Spanish translation: *O Theatro da vida*), new revised edition in preparation, 1999.

Schützenberger, A.A. (1990a) *Le Jeu de role et le psychodrame*, Paris: ESF (A cook book for role-playing and psychodrama).

Schützenberger, A.A. (1991) 'The drama of the seriously ill patient: fifteen years' experience of psychodrama and cancer' in Holmes and Karp, *Psychodrama Inspiration and Technique*, London: Routledge.

Schützenberger, A.A. (1993) 'Cancer patients and family repetitions' in *Aïe, mes Aïeux, liens transgénérationnels, secrets de famille, genosociogrames*, Paris: DDB. trans. (1998) *The Ancestor Syndrome*, London: Routledge.

Schützenberger, A.A. (1997) 'Health and Death: Hidden Links through the Family Tree', *Caduceus*, March pp. 40–45.

Siegel, Bernie (1986) *Love, Medicine, Miracles*, New York: Dutton.
Starr, Adeline (1977) *Rehearsal for Living: Psychodrama*, Chicago: Nelson Hall.
Toffler, Alvin (1970) *The Future Shock*, New York: Random House.

Index